How to Find the Right Fit and Save Big Money

BARB PYTEL
Licensed School Counselor and Private College Consultant

Works
America's Career Publisher

Best College for You
How to Find the Right Fit and Save Big Money

© 2010 by Barb Pytel

Published by JIST Works, an imprint of JIST Publishing
7321 Shadeland Station, Suite 200
Indianapolis, IN 46256-3923

Phone: 800-648-JIST   Fax: 877-454-7839
E-mail: info@jist.com   Web site: www.jist.com

Visit www.jist.com for tables of contents, sample pages, and ordering information on our many products.

Quantity discounts are available for JIST products. Please call 800-648-JIST or visit www.jist.com for a free catalog and more information.

Acquisitions Editor: Susan Pines
Development Editor: Gloria Jasperse
Cover Designer: Alan Evans
Cover Image: © Getty Images Stockdisc / College Education
Interior Design and Layout: Toi Davis
Proofreader: Jeanne Clark
Indexer: Jeanne Clark

Printed in the United States of America

14 13 12 11 10 09   9 8 7 6 5 4 3 2 1

Library of Congress Cataloging-in-Publication Data
Pytel, Barb.
  Best college for you : how to find the right fit and save big money /
Barb Pytel.
    p. cm.
  Includes index.
  ISBN 978-1-59357-617-2 (includes cd-rom : alk. paper)
  1. College applications. 2. Universities and colleges--Admission. 3.
College entrance achievement tests. 4. College preparation programs.
I. Title.
LB2351.5.P97 2009
378.1'61--dc22
                              2009021681

We have been careful to provide accurate information throughout this book, but it is possible that errors and omissions have been introduced. Please consider this in making any career plans or other important decisions. Trust your own judgment above all else and in all things.

ISBN 978-1-59357-617-2

Streamline the College Selection Process and Get the Best Financial Aid

Choosing, applying for, and getting accepted at the right college can be overwhelming. *Best College for You* simplifies this process. As a licensed school counselor and private college consultant, I have helped many college-bound students and now show you

- How and when to begin your college search
- How to find your best-fit college
- What to do in high school for a smooth college admissions process
- How to predict where you'll be accepted and succeed
- How the right timing is key to getting accepted and making college affordable
- How to get the best financial aid and save thousands of tuition dollars
- Mistakes to avoid along the way

If you follow my suggestions, you will get into a college that matches your abilities and interests, plus save big money on tuition bills.

The CD-ROM packaged with this book provides convenient worksheets, timelines, and examples to print out and use during your college search.

Good luck.

Contents

Part III: College Visits: A Key Step in Finding the Best School for You 188

Part IV: Applying to the Best Colleges for You.............. 222

Part V: How You Can Afford the Best College for You ... 283

Appendix: Using the *Best College for You* CD-ROM 372

Introduction

"I don't know which college I like!" If you feel this way, you're not alone. What's more, no one expects you to know the college of your dreams right away. The decision is a significant one, and the process takes time—and effort.

Think of people you know who have purchased a home. They might tell you that at first the whole idea seemed overwhelming. After all, there are so many homes to choose from. How could they figure out which one was right for them and their family? They might have started with the drive by, to see which homes were available and which ones had the most appeal. Before long, they probably narrowed down their choices and began to focus on the handful of homes they wanted to tour. No doubt, finances played a large role in their selection, because affordability is very important. Eventually, when all the criteria were considered, one home emerged as the perfect fit.

Selecting a college is very much like this. College is so different from high school. What kind of college will meet your needs? Will it be a one-year, two-year, or four-year school? Will it be a college far away from your home or one right in your neighborhood? As you learn about the different schools, some will interest you more than others. You will begin to rule some out as you become more serious in your search. Eventually, you will select the college that seems to be just the right fit—and that is affordable, too.

This book is designed to show you what to look for in your perfect college match—including financial aid—and how to go about the process of selecting just the right school. In addition, you learn what to do in high school to make the steps easier. I include examples of real students so that you can learn from their experiences.

- Part I helps you to prepare for college while you're still in high school. What should you do during each of your high school years? What are ACT, SAT, AP, and IB exams? How can you present yourself in the best possible light?

- Part II offers help with the college search journey. Where and how do you begin looking so you won't waste time and money?

- Part III will help you understand how to make the best use of your time on those important college visits.

- Part IV is a guide to the application process. It isn't as tough as you think.

- Part V explains that dark, muddy bog of financial aid and the affordability of college. You can tip the odds in your favor.

- Use the CD-ROM to print out examples, worksheets, and other documents to help you in the process of finding the best college for you.

If you think you are college bound, or if you might want to be, there is finally a guide to simplify the process. You have it right here in your hands. Read it, enjoy it, and use it to prepare for your fantastic college journey.

PART I

High School Classes and Tests: The First Steps Toward the Best College for You

CHAPTER 1

Where Do You Start?

Every good plan requires thought and research. As you will soon see, your plan for college will be no different. Your college education may represent your first real-world purchase. It might even involve taking out a sizable loan and incurring debt. Many young people find themselves ill-equipped as they approach the challenge of college. But with preparation and planning, it doesn't have to be that way.

Begin Early

It's never too early to start to plan for college. In fact, eighth grade is really the place to begin. No, I'm not kidding! It's likely, though, that if you're reading this, eighth grade for you has come and gone. Is there still time to prepare for college? Of course! You can start right now, honing some of the skills you will need to make your college experience successful.

Manage and Organize Your Time

It's no secret that many high schools are raising the academic bar, and students are finding that more and more classes are mandatory for graduation. How can you manage to do everything you need to do—and do it all well? What's the key to becoming efficient? Here's the simple answer: time management and organization.

Note Being organized is the key to getting things done on time.

Most students who are efficient have learned to look at their workload in a realistic way and estimate how much time they will need to complete any given task. Take homework assignments, for example. If you think of your workload as large and unmanageable, it probably will be. Instead, try to think of individual assignments and what is involved in completing each one. You might be surprised at how efficient you can become simply by changing your perspective!

To enhance your efficiency, try this for a few weeks:

- List the homework assignments to be done at the end of the school day.
- Estimate how long each assignment will take.
- Schedule a time to do each assignment, working around appointments, practices, and family obligations.
- See how close you came to being accurate each night.
- Place all completed work and textbooks in your book bag for the next day.
- Place your book bag in the same spot every evening for a quick morning pick-up-and-go.

Students who learn to accurately estimate homework time begin before they are tired and complete assignments in time to get a good night's rest. The next morning there is no mad scramble to find assignments, books, and book bags. This reduces stress in the morning and sets a calm and confident tone for the school day.

Boys vs. Girls

Did you know that your gender may influence how you approach homework assignments? Believe it or not, it's true. Studies show that, in general, girls are better at estimating how long homework is going to take. On the other hand, boys overestimate how long it will take, get discouraged with how much homework they have, and are more likely to not do homework at all as a result. What can we learn from this? Boys, it is important for you to learn the skill of accurately estimating homework time! If you do, it is more likely that you will complete assignments and move more smoothly along the path to college.

But the gender differences don't stop there! Boys are also less likely than girls to be organized. Girls tend to coordinate their outfits even in elementary school, making sure socks and ribbons match the clothes of the day. Often, boys just want to get to school with little regard to whether anything matches. Girls will often coordinate book covers with book jackets and know that the color blue means math, red is language, and orange is science. Boys tend to throw everything into a locker or bag and hope for the best. Girls rearrange bedrooms and enjoy changing the color scheme. Try to find a boy who will be coordinating his bedroom after school.

Note Being organized often is easier for girls than it is for boys.

Organization Tips

Ana Homayoun has made a career out of organizing boys. Homayoun graduated from Yale in 2001 and formed a business, Green Ivy Educational Consulting. Her operation is twofold: She provides tutoring and helps young people to improve their organizational skills. While some girls do need organization tips, 75 percent of her clients are boys.

Homayoun requires each subject in school have a corresponding three-ring binder with these dividers for each class:

- Notes
- Handouts
- Homework

- Tests and Quizzes
- Blank Paper

Students are to estimate homework time and list each project in order of difficulty with the most difficult listed first. Then, they reserve time to do the homework. And reserved means reserved.

Homework time is to be uninterrupted. If homework is estimated to take two hours, for that two hours Homayoun insists on

- No distractions
- No music
- No cell phone
- No television
- No instant messaging
- No iPod

Students emerge from the study area when work is completed.

Register for Classes

With an organizational plan in place, you're ready to think about the classes you will take. Keep in mind that some of these decisions will not be in your hands. Quite often, specific classes are required during freshman year, leaving you with few electives or choices. Still, freshmen often are asked to fill out a four-year plan outlining a complete course of study. Yikes! How in the world do you know what to select? Take heart. It isn't so overwhelming.

First, consider all the classes required for graduation. This is a no-brainer. If you want to graduate, you will take these classes, right? So first fill in the **required** blanks. Now, after this, you may need to choose to go in one of two different directions. Many students will choose to go to a four-year college. Others will go to a vocational college. This is where tough decisions have to be made.

Quote "It is the first of all problems for a man [or woman] to find out what kind of work he [or she] is to do in this universe."

–Thomas Carlyle

Vocational Careers

Most parents, when polled, state that they want their son or daughter to get a four-year degree. Clearly, this is out of caring for their child and wanting the best future for him or her. But hold on there. Did you know that some of the hottest jobs out there today are reserved for graduates of two-year colleges? That's right! Did you know that various vocational jobs (some requiring as little as one year of education) offer starting wages that surpass the earnings of many four-year grads? This is no exaggeration!

Note The fork in the road is the four-year college route and the two-year route.

Students who are creative and enjoy hands-on activities have the advantage here. What are the options for these students who are on the cutting edge? They might select majors that fall under the heading of Applied Science and Technology.

Some of these majors are listed here:

- Automotive Technology
- Automotive Collision Technology
- Biofuels Technology
- Carpentry
- Computer Repair
- Dental Hygiene
- Diesel Technology
- Emergency Medical Services
- Graphics Technology
- Industrial Electrician
- Industrial Mechanics

6

- Maintenance Electrician
- Manufacturing Technology
- Media Technology
- Medical Assistant
- Medical Laboratory Technician
- Radiologic Technology
- Sustainable Energy
- Web Technology
- Welding Technology

Many employers in these fields find that they have more jobs than applicants, and they cannot fill the openings that occur annually. With a shortage of qualified applicants, jobs go unfilled and salaries go higher and higher each year. Some employers find themselves recruiting from neighboring states to fill available positions—positions that are essential to the economy and necessary to keep plants operating at full capacity. Companies are seeking students at junior colleges, often offering them jobs one year before graduation.

A Changing Workforce

What has sparked the sudden emphasis on these vocational jobs? You may be surprised to learn that nationwide the average age of workers in these fields is between 55 and 65. When these workers retire, very few men and women are waiting to fill their shoes. Many jobs have been exported offshore as companies fill available jobs with individuals who live outside the United States. This isn't always the best solution, however; while someone far away may be able to fix your computer, the same approach doesn't work when it is your car that needs repair. Some services cannot be outsourced.

One important and relatively new area of interest is energy and green jobs. As our nation looks toward sustainable and self-sufficient sources of energy, it is focusing on ethanol, bio-diesel fuel, wind, sun, and all renewable sources of energy.

Hands-on learners who have strong mechanical abilities will find themselves sitting in the front seat when it comes to career selection here. Some of these careers (biofuels, wind energy, and solar) may have seemed futuristic a few years ago, but keep in mind that the world is changing quickly. Those who are ready when the tide comes in will ride the waves.

Traditional Careers

What about the traditional careers? They will always be with us. We will continue to need nurses, lawyers, doctors, teachers, human relations professionals, counselors, and funeral directors. However, new fields are opening, bringing brand-new options to consider. Many jobs you may find in the future do not even exist today.

So, as you consider your college plan, there are many things to think about! What do you see yourself doing a few years from now? Talk to parents, friends, teachers, and members of your extended family, and explore career assessment possibilities. Ask those who know you about what they see you doing later in life. If nothing else, it would be interesting to see how they might envision your career choice. In the end, however, remember to follow your own heart!

 "Go ahead and do what you really love! "
–Neale Donald Walsch

CHAPTER 2

What About Your Schedule?

Y ou can't wait to graduate from high school and go to college! Life will be perfect in college, right? You'll have freedom from your parents! Fewer hours in class! Parties! Well, you might be right. College will be different—but it probably won't be perfect.

In high school you are in classes most of the seven to eight hours spent in school. A bell rings and you have five minutes to get to your next class. This happens eight or nine times per day. Teachers are on your case to finish assignments and to use your time wisely, and they suggest you stop socializing. Detentions are given when you're late, and hall passes make sure you've gone where you said you were going. It feels like a prison.

This chapter highlights how your high school and college schedules will differ, so that you can start thinking about building good time-management habits now.

Manage Your Class Time

College is different. But all of those habits high school teachers tried to enforce will be to your advantage if you have taken their suggestions to heart. Yes, there is more freedom in college, but with that freedom comes more responsibility.

Note College does require less class time but it also requires more study time.

College requires time-management skills. You're thinking, "What? We'll have so much free time in college. Time management shouldn't be an issue." Well, it is!

Understand Hours and Credits

In high school, you attend a class five days a week for one semester to earn one credit hour. In college it is figured differently. The typical college student carries approximately 15 credit hours per semester. What does this mean? Let's take Psychology 101—a three-credit class. This means that Psychology 101 is likely to meet on Monday, Wednesday and Friday, each time for 50 minutes. The class meets three hours a week so it is a three-hour class. Therefore, students are likely to take five classes instead of the six or eight in high school. So college is easier, right? Not so.

College assignments are more challenging than those in high school. A high school teacher may assign ten pages to be read for the following day. A college professor may assign three chapters for the following class. Your free time is quickly slipping away, isn't it?

What about arriving for classes late or skipping them altogether? Missing a class in college has been compared to missing an entire week of high school. The college pace is faster. High school teachers may seek you out and arrange a time for you to do make-up work. In college, professors post office hours and it is up to you to get in touch with them. And professors have the privilege of dropping a student who misses too many classes. That is usually done past the refund date, so you end up paying for the class but having to retake it. And if you have a hard time getting around on time, think about this: Some professors lock the classroom door when class begins. It is best to go to all your classes (and get there on time), even if people tell you it is unnecessary.

Study Time Rule of Thumb

There is an unofficial rule among college students for success in classes. Students are likely to do two to three hours of studying for each hour of class attended. So a three-hour class can easily demand six to nine hours of reading, note taking, and writing per week. Now, take this figure times five classes. You can easily spend 45 hours a week or more in preparing for classes. Add in the 15 hours of class time and you are up to 60 hours a week, and you have just begun calculating.

 Note College students spend two to three hours or more preparing for each hour of class time to be successful.

What about meals? Students often skip breakfast, but if you don't, add 10 hours for eating the meals. The total is now up to 70 hours per week doing something.

Work-Study

Many college students who qualify for substantial financial aid will be awarded work-study. Work-study is a type of job on campus, usually at minimum-wage pay. Students receive varying numbers of hours per semester, based on need. Often, students are allowed to work 8–15 hours per week if the hours are available to them.

A work-study job is often awarded without regard to class schedule. So there could be a conflict with classes. Let's take one popular work-study job—helping out in the campus mailroom. If you have an 8 a.m. class and a 10 a.m. class three days a week, this is going to conflict with placing mail into student mailboxes. When you show up to work at 11 a.m., the sorting has already been done. You are no longer needed. As a result, there are no hours worked—and there's no money coming in. So a choice must be made. You must decide whether working on Tuesdays and Thursdays will generate enough money for your needs. It probably won't. So you may want to petition to change jobs.

Students are responsible for finding a job that fits their class schedule.

If you receive 10 hours per week of work-study at college, the weekly hours are now at 80 and counting.

> **Note** Work-study jobs in college must be adjusted to fit your class schedule.

What are some other potential work-study jobs?

- Entering data for a professor in the science department
- Answering the telephone in the admissions office
- Planning intramural events
- Clearing tables or cleaning dishes in the cafeteria
- Tutoring other students in writing or math
- Returning books to the shelves in the library
- Assisting students in the computer lab

Just a little tip about work-study hours: The college is not obligated to provide you the income from work-study hours. If you do not work the hours, you do not receive compensation. In other words, no work, no money. If there is a conflict, you must find another job that works or the funding allowed will not be earned. And you cannot go over the amount given. If $1,000 per semester is the maximum, then that is it. Even if other students don't work all their hours, you are limited to your allotted figure.

Time for Yourself

In the college guidebooks, you might see pictures of students sitting on the lawn, enjoying the sun. It looks like they have nothing to do but catch some rays. Some pictures show students enjoying a picnic. And there is the snowman competition where winners receive great prizes. Sure looks like fun! But keep in mind that this time also comes out of the time bank. Manage your time wisely or it will slip away and leave you short. Decide what you need to be successful and not what others need.

"To get to nowhere, follow the crowd."

–Charlie Brown

Hanging out with other students in the dorm is how lifelong friends are made. Research shows that students living in the dorms do better and are more likely to graduate than those living off campus the first few years. This is why many private colleges require students to live on campus the first three years or even all four years. Colleges often show movies, organize events to keep students on campus for the weekends, and hold study groups. These events provide social time for students, allowing them to build community. The cafeteria is a good place to meet people and make friends. It is handy for meals, and students are more likely to eat a balanced diet when on the meal plan.

Sports

You may find the college athletic schedule to be different from the high school schedule you have known. High school out-of-town games are often held at locations within one hour's travel time of the school. A long trip might be two hours away. In college, students may travel from four to eight hours, stay overnight, and miss an entire day of classes because of being on the road. Professors appreciate and often demand advance notice of away games, and student athletes could be expected to download a lecture onto an iPod and be responsible for all information missed prior to the next class. Missing notes because of a game is no excuse! Add all this to a busy week and you can see that your free time is shrinking away.

Sleep Time

While high school students are often in bed by 11 p.m. to be ready for the next day, college students often are still up at 2 a.m. working on a research paper, catching up on e-mail, or just socializing over popcorn with other students on the floor. Late evening is also a great time to call friends at other colleges to catch up on news. You may not have a class until 10 a.m. the next day, so staying up does not mean you won't get your sleep. Again, time management is very important.

It's Up to You Now

Not everyone is on top of the game all the time. The changes from high school to college may leave you a bit overwhelmed. You may need time alone to cope with the changes.

Some students may decide to go home after one semester. Many times, students go home for Christmas and refuse to return. Many who have "helicopter moms" doing everything for them find the responsibilities of college life overwhelming. Clothes no longer magically appear clean in the closet. Wrinkled clothes remain wrinkled. No one reminds these students to get that research paper done on time, and no one reads it over for typos. Bed time is up to them and if they don't get enough sleep, they may perform poorly during the day. There is no one to blame but themselves.

In high school it is so easy to blame parents, calling them "lame" and "out of it," but once you are in college, all the responsibility for your success or failure falls on you. There is no one else to blame. Sure, mistakes may be made, but the majority of college students who give it a good try are successful and graduate. Decide what you want and go for it!

 "Never let the fear of striking out get in your way."

–Babe Ruth

CHAPTER 3

What Should You Do During Your Freshman Year?

Suppose you have graduated from middle school and are just entering high school. This is the last step before going on to college. Up with the big kids! Unfortunately, you are the bottom on the totem pole—again. Life is a series of ups and downs, a roller coaster ride that starts at the top and plummets right to the bottom. Being a high school freshman may feel very much like being at the bottom. Here's the bad news: This will not be the last time you feel this way. As a college freshman, you will find yourself at the bottom once again, ready to work your way up. Even when you enter the workforce, it's not over. Your first job will represent a good opportunity to start at the bottom and work your way up the corporate ladder. It all starts in high school!

What can you do to prepare for college and the days ahead if you're just starting high school?

Establish a Solid Grade Point Average

Take all the required classes and do your best in them. If you find that you need tutoring, get it. If you need to ask the teacher a question before school, ask. If you have to miss some fun with friends in order to stay after school to understand algebra, do it. Your major goal as a high school freshman should be to begin building your grade point average. That grade point average will change less and less each year during high school. Get a good start in your freshman year.

Get Involved in Extracurricular Activities

Do you really need to think about extracurricular activities at this point? Absolutely, yes! Here is why: Colleges are looking for students who get involved and who don't just sit behind a book and study. Colleges also are looking for students who do things on a consistent level. If you join the band, stay in band all four years of high school. If you join speech, stay in speech for four years. It is more important to participate in an activity throughout your high school years than to join many different activities and drop them after one year. Hopscotching through high school is exactly what colleges don't want to see. Be consistent. After all, in middle school you got to try out many activities to see what you enjoy. Pick several in high school and stick with them.

Are you an athlete? Be careful to not select only one sport and expect to have athletic scouts looking for you. Many athletes who are starters in high school just don't seem to get off the bench in college. Remember to always have a "Plan B." Get involved in more than just one thing.

Do Volunteer Work

Don't forget volunteer work. Why? It is impressive on a resume, and it indicates that you are willing to give back to the community that contributed to you and your education. Volunteerism doesn't have to be boring. Again, find something you like and try to stick with it for a few years.

What are some activities that you might enjoy? Consider these suggestions:

- Working as a Big Brother or Big Sister
- Tutoring
- Coaching or working as a referee for Little League teams
- Working with Habitat for Humanity
- Singing or playing the piano at your church
- Helping with community landscaping and/or maintenance
- Volunteering at a local nursing home
- Reading with children at your local library

Why is volunteering such a big deal? In your senior year, you will be submitting a professional-looking resume with your applications for college admission and scholarships. Every application will be reviewed carefully. Look at the following two examples.

Student A	Student B
Four years of lettering in track	Four years of lettering in basketball
Four years in band, first chair	Mission trip to Appalachia past two years
3.75 grade point average	3.68 grade point average
Coach for Little League past two years	Four years in choir, All-State
	Six years pianist in church
	Big Brother past three years
	Habitat for Humanity three years
	Meals on Wheels two years

These two students are about the same academically. They are also about the same in the areas of sports and music. But, when it comes to the volunteer work, Student B is far more active. If you were on the committee to admit a student into your college, or if you were to decide on the student to receive a more generous scholarship, which one would you choose? Did you say Student B? Student B is head and shoulders above Student A because of the volunteer work.

Quote "The only ones among you who will be really happy are those who have sought and found how to serve."

–Albert Schweitzer

With that in mind, though, be careful not to get too involved and let your grade point average slide. If school is not easy for you, you may want to focus on summer volunteer activities and stick to academics and extracurricular activities from September to May.

Become a Leader and Stretch Yourself

Bob was a terrific student. Some would call him a genius. He had a photographic memory, so, as you would guess, the ACTs were a breeze for him. His first ACT score was 33 and his second was 35. (The best possible is 36.) Bob was definitely Ivy League material and, with his low family income, Bob was sure to receive his education at no cost to him or his family. Bob confidently submitted his applications to several Ivy League schools and was rejected by all of them. This was a great shock to the community that knew of Bob's great college entrance scores and his 4.0 grade point average. What was the matter with Yale, Harvard, and Stanford for rejecting Bob for admission? The simple answer is that Bob did not participate in any sports, speech, music, or volunteer work. Bob was a bookworm and studied all the time. Bottom line: Bob was not a balanced individual. He was not a leader. Bob was a great student, but, today, colleges are looking for more than that.

Tamika was a great example of a high school student. She signed up for everything available to her in her very small school in the Midwest. She did volunteer work, participated in jazz band, won awards in music, and was the squad leader of her drill team and a cheerleader for three years. She led singing in her church, lettered in volleyball and basketball, participated in softball and track, edited the school newspaper, and maintained a 3.2 grade point average on a scale where an A was 93–100 percent.

Compare Tamika with another student, Stephanie. Stephanie did not assume the type of leadership roles that Tamika did, but she maintained a GPA of 3.6. At her high school graduation, Tamika was surprised to learn that she had received more scholarships than Stephanie, who had the higher grade point average. Why was this the case? Tamika was a leader.

Colleges are looking for leaders and are willing to pay for leadership by way of scholarships.

Emily was a very focused student and had been this way from her first day in high school. She did all the right things. She was involved in school activities, took on leadership roles, and participated in church activities. However, she was so anxious about her grade point average that she avoided taking the most challenging classes. She guarded her 3.9 GPA like a prized jewel and in her senior year was named valedictorian. However, her ACT score was not much to write home about. Emily earned an ACT of 23, which is above average nationally but rather lackluster for a valedictorian. She was admitted into a moderately selective college and did earn some scholarships.

In the same school, Brandy was named salutatorian with a GPA of 3.85, because academic awards are based on grade point averages. Brandy earned an ACT of 33 and was accepted to Notre Dame. Why did Brandy do so much better on the ACT? Brandy took the more challenging classes that would boost her ACT score and increase her chances of doing well at a highly selective college. She took calculus, chemistry, advanced biology, physics, and math classes at a local college for college credit.

Brandy took the risk of receiving a lower GPA but knew it would be best for her in the end. Emily took the safe route and guarded her number one position in her small class with safe courses. Some students put too much emphasis on high school glory.

Emily and Brandy were typical high school students. Some students take safe classes and some take challenging classes. Emily was capable of taking challenging classes; however, she didn't want to risk getting a B or a C in a difficult class. Being valedictorian was more important that stretching herself academically.

Quote "There are costs and risks to a program of action, but they are far less than the long-range risks and costs of comfortable inaction."

–John F. Kennedy

Take challenging classes if you are capable. Many colleges would rather see a B in a difficult class such as chemistry than an A in a less-challenging class. High school is preparation into the world of higher education. The glory earned in high school quickly fades.

The freshman year should be the time to select activities and then follow through. Participate and watch the leaders. See how they juggle activities and how they lead. Have a tentative action plan for what you want to do, because if you don't, it will be too late to catch up midway through your junior year.

Note Have a plan. Avoid regrets and catching up.

CHAPTER 4

What Should You Do During Your Sophomore Year?

Congratulations! You are no longer at the bottom of the food chain in high school. You are definitely moving up. But just how important is your sophomore year?

Check Your Grade Point Average

Think of beginning your sophomore year with the solid grade point average you earned the year before. What is "solid"? Colleges are not very interested in students who earn below a 3.0, so try to keep a minimum GPA of 3.0–3.2. Of course, higher is better.

Note Set a goal to keep your grade point average above 3.0.

Does this mean that you won't be admitted to college with a lower grade point average? No, not at all. But you will have less leverage when seeking financial aid, and you'll have fewer choices regarding which college to attend. A higher grade point average will give you access to a larger selection of colleges and increase the odds of receiving scholarships. But taking fluff classes to elevate a grade point average isn't wise and isn't to your advantage in the end.

Focus on Curriculum

You may have noticed that certain classes appeal to you more than others do. If you're like most students, the subjects you like best are those at which you're most successful. For example, you might like science if you are good at science. And you might like math if you're good at that. Sophomore year is the time to begin focusing in on the subjects you like.

First, though, visit with your guidance counselor and see if you are on track with all your required classes. Making sure everything is on target is part of being responsible as you look toward your future.

 Note Visit with your counselor to see if your original class choices may have changed.

Ask your counselor about taking an assessment to help in developing a focus and direction for your educational plan. Very few students know what they want to do after high school, but an assessment tool such as CHOICES can help narrow the options down to a career cluster. After a quick inventory, you'll see that careers will probably be grouped into one or two specific areas.

 Quote "The indispensable first step to getting the things that you want out of life is this: Decide what you want."

–Ben Stein

Careers may fall into the following clusters:

- Agriculture and Natural Resources
- Architecture and Construction
- Arts and Communications
- Business
- Education
- Finance
- Government

- Health
- Hospitality and Tourism
- Human Services
- Law and Public Safety
- Manufacturing
- Marketing and Sales
- Science and Engineering
- Transportation and Distribution

Prepare Your Resume

Don't let the idea of a resume frighten you. It isn't that difficult if you begin collecting items early. Think back on your school experience so far. Have you received any awards? Have you been involved in community activities? Create a list including every activity like this, even if it seems unimportant to you now. Then, put the list in a special drawer or envelope.

Note Collect information in a special spot for your resume.

If your name appears in an article in the newspaper, add that to the collection. Were you the school's most improved basketball player? Did you coach Little League this summer? Did you win an award for an art project? Did you hold down a part-time job? Date everything as you collect it. This will all make sense later when you begin building your resume.

Take the PSAT

The Preliminary SAT/National Merit Scholarship Qualifying Test is administered during the sophomore year of high school. Students who do well on this test have a chance to be considered for National Merit Scholarship Corporation (NMSC) scholarships. It is a huge honor to be eligible for this, so if you qualify, you might want to throw your hat into the ring.

Note Take a chance and register for the PSAT.

Even if you don't do all that well on the PSAT, you will have your first experience in taking a college entrance exam. Don't worry. Everyone leaves the testing hall feeling not too smart. The tests are meant to be challenging. Keep in mind that you are just testing the waters with this exam.

What does the PSAT measure?

- Writing skills
- Math problem-solving skills
- Critical reading skills

You will receive the results in December, and they will show your strengths and weaknesses in the categories listed above. You will also learn how you compare to other students across the nation who have taken the PSAT. If nothing else, you will learn what the SAT or ACT format will be when you take those tests later in your junior year. Your score will show where you fall only among students who took the test—not among everyone in the nation. Usually, only the top half of the students take the PSAT. So if you fall in the mid-range, you are actually in the 75th percentile nationally.

Register for the SAT or ACT

You are now in the third or fourth quarter of your sophomore year. It is time to register for the SAT or ACT for testing in the summer or early next fall. If you live in the Midwest or South, you are likely to take the ACT. If you live in the eastern or western states, you probably will take the SAT. Both tests are used for college entrance and most colleges accept both. The ACT is growing in popularity while the SAT has hit some speed bumps in the past few years because of errors in scoring. But both are going strong.

Note Register for the ACT or SAT for the summer before your junior year or very early in the fall.

Why do you need to take the ACT or SAT so early? The test results will show you your academic range, which will determine the colleges you will want to visit in the fall of your junior year. There is no need to visit colleges until you know your academic range. You could be wasting time and money by visiting the wrong colleges.

Think About Advanced Classes

Talk to your counselor about taking advanced classes next year. There are several options for advanced classes, and your school may offer one or two—or all of them.

 Quote "In the long run you hit only what you aim at. Therefore, though you should fail immediately, you had better aim at something high."

–Henry David Thoreau

Here are a few options for advanced classes:

- **Advanced Placement.** Available in select areas. Colleges accept AP classes for college credit.
- **Dual credit.** Classes taken in high school also qualify for college credit. One class counts for both high school and college credit.
- **College credit.** Instructors holding a master's degree may teach college-level classes within a high school setting.
- **College campus classes.** Students may attend classes at a local two-year or four-year college while still in high school. These classes would be taken online or on the college campus with college students.

 Note Consider taking advanced classes in your junior and senior years.

For more information on these options, see Chapters 8–11.

Sign Up for Volunteer Work

Analyze your current volunteer options and see if you can add one or two more activities.

For example, summer is a great time to do volunteer work with children. Perhaps summer Bible schools need volunteers. Cities have day camps or activities in the parks, and these programs might be in need of high school volunteers. Some cities have a volunteer community band, and band members are paid a small fee to participate for six or eight performances. Just remember to volunteer every year to be consistent.

 Note Remember to be a volunteer and document all your volunteerism.

Keep track of everything you do with specific dates. This will be very helpful when you begin to organize information for your resume next year.

 Quote "Hold yourself responsible for a higher standard than anybody expects of you. Never excuse yourself."

–Henry Ward Beecher

CHAPTER 5

What Should You Do During Your Junior Year?

You are now a junior in high school. This is the big year for college planning. That's right! Your senior year is important, but it takes a back seat to your junior year when you're thinking about college. So what should you be doing? Hang on!

Schedule ACT or SAT

At some point during the summer or very early in the fall, you will be taking either the ACT or SAT. Then, first thing next fall, schedule to take the test again. Why? Because many students raise their scores significantly by taking it a second or even a third time. Experts seem to agree that taking it a fourth time is not helpful.

What if your score goes down? That is a possibility. Perhaps the reading score will drop one point or so. But you may be pleased to know that colleges usually take the highest scores in each section. So, if you received a 23 in science on the first test and then dropped to a 22 on the second test, colleges will use the 23 ACT score to evaluate you as a student.

Research Colleges

After you receive your ACT or SAT scores, the next step is to find a college match. A good match for you will be a college at which your ACT or SAT score falls in the mid-range of students there. For example, suppose your score is 23. A college that has the middle 50 percent of students falling between 21 and 24 is a good match for you. You would place in the top half and not in the lowest 25 percent. More information on this topic is presented in Part II.

Note Use ACT and SAT scores to determine which college is a good fit for you.

Sam was one of the nicest high school boys you would ever want to meet. In addition, he was built like a brick wall and was a fabulous football player. His dream was to play football for Notre Dame. Having no knowledge about ACT score averages at a college, Sam set his dream for one college and one college alone. Sam waited until his senior year to take the ACT, and he scored a 19. Many colleges will accept a student with a score of 19, but Notre Dame is not one of them. The average ACT score at Notre Dame falls between 30 and 33. With his score, Sam would not be seriously considered even on a slow application day. His dream disappeared. He had no back-up plan. Eventually, he attended a small local college and played good football there. Sam's college experience was very positive, but it wasn't the experience he had anticipated. Research prior to setting your goals is very important.

Do thorough research on a college. What are your interests? Does the college offer you what you are looking for? Don't assume that a particular college offers what you want to study. You may be surprised to learn how many colleges do not offer all majors. For example, College A has a beautiful campus and a great football team and many of your friends have selected it as their top choice. You put it on your list to visit. Hold on! You are interested in engineering. Does College A offer that major? Look through college guides and find out the most popular majors. If it isn't there, look and see if it is offered in the long list of other majors. If it isn't, move on to another college. A limited number of colleges offer engineering, so you may have to do some research.

Note Research your college to make sure your likely major is offered.

Check the other activities on campus, such as drama, swimming, baseball, student government, and sororities or fraternities. Are these available? Consider the story of Andy.

Andy loved baseball. While he performed respectably at basketball and track, baseball was his favorite sport, probably because he could hit the ball out of the park! He selected a college and had plans to play with the team. He was really pumped. It was on the second visit and after non-refundable fees were paid that Andy discovered his college did not offer baseball. He assumed every college had a baseball program. They do not.

Researching a college prior to a trip on campus can save you time and money. Also consider that many high schools limit the number of days you may take off for visiting colleges. You don't want to waste a day!

A way to get more college visit days is to check your high school calendar against the college calendars. An in-service day at your school may just be a perfect day to visit a college. High schools often take fall and spring breaks at times that colleges are in session. Take advantage of a mismatched calendar.

Note Plan college days for times when you don't have school but the college does.

Prepare Essays

While very few students enjoy writing about themselves, essays are a necessary component of most college applications. In fact, 99 percent of private colleges have an essay topic at the end of the application form. Seems like they've saved the worst for last, doesn't it? Be encouraged that there is a way to make this process much less painful.

You have begun inquiring at some colleges the summer prior to September of your junior year. You probably never knew a person could get so much mail! Colleges are very assertive in recruitment, and it may seem like all colleges want you. You will probably receive a guidebook and, later, some promotional material on specific programs. Then, eventually, a college will send you an application form. Turn to the back page. There you will find the essay questions from which you will need to select one topic. Most forms offer two or three choices.

 Note Collect essay topics on application forms and begin writing them early.

Now, check out the next college application form, and the next, and the next. You'll see that some colleges will have nearly identical essay questions. Try this strategy: Begin writing an essay every four or six weeks on the most popular topics. Save these on your computer. By the end of your junior year, you could easily have a pool of six or eight essays. In the fall of your senior year, when you decide to apply to several colleges, chances are very good that your essay will already be written.

Then, in the fall of your senior year, all you will need to do is ask a teacher (preferably an English or creative writing instructor) to check it over for you. If the teacher does this favor for you, thank him or her in some way. The toughest and most time-consuming portion of the admissions process will be behind you. This greatly relieves senior year stress at a time when you are busy planning your graduation, making a second trip to a college, competing for scholarships, and taking those tough advanced classes.

Oh, those essays often can be used again for scholarship competitions, either locally or on the Internet. Essays can constitute up to 30 percent of an admissions package.

Plan College Visits

A college visit is not merely a "drop in" idea but, rather, an event that should be planned. There is a very good reason for this. The admissions director takes inquiries and assigns students to counselors within the admissions office. This is done according to territory. Each counselor has a specific turf for recruitment, and he or she attempts to bring in as many students as possible from the designated area. It is particularly important to contact the counselor assigned to you for every question regarding the college visit.

 Note Always carefully plan a college visit to make sure classes are in session on campus and your personal counselor can be there.

Plan to visit four to six colleges. Why so many? You're looking for a good fit and financial aid. You want to make sure that the college you attend has what you need and that it is affordable. Colleges differ widely in what they will offer in financial aid. Don't put all your eggs in one basket, because that basket could be the most expensive one!

Make a List for Each College Visit

Have a list of things to review on each college visit and take notes while visiting. By the time you get home, you won't remember the details and will probably get confused about which college is which. Be sure to jot down information and compare one college to another. By the time the financial aid letters come rolling in, one or two will begin to look like winners.

Note Don't set your heart on one college. Other colleges may give you a better package.

Remember Those Grades!

Remember to keep those grades up so you look interesting to a college. Your junior year may open you up to taking more electives that allow you to learn more about yourself. Junior classes can also be very challenging as advanced math and science classes push you to a new and higher level. Take time to seek help if needed and hire a tutor if necessary.

Create Your Resume

The resume you've been hearing about can be constructed in your junior year or the summer between your junior and senior years. Part IV of this book explains how to construct a resume and how to use it.

Your resume should be ready to submit when you begin sending applications to colleges and applying for local scholarships. Resumes give a professional touch to the process. Not everyone will use a resume but those who do will have a competitive edge. On the application forms, you will be asked to list all your activities and honors. You may merely write "see resume" and attach it. It will always be professional-looking, and once you check the spelling, it stays perfect. There is no chance for typos.

Note Resumes have many purposes and are worth the effort.

Resumes also may be used to apply for jobs and may be included when you ask a teacher for a letter of recommendation. Resumes are just a good thing to have on hand.

Your junior year is a major year in the college journey. Your senior year will flow much more easily if you do your homework as a junior. You will tip the odds in your favor by doing the necessary groundwork.

CHAPTER 6

What Should You Do Before Your Senior Year?

The summer just before your senior year is the last time to check, check, and double-check before you enter the straightaway of high school.

Follow this checklist and see whether you need to get some things done before you begin school in the fall:

❏ Register for Advanced Placement classes, classes that offer college credit, or dual-credit online classes. Check with your counselor long before classes begin in the fall to see whether you are a candidate for these advanced classes. If you are, get registered.

What's the big deal about college-level classes? Well, taking college-level classes sends the message that you are ready for college-level work. This is a good way, also, to earn college credits free. That's right, these credits are free of charge to you. Some students are so focused that they earn one or two years of college credits by the time they graduate from high school. And it costs them absolutely nothing!

Note Take advantage of dual-credit classes and college-credit classes.

❑ If you have taken the ACT or SAT once or twice and are dissatisfied with your scores, you may want to take some ACT or SAT prep classes. Companies such as Kaplan and Sylvan offer these classes. The classes clear up some mysteries that get students confused when thinking about the exams. Kaplan and Sylvan can teach you how to sift through the confusing verbiage and formats and do better on the exams. In fact, they offer guarantees: If you do not raise your previous score by several points, you may either receive a refund or take the classes a second time at no charge. These classes may be especially helpful for students with test anxieties. Knowing how the format works and practicing taking the exams may be just what a poor test taker needs.

Note Take the ACT or SAT one last time if needed first thing in the fall.

❑ Go on the ACT or SAT Web site and sign up for a question of the day or preps online. For online prep information on the ACT, see www.actstudent.org/onlineprep/index.html. SAT offers a question of the day. The question comes to you, you select an answer, and you get instant feedback. The site keeps track of how many answers you have gotten correct. See http://apps.collegeboard.com/qotd/question.do.

❑ If you don't have a list of five or six colleges in mind for fall, you must put that together yet this summer. This will be the list of colleges that you have visited and that you are considering attending. Summer is not the best time to visit a college because the students are gone and so are the instructors, in many schools. You won't get a true feel for what the campus is like on a typical day, and you won't be able to eat in the cafeteria unless you are visiting a large university. However, while it isn't the same as visiting in the fall, a summer visit is better than entering your senior year with only one or two college options.

Note Have a list of five or six colleges and applications in hand by fall.

❑ Get your essays in tip-top shape. During the lazy days of summer, check over all your essays and see if you have them the way you want them for submitting to a college. Teachers have more time in the summer than during the school year. Call a teacher and see whether he or she would be willing to look over a few essays. (This is something that can be done while sitting on a patio, drinking iced tea.) In the fall, when all the other students are scrambling to get organized, your essays will be finished and the teacher(s) will appreciate your planning.

❑ Update your resume. Make sure all the data is easily understood and easily scanned. College representatives want to be able to quickly scan a one-page document. They don't want to be flipping pages and wondering what CYO stands for (Catholic Youth Organization). Spell it out for them!

Note Have your resume completely updated and ready for fall.

❑ Make up your mind to prevent Senioritis. This is a "disease" that seems to set in for some high school seniors when they think they are 99 percent of the way through high school and don't need to work as hard any more. It would be so wrong to think that way! If you are taking college-credit classes, you need to give them your all until the final bell rings. While high school classes will stay in high school, college-credit classes will transfer to a college and be on your transcripts forever. Don't get too confident and end up with a C or D in a college-credit or dual-credit class. You may apply for a new job at the age of 40 and those transcripts may be requested, even then, with all classes and all grades. Don't have regrets later in life. Keep up with your work all year.

Note   Don't catch Senioritis!

❑ Make a list of the teachers to write letters of recommendation for you. (More on this will follow in Part II.) It is very important to select someone who can write a quality letter for you. Don't pick just any teacher. Instead, give this some thought. In September, ask selected teachers to write these letters. Why so early? If you ask before everyone else does, you may well get better letters because the teachers don't have eight others to write as well. Ask each teacher to save the letter on a computer so if you need another letter, it will be ready to go.

❑ Go to www.fastweb.com. If you haven't already registered on this site, do so now. To register, fastweb.com will ask you to complete a questionnaire, which could take some time. After that, scholarships that you might be eligible for will appear in your e-mail inbox. It is free, and the applications come to you! Get registered and act promptly when possible scholarships appear on your computer. You can't apply for too many scholarships!

Note   Sign up for scholarships online.

❑ If you need to take the ACT or SAT one more time, don't wait until late fall. Schedule the test in summer for the first testing date in the fall. Why? You want the results back before you send out your college applications. What if these scores are your highest yet? You may have just qualified for $4,000 more in scholarships. Isn't that a good reason to test early and wait for your scores?

❑ Get your physical exams if you need them for the colleges you select. Getting a physical in the summer is so much easier than trying to make time for it during your senior year.

❑ Save your money. Don't get carried away in buying a fancy car or something else that you don't need. If you do, you will wish you had that money back later. The senior year is expensive. For one thing, you might be asked to compete in a scholarship weekend in February and may need to fly out to the college. Senior pictures can be very expensive, too. Books for college can cost over $700 per semester. Out-of-pocket expenses can easily pile up on campus. Be tight with your money in the summer and enter your senior year with a surplus. You won't be sorry.

Quote *"A penny saved is a penny earned."*
–Benjamin Franklin

❑ Be thinking of what you will give those teachers who write letters of recommendation for you or who check over your essays. A thank-you card is the bare minimum. Some students give a gift card to a local restaurant or coffee shop. Other students prefer to bake cookies or buy a scented candle or a gift card to a local movie gallery. Think about it and have something in mind for teachers who go the extra mile.

Note Show some form of gratitude to teachers who help you with essays or letters of recommendation.

CHAPTER 7

What Should You Do During Your Senior Year?

Wow! You are a senior and at the top of the totem pole this year. You will soon be on your own at college, enjoying a great campus, meeting new friends, and experiencing new freedom. But hold on. You aren't there yet. You still have many things to finish—and finish well—before that great college experience.

If you have followed the guidelines for your junior year, you are all set to enjoy your senior year. If you haven't, you have a very busy year ahead.

Fill Out College Applications

Do you have five or six colleges selected? Do you have the applications in hand? Do you have the essays ready to go with the applications? You may wonder, "Why the hurry?" Can't you just apply after Christmas like some other students do? No. Here is why: The early bird gets the worm.

Some colleges are endowed beyond our wildest imaginations. Translation: They are rich. However, you don't know exactly how your college is sitting financially. So, to be on the safe side and tip the odds in your favor, apply early to all the colleges on your list and be in the best position.

Preferred deadlines are often in November. Yes, a college may accept students in March or later, with a rolling admissions policy, but the scholarships may be earmarked for the early applicants in January and you will get loans instead of grants and scholarships if you wait to apply. That is not a good thing. You want to be early and be a candidate for all the opportunities available.

Keep a copy of everything you send out. Have a file for each college. Colleges may write to you saying they didn't receive something. If you have a copy of what you sent, that problem is easy to remedy. Things do get lost.

 Note Your goal should be to get applications out before the end of November.

Letters of Recommendation

Colleges will expect two or three letters of recommendation to accompany your application. The letters are likely to be requested from your counselor, the principal, and a teacher. Some colleges may ask for a letter from a person in your community or even from a parent. Since you should allow individuals three to four weeks to write a letter for you, ask if they would be willing to do so two months prior to the November deadline. If they don't want to do this, move on to someone who is happy to write a letter for you. The counselor and principal letters might not be optional.

 Note Carefully select teachers to write letters of recommendation.

Your Resume

Update your resume at the last minute to make it as current as possible. Use it for local scholarships and college applications and for requesting letters of recommendation. It will save you so much time. Part IV of this book gives details on constructing a resume.

You should submit a resume even if others do not.

Essays

Review the essays and select which one will be used for which application. Double-check the word length. If your essay contains 750 words and the college wants 500 words, your essay will need to be cut down. If the essay is 500 words and the college requests 800 words, you will need to augment. You will want to have a teacher check your essay, again, after your revision.

 Write essays months before you apply to colleges.

Contact Your Admissions Counselor

Contact your personal admissions counselor at each college and verify the priority deadline for admission. It can vary from November 15 to March 15. Ask whether your application has to be received by the deadline or whether it must be postmarked by that date. You may also ask other questions at this time. It's a good idea to keep in touch. Each phone call is a positive for you. You've made another contact with the college, and they know you are still interested. If you show you are interested in them, the college is more likely to be interested in you.

Schedule Campus Visits

If you still have questions about a college after your first visit, plan on visiting once again. If you visited a college for the first time in the summer, with no students on campus, you may want to visit while classes are in session. This is especially appropriate if this particular college has risen to the top of your pile of possibilities. Have a list of questions that need to be answered in order for you to make a good decision in the spring. Make the visit prior to the time that award letters are mailed in April.

Apply for Scholarships

If you applied to colleges by the end of November, you will be receiving scholarship applications in late December or early January. You will be asked to write more essays for scholarship competitions.

Strongly consider attending a scholarship weekend if invited. Keep in mind that you probably wouldn't be invited if you didn't stand a good chance of receiving a scholarship. More on scholarship weekends follows in Chapter 56.

Maintain Strong Grades

Keep your grade point average solid. It is really easy to relax a bit too much and let the academics slide during your senior year. Don't catch the Senioritis bug. Keep those grades up! If your grades drop significantly, colleges may rescind their offers, assuming that your falling grade point average means that you are no longer the student they accepted in the fall. After all, your grades are now lower, and other students have applied who look more interesting. You may eliminate yourself from scholarships and even admission by not keeping up your grades.

Note Reminder again: Don't catch the Senioritis bug!

Update Your Awards

Many awards are given late during your senior year. If you should receive an honor after your college application has been mailed, let your personal admissions counselor know. It could make a difference. You may call or e-mail your counselor with the information and at the same time update your resume to reflect the added honors. Colleges want you to look your best. Be sure your admissions counselor has the information that will justify giving you a better financial aid package. This will increase your chances of attending the college of your choice.

> **Note** Don't miss any college deadlines.

Complete FAFSA Forms

The Free Application for Federal Student Aid is probably one of the most important forms you will fill out throughout the college process.

You can follow this timeline:

- **November.** Go online to www.fafsa.ed.gov and obtain a PIN number. You will need a PIN number, and your parents will also need a PIN number. Print out the FAFSA form and review what documents you will need in January to file online. You may pencil in all the data and use the form as a worksheet for when you file electronically.

- **December.** In December, and even November, high schools offer a financial aid night during which the financial aid process is explained. You might find it helpful to review the FAFSA form prior to attending a financial aid night, to prevent the possibility of becoming overwhelmed. If you have studied the FAFSA form, you will know which questions to ask. Save all year-to-date payroll stubs.

- **January.** Try to have income taxes filed as early as possible in January and file the FAFSA with the data on the 1040. Each college has a different financial aid deadline. Make sure you know all the financial aid deadlines for your colleges. Some may be February 15 and others April 15. Don't miss a deadline and disqualify yourself from financial aid.

- **February.** You should receive your SAR (Student Aid Report) quickly after filing the FAFSA. If you don't receive it within four weeks, call the Federal Student Aid Information Center at 1-800-4FED-AID. More on the SAR follows in Part V.

- **March.** Colleges may send you verification forms to confirm your FAFSA information. Often, copies of student and parental income tax forms are requested. If you are asked to submit a form like this, don't be concerned. You are not suspected of fraud! This is a common request.

> **Note** Be sure to file the FAFSA prior to any college financial aid deadline. It is the mother of all financial aid.

Make the Final Decision

In May, the final decision about which college to attend will probably have to be made. Colleges will submit award letters with deadlines. Look at all the offers carefully and decide which one is for you. The best offer could be a huge surprise, so leave yourself open until you have all of the offers on the table. If you receive an offer from College A and this is not your first choice, feel free to fax College A's offer to College B to see if they will match it. Colleges often leave room for negotiating.

> **Note** Base your college decision on where you want to go and not where friends are going.

But it isn't just about money. It may be worth it to pay more for the right match. For $250 or $500 more, you may receive better food, better dorms, a better location, or a major with a better reputation. Sit down with your family to weigh all options and then decide.

Prepare During the Summer

Here are some things to do during the summer after high school graduation:

- Save money for college with a summer job.
- Set up a budget for anticipated college expenses. How much is it going to cost for laundry, food (other than cafeteria food), computer expenses, gas (if you have a car), and so on? Figure out what you will actually need to live. Remember, nearly all your expenses are covered when you live in a dorm. The expenses you're considering here are all extras, and some may be unnecessary.

- Visit with your dorm roommate and decide who is supplying what to avoid duplications or voids.

- Notify your college of any scholarships you may have received. The college will make adjustments to your financial aid package. More on this will follow in Chapter 57.

- Attend college orientations. Not only will you feel more at ease when you make the move, but you will meet students and have friends when you arrive on campus, as well.

- Send thank-you cards for all graduation gifts.

- Don't get misled by credit card offers. You will have enough debt at graduation with student loans. Make your budget work without credit cards.

 Summer is for saving money, planning for fall, and saying goodbye.

CHAPTER 8

What Are AP and IB Classes?

Y ou probably have heard of classes that are labeled "AP" or "IB." Just what are these classes, and are they for you?

AP *(Advanced Placement)* and IB *(International Baccalaureate)* classes are designed for students who are planning to attend upper-level selective colleges. Successfully completing these classes is a way for students to demonstrate their ability prior to admission. AP and IB tests are used to assess and screen students.

AP Classes

AP classes are for students who enjoy a challenge and who are willing to work hard. In an AP literature class, for example, the teacher might expect students to read several books during the summer months before school starts. AP classes provide the opportunity for students to push themselves to a high level of achievement and to demonstrate readiness for college-level work.

Note Higher-level colleges are more likely to require AP classes.

Upper-level colleges typically require high grade point averages and ACT and SAT scores that are higher than those required by colleges ranked as average. Level 1 and level 2 colleges are likely to demand AP classes. Chapter 22 explains the five academic levels of colleges.

Advanced Placement classes are for four-year college-bound students. These classes are different from regular high school classes or other college-credit classes. AP classes cover limited topics, and each class must follow a strict syllabus. Not every college-credit class is an official AP class. The College Board requires that official tests be administered to students showing proficiency. Scoring falls within the range of 1–5. Most colleges consider a 1 or a 2 unacceptable. Ivy League colleges expect a student to score a 5, although they will perhaps accept a 4. Other colleges will accept a score of 3 for college credit.

The scoring code is

1—No recommendation

2—Possibly qualified

3—Qualified

4—Well qualified

5—Extremely well qualified

Your high school guidance counselor or your AP coordinator should have a complete list of AP classes offered at your school. Unless your school is large, do not expect many choices to be available. There are online options for taking AP classes if your school does not offer the subjects you desire.

Approved Classes

Following is a list of classes approved nationally for AP credit.

- Art History
- Biology
- Calculus AB
- Calculus BC
- Chemistry
- Computer Science
- Macro- and Microeconomics
- English Language and Literature
- Environmental Science

- European History
- French
- French Literature
- German
- Comparative Government and Politics
- U.S. Government and Politics
- Human Geography
- Italian Language and Culture
- Latin Literature
- Latin: Virgil
- Music Theory
- Physics
- Psychology
- Spanish Language and Literature
- Statistics
- Studio Art
- U.S. History
- World History
- Chinese
- Japanese

 Note Scores of 4 and 5 are most respected on an AP test.

Enrolling in AP Classes

If you decide you want to take an AP class, you must register at www.collegeboard.com long before the beginning day of the class. The deadline for fall is March 15 of the same year, and the phone call to initiate the process has a March 1 deadline. Start the process far before this deadline. The cost for 2008–2009 classes was $84 per class. Fees may be reduced to about $25 if the need for financial assistance is verified.

Students with a learning disability may petition for accommodations prior to registering. This should be done substantially ahead of the March deadline because the process may involve gathering and reviewing a significant amount of data.

Note Students with learning disabilities need to call far in advance to process the request for accommodations.

The AP Test

Taking an AP class with a final exam is not enough. You must also take an official AP exam. These exams vary in length from two to three hours. They include multiple-choice sections that are scored by computer and free-response sections that are evaluated by experienced AP teachers and college professors called "readers." These readers spend a week in June scoring tests. Most AP grades are released to colleges in mid-July if authorized by students. For more information about AP tests, see www.collegeboard.com/apstudents.

Do not assume that colleges will accept all AP classes. Contact the AP coordinator at each college and get approval for each class. Keep in mind that verbal approval is not enough. Get it in writing!

IB Classes

Explaining the differences between AP and IB is like trying to discuss the differences between Chevrolet and Ford! The AP and IB programs are quite similar. The AP is a very established, common name in high schools, while the IB name is at the start of its already rapid growth. Colleges love both of these advanced classes, but each has a slight preference. In fact, the preferences may differ from department to department within a given college. At College ABC, for example, the engineering department may prefer the AP, while the English department may prefer the IB.

Class Offerings

IB classes are offered in six areas in English, French, and Spanish:

- Language
- Individuals and societies
- Mathematics and Computer Science
- The arts
- Experimental sciences
- Second language

Core Requirements

The three core requirements are

- **Extended Essay.** Essay is limited to 4,000 words, requiring independent research and writing skills at a college level.
- **Theory of Knowledge.** TOK is designed to explore the nature of knowledge and to encourage an appreciation of other cultural perspectives.
- **Creativity, Action, and Service.** CAS encourages artistic pursuits, sports, and community service work, which fosters an appreciation of life outside the academic arena.

Other Considerations

The IB curriculum is more expensive than the AP in that it covers a wider range of content. Many people believe that the IB is more thorough. On the other hand, the IB doesn't deliver college credits with the consistency of the AP. Before taking either test, contact the colleges you are thinking of attending and see which they prefer. And be sure to check the various departments, because opinion can vary there as well.

AP and IB classes both represent challenging steps to take in high school as you prepare to move to the next level. If your counselor thinks you are a good candidate for these classes, go for it!

CHAPTER 9

Should You Earn College Credits in High School?

Some in the field of education are not in favor of providing the opportunity for high school students to earn credits by taking college-level classes. Who are those people, why do they feel this way, and how should this influence you?

Opponents of High School College Credit

One group of opponents is made up of four-year college professors who believe that college-level classes do not prepare high school students for the rigors of college life. These professors fear that, instead, taking such classes may lead students to a false sense of security about their ability to do well in college. Since there is no uniform standard from one high school to the next, these concerns may well be valid in many cases. However, high school teachers who teach college-credit classes usually have advanced degrees in their areas of expertise, and they typically approach these challenging classes with high expectations for student achievement.

Some people would like to see a type of test administered to evaluate a student's readiness for taking a college-credit class. Others oppose a test format, pointing out that there are more effective methods to indicate student readiness. In fact, each year more colleges are added to the list of ACT- and SAT-neutral colleges. These colleges do not require incoming students to take the ACT or SAT. Instead, they will accept applicants with or without these exams. Colleges are finding that the ACT and SAT tests may, in fact, be serving to weed out the creative students who tend to score lower on standardized tests. See Chapter 13 for more information, including a Web site address and a list of colleges not requiring the ACT or SAT.

> **Note** ACT and SAT tests are gradually losing favor among colleges.

Types of College-Credit Classes

Several types of college-credit classes are available in high school:

1. One form of college-credit classes involves a trip to the local college. Students jump in their cars or take a bus to attend a class three days a week at the local college. It may be either a two-year or a four-year college. In either case, high school students are eligible to attend. They take the class with students older than themselves, and they have a true college experience. Some rules usually go along with this situation. One stipulation often is that the high school does not offer the same class that students are able to take at the college. Another typical requirement is that each participating student must be recommended by a teacher who believes that student is capable of success.

    This is a good option for those students who are qualified to take courses not offered at their high school. For example, a student may be ready for calculus but the high school does not offer it. This student would be eligible to take calculus at the local college at no cost to him or her. Who pays the bill? The local public school picks up the tab. Many high schools are glad to do this, but some find themselves discouraging students from taking the advanced classes because of a tight budget that limits spending.

2. Another form of college credit is dual credit. Here, the student does not leave the high school building or campus.

Instead, certain classes at the high school are earmarked as "college-credit classes" because the instructor holds a master's degree and the curriculum qualifies as college level. Students follow a normal schedule, going to the next class when the bell rings and attending every day, but they receive college credit at the end of the semester. The college-credit classes count toward high school graduation and the student earns college credit at the same time—two birds with one stone! An agreement between the high school and the local junior college typically paves the way for dual-credit classes. And there are no transfer issues if the student goes on to attend the junior college that offered the classes.

Note Dual-credit classes are becoming popular.

Colleges and state departments of education don't always speak well to each other. If they did, state agencies would realize that colleges are not in favor of some of the high school requirements. A good example of this is the math curriculum. States mandate many math concepts to be taught in short periods of time. What colleges prefer is that fewer concepts will be taught over a longer period of time. Colleges want students to be solid in the basic concepts so these students can go on to advanced stages. However, quite often high school curricula are pushing students into higher-level math courses before they have mastered the lower-level concepts. There is a major disconnect here and colleges are complaining.

3. "Early bird" classes represent another offering at the high school level. Because many students have schedules that are already full eight periods out of eight—with no study halls—high schools sometimes offer college-credit classes an hour prior to the official beginning of the school day. A teacher holding a master's degree might teach the class at

7:30 a.m. or earlier for college credit. While having an 8 a.m. class on your college schedule is considered extremely bad luck, try getting to class before 7:30 a.m., particularly if you had basketball practice until 10 the night before and then had two hours of homework after that!

Note Early bird and online college classes are creative ways to take college classes even if you have a full high school schedule.

4. Online college classes are becoming very popular for busy high school students. This type of class does require students to be very motivated and have excellent time management skills. Since these classes do not meet at a specific time, students often get behind in the schedule and have to pull several all-nighters to finish on time. One drawback is that other classes may suffer as a student completes an online course, and this could result in lowering the grade point average. As with other college-credit classes, make sure credits transfer prior to spending the money on an online course.

Note Get college credits approved in writing from the college that you plan to attend after graduation.

The Glitch

Students work above and beyond typical expectations to earn college credits. How can this be a negative?

The rule is to always check with prospective colleges to see whether they will accept college credits from high school or from another college. They may, but many don't. Why not?

There is academic prestige with higher-end colleges. The Ivy Leagues are not popular merely because they have deep pockets and beautiful buildings. The ACT and SAT scores of students attending these colleges are in the top 10 percent in the nation, and there is a strong desire on the part of the schools to maintain academic exclusivity. Prestigious colleges just don't think that all college credits are the same. Level 1 and level 2 colleges may reject all dual-credit classes and even credits earned at another college. Even level 3 colleges may reject classes from lower-level colleges if the catalog descriptions for these classes are not the same as those offered at a particular college.

Alicia was a gifted student attending a local public school. She quickly completed the minimal graduation requirements and spent most of her junior and senior years in high school taking college-credit classes. Except for a government class as a senior, she was considered a college student. In order to allow for this, Alicia dropped out of sports and music events because some of her college-level classes were held at the local junior college in the evenings. She also took early bird classes before school and even took college classes in the summer. She did well in these classes and applied to level 2 colleges with over 50 credit hours. Go, Alicia!

Unfortunately, Alicia never contacted her pool of colleges about transferring these credits. She assumed that it was a good thing to have over 50 college-credit classes and she assumed also that all would be accepted. Her plan was to begin as a junior, and she and her parents would save two years of college expenses, because the local public school was paying for most of her college classes. Alicia applied to her top choice college, sending along her college transcripts. She was surprised and horrified to learn that her top choice college rejected most of the college credits she had already earned. Why? A panel that protects academic integrity determined that, in terms of academic rigor, the classes were not equal to those of the college. It was also determined that some of the catalog descriptions did not match perfectly from one college to another, and Alicia would need to take her courses again.

Since Alicia was in love with one particular college, she decided to attend there anyway and began as a freshman. Of course, news spread quickly throughout the high school that Alicia was starting from scratch, and while all that sacrifice may have built character, it didn't do much else. And since she had given up extracurricular activities, Alicia had little on her resume for scholarship competition other than a high ACT score. Alicia had missed out on art classes, music, sports, volunteer work, and many social activities that can be the most cherished memories of high school. She also had no work experience because there had been no time to hold a part-time job with her academic load.

As you would imagine, the counselors at Alicia's high school now tell students to contact colleges and learn whether their college credits will transfer. Even if a junior college assures you that these credits will transfer everywhere, get it in writing from your future college.

Electives and Transfers

Colleges may accept all your college credits but may require you to take the same classes over anyway. For example, suppose you took Sociology as a senior. A college may determine that the class description does not match theirs. They will accept Sociology as an elective, but you will not be granted credit for taking the class. Instead, you must take Sociology again on their campus. You didn't lose the credits, but your elective pool is now filled with high school classes that you must take again. This means you will have less opportunity for taking interesting or unusual electives. You might find this especially frustrating when you go to the bookstore to buy your expensive textbook for Sociology, and it is the same book you used in high school!

Note Know whether your classes will transfer toward your major and not as electives.

So reach for the stars! Set high goals. Be cautious. College-credit classes in high school can be a good thing, but always check ahead with prospective colleges to see whether the classes will be accepted and how they will be transferred.

CHAPTER 10

How Are the ACT and SAT Different?

While the ACT and SAT might appear to be similar, there are some subtle, but major, differences between the two exams.

Colleges use both the ACT and SAT exams for college admission and placement. Students suffer anxiety before, during, and after both tests. And both leave students thinking they did not do well. This is because the tests are designed to be so difficult that a perfect score is rarely achieved. If a student does get the top score possible, it is state or national news! Please note, though, that while the two standardized exams are used for the same purpose and are much alike, there are some very clear differences.

Note The ACT and SAT have subtle differences.

The ACT

The letters A-C-T stand for "American College Testing." However, when you hear "ACT," you probably think of the test, not the group that created it. The ACT exam is a standardized series of tests administered to secondary school students and used by colleges and universities in determining admission and placement. Used predominantly in the Midwest, the ACT is becoming more popular nationwide.

Note The ACT is dominant in the Midwest.

The ACT actually tests material covered in the high school curriculum. A student is likely to improve his or her ACT score by taking rigorous classes in high school. The ACT emphasizes grammar, scientific reasoning, and trigonometry but has less math, overall, than the SAT. Still, math and science classes are especially helpful in improving ACT scores.

Science

The ACT organization has conducted research that reveals a correlation between science scores and classes taken in high school. For example, if a student takes biology only, he or she can expect to receive a score of approximately 17.7 on the ACT. Because colleges prefer to see minimal scores in the 18–19 range for admission, this student may not be accepted at the college of his or her choice.

If ACT tests predict success in college, as some believe, a student with a 17 in science is not likely to pass a college biology class. On the other hand, the student who takes both biology and chemistry is likely to score a 20.5 in science. What if a student takes biology, chemistry, and physics? He or she is likely to score a 23.1.

Math

Math classes are not the same in every school. A pre-algebra class at School A may be more difficult and more advanced than an algebra class at School B. Expectations, grading scales, and standards differ from school to school and from state to state. The higher the standards at a particular school, the higher the students' scores may be on the ACT.

Students taking the minimal high school math requirements, including general math I and II, can expect to score a 17 or lower on the ACT. Students taking the minimal core classes of algebra

I and II and geometry can expect to score 18 or 19. Taking one additional advanced math class can raise the score to 20 or 21. Add trigonometry and the score jumps to 22 or 23. With calculus the student could expect a 25 or much higher.

> "Perhaps the most valuable result of all education is the ability to make yourself do the thing you have to do, when it ought to be done, whether you like it or not."
>
> –Walter Bagehot

English

In English, students taking the bare minimum can expect to receive an 18 on the ACT, but students who take higher-level classes can expect a 22. Minimal reading classes produce a 20, but college prep classes produce a 22. Overall, the difference between minimal curriculum courses and more rigorous courses is 2 or 3 points on the ACT. Taking more math, English, and science classes is more than worth it, not only in earning a better ACT score but in better preparation for college work, as well.

> "The truth of the matter is that you always know the right thing to do. The hard part is doing it."
>
> –H. Norman Schwarzkopf

Average Scores

What is the average national ACT score? The average scores have not changed much over the past five or six years. In 2005 the average ACT scores were English 20.4, math 20.7, reading 21.3, and science 20.9, with a composite average of 20.9. In 2008, the scores were nearly the same.

Now, keep in mind that this average is for students taking the test. Many high school students do not take the test. In some schools, only the top third take the test, while in other schools nearly all the students take it. If you assume that half the students on average take the ACT, a student with a score of 22 is not in the middle of the nation. This student is in the middle of the top half of the group of students who take the test.

Research shows that an English score of 18 will produce a grade of C at a college. An ACT math score of 22 or higher indicates readiness for college algebra, and students scoring in the 17–19 range will struggle in the areas where scores are low. The only way to truly prepare for the ACT is to take the most challenging high school classes available.

The Questions

The ACT is not arranged in any order of difficulty. You may find a difficult question followed by a much simpler one. There is also no penalty for guessing. On the ACT you are wise to eliminate the obviously incorrect questions and choose among the remaining questions. It is to your advantage to complete all questions in the time allowed.

The SAT

The SAT I (Scholastic Assessment Test), like the ACT, is a standardized series of tests administered to secondary school students and used by colleges and universities in determining admission and placement. The SAT is compiled by the College Entrance Examination Board and is popular in the eastern and western United States.

The structure of the SAT is somewhat different from that of the ACT. The SAT emphasizes vocabulary, math, and abstract reasoning. In 2005, the SAT was renamed the SAT Reasoning Test and a writing test was added, increasing the maximum score potential and the length of testing time.

The SAT II is a cluster of subject tests that are used to measure academic achievement in specific areas. Once a student applies for admission to a college or university, he or she may be asked to take an additional SAT in a particular subject area such as writing. The results of this test will then be used for admissions and placement purposes.

The SAT is arranged in order of difficulty. Students taking the test experience more difficult questions as the test progresses. And there is a penalty for guessing.

Average Scores

SAT scores range from 600 to 2400, with an average score in the range of 1000–1050. (Prior to the addition of the writing portion, the SAT score range was 400–1600.)

 Note The SAT score range is 600–2400 with the new writing component.

SAT Scandal

Over the past few years, errors in scoring have been uncovered, and the SAT has issued apologies. However, in many cases, the faulty scores were not corrected. This resulted in some students getting into Ivy League colleges and receiving scholarships based on inaccurate scores. It also resulted in at least one court case when a student in Minnesota filed a lawsuit against the scoring agency, The College Board.

The SAT is the test of the Ivies. Since it is quite popular on the East Coast, where the Ivy League colleges are located, the SAT is a very important tool for admission into the top colleges. Some people believe the SAT is used to foster inequality in admissions, as affluent families can afford to spend thousands of dollars on preparation classes and coaching for the SAT. There is some controversy concerning whether the SAT and ACT should even be used for college admission.

 Note The SAT is dominant in the coastal areas of the United States.

Taking the Tests

Kaplan and Sylvan are two well-known names in the standardized test prep business. These companies teach students how to take the ACT and SAT. Students learn how to select the best answers on the tests, and the practice tests give them experience in the format.

Good results could also be achieved if students were to take the practice tests individually and study the manuals. Unfortunately, most students taking the college entrance tests do not prepare in this way. They simply take the tests cold and hope for the best.

Quote "You miss 100% of the shots you don't take."

–Wayne Gretzky

How Many Times Is Best?

While there is no magic number, most students are pleased to find out that their scores improve if they take the exams two or three times. Taking the exams without any preparation creates stress for students getting acquainted with the format in a timed situation. In fact, students are often so overwhelmed with the format that they find this works against their score. Taking the test a second and even a third time may lead to greater relaxation for the student, and a more relaxed brain is likely to do better and retain more information.

Note Take the ACT or SAT twice and perhaps even three times.

Colleges figure the scores in two different ways. Some colleges average the two scores together. Other colleges take the best of the scores. Let's pretend that Juan took the ACT three times and received scores of 19, 23, and 22 in math. One college may just use the math score of 23 and ignore the fact that Juan dropped down on the third test. A different college may average the three together and assign him the score of 21.3.

The Same But Different

Some schools wanted to be efficient with testing time and requested the use of the SAT as a high school assessment tool. While the ACT was approved for this purposes, No Child Left Behind officials denied the SAT as an assessment tool. Why? The SAT is not testing for knowledge taught in high school. Instead, the SAT is a reasoning test evaluating students' problem-solving and reasoning skills. An analogy would be this: The SAT is to the ACT as thinking is to knowledge.

While the ACT and SAT are both college entrance exams, they are different in scoring and purpose. Most college-bound students do take the ACT or the SAT or both. The scores are not magic numbers. Make the most of the score you have.

 "We cannot choose the things that will happen to us. But we can choose the attitude we will take toward anything that happens. Success or failure depends on your attitude."

–Alfred A. Montapert

CHAPTER 11

Should You Take the PSAT, ACT, SAT, or ASVAB?

What a loaded question! And, for each exam, the answer is both *yes* and *no*. Each test serves a different purpose.

The PSAT

The PSAT is a practice SAT test administered during the sophomore year in high school. It is just that—practice. You can't study for it, so don't sweat bullets over it. The PSAT is similar to the SAT, which is a reasoning test and not a knowledge test. The SAT format is less about what you know and more about how you think. It is a good idea to take the PSAT as an introduction to the SAT, because of the format. These standardized tests can be quite confusing, especially for the right-brain learners!

> **Note** The PSAT can serve as a practice test for the SAT or the ACT.

It does pay to review practice tests and get used to the question-and-answer format. By doing so, you increase your odds of being relaxed and thinking more clearly when you take the "real" test. After all, it can be stressful trying to work in an unfamiliar test format. Keep in mind that if you do quite well on the PSAT you are a contender for National Merit Scholarships. In fact, if you are a strong student and your PSAT scores are high, you might have a very good chance to be named a National Merit Scholar in your junior year. On the other hand, if your academic record is better described as average, the PSAT will be a good trial run for the SAT or ACT.

> **Note** National Merit Scholars emerge from the PSAT.

The ACT

If you live in the Midwest or plan on attending a college in the Midwest, the ACT is probably for you. Plan on taking it twice in your junior year and once more either in the summer just prior to your senior year or in early fall at the start of the year.

> **Note** The ACT is common in the Midwest and South.

If you are strong in math, you may want to take the ACT along with, or instead of, the SAT. On the ACT you will find more math, including math that is considered advanced. If math is your shining star, you may want to give the ACT a try, to see what type of score you can attain.

The ACT II includes a new writing test. It is optional, but some colleges are asking students to take this test. Call the colleges you plan to visit and ask whether they require this. If not, decide for yourself. If writing is a strong area for you, you may want to take the test and show your strength.

The SAT

The SAT may be the test of choice for you if you live along the eastern or western shore of the United States. If you are planning on applying to a college on the East or West Coast, you will want to consider the SAT. Some colleges specifically require the SAT or an SAT II Subject Test. However, most U.S. colleges will accept both the ACT and SAT. Even if a college is predominantly accepting students taking the ACT, it may have conversion charts showing that an SAT of 1100 is probably in the 22 range on the ACT.

If you live in Virginia, you are likely to take the SAT. If you live in Iowa, you will probably take the ACT. If you are a strong student or want to practice the SAT or ACT format, take the PSAT.

Note The SAT is common on the West Coast and East Coast.

For both the ACT and SAT, you will want to register far in advance. Six to eight weeks is not too far ahead. There are penalties for late registration. Note that it usually takes a while for students to get their scores. So, from the time you register until you receive your scores, three months may pass. If you are waiting for those scores to determine which colleges to attend, or if you're waiting to apply to a college, you need to plan for a three-month delay. There is more information on the ACT and SAT in Chapter 10.

Note Taking the ACT or SAT is usually a geographical matter.

ASVAB

If you want to get a general idea of your areas of strength—areas that schools may not test—take the ASVAB.

ASVAB is an acronym for the Armed Services Vocational Aptitude Battery. While some may take this test in the junior year because the military is a career consideration, there are other reasons, as well, for taking the ASVAB:

- It is free. While AP classes, the PSAT, the ACT, and the SAT require registration fees, the ASVAB does not.
- It helps those who are undecided to explore some strength areas. The ASVAB just may help you find a major to pursue in college.

- It may result in your receiving a very expensive education at no cost by joining a branch of the military.

The ASVAB is broken up into eight tests:

- General Science tests the ability to answer questions on a variety of science topics drawn from courses taught in most high schools. Areas are life sciences, earth and space sciences, and physical sciences.

- Arithmetic Reasoning tests the ability to think logically and to solve basic arithmetic problems encountered every day.

- Word Knowledge tests the ability to understand the meaning of words through synonyms.

- Paragraph Comprehension tests the ability to synthesize information from written material.

- Mathematics Knowledge tests the ability to solve problems by applying knowledge of mathematical concepts and applications, including algorithms, number theory, numeration, algebraic operations and equations, geometry, and probability.

- Electronics Information tests understanding of electrical current, circuits, devices, and systems, electrical tools, symbols, devices, and materials.

- Auto and Shop Information tests aptitude for automotive maintenance and repair and wood and metal shop practices.

- Mechanical Comprehension tests comprehension of the principles of mechanical devices and properties of materials, including simple machines, compound machines, mechanical motion, fluid dynamics, properties of materials, and structural support.

 Note The ASVAB is more than a military test.

The Military Careers Connection

The military has 140 career areas and the ASVAB scores will indicate the best choices based on aptitude. The career choices may be reviewed at www.militarycareers.com. The military often has requirements for entering a specific field. The ASVAB scores may be used in addition to grade point average and even ACT scores in making admission decisions. Top career choices require higher scores. The higher-ranked positions are chosen early in the process and high school students should begin inquiring into the military early, as well, if they want to pursue a specific career. Career slots are rationed to a geographical area and, when filled, those careers are closed until the next recruiting season.

Not everyone is able to pursue a military career. If you have been in conflict with law enforcement, you could be disqualified from the military. A speeding ticket is not likely to eliminate you, but an assault charge probably will. In such cases, military recruiters would want to know the details of an incident because there is a wide range of severity within the definition of assault. Defending yourself in a hallway scuffle at school is different from an incident involving a weapon in the park. Decisions are made on a case-to-case basis.

Other factors, such as physical and emotional histories, can lead to disqualification, also. If you have had a recurring knee problem, for example, that may be enough to disqualify you. If you have been on certain types of medication throughout high school, that may also be enough to disqualify you.

The ASVAB Career Exploration Guide

The ASVAB Interest-Finder is not a test with better or worse scores. Instead, Interest-Finder helps students to identify their work-related interests. The results belong to the student alone and make up a profile of the student's likes and dislikes. It takes about 20 or 30 minutes to answer all the questions, but there is no time limit.

Results show that students will fall into one or more of six categories outlined by John R. Holland, Ph.D. See how these six interest groups connect to career clusters for the best job satisfaction. Individuals might take a job outside their interest area, but most will probably be happier if they don't.

- Realistic individuals enjoy working with their hands and using machines, tools, and equipment.

  A Realistic person may choose to become a pilot, mechanic, desktop publisher, engineer or engineering technician, firefighter, conservation worker, woodworker, or dental laboratory technician.

- Investigative individuals enjoy solving problems and creating things and ideas.

  An Investigative person may choose to become a dietitian, forensic science technician, doctor or surgeon, systems analyst, veterinarian, meteorologist, or respiratory therapist.

- Artistic individuals enjoy writing, painting, music, or creative work.

  An Artistic person may choose to become an actor, architect, graphic designer, photographer, radio/TV announcer, writer/author, musician, or reporter.

- Social individuals enjoy interactive skills, working with and helping others.

  A Social person may choose to become a dental assistant, paramedic, nurse, teacher, social worker, physical therapist, or childcare worker.

- Enterprising individuals take leadership roles, speak to groups, and take on many responsibilities.

  An Enterprising person may choose to become a coach, lawyer, paralegal, real estate agent, travel agent, financial manager, private detective, sales representative, or business owner.

- Conventional individuals are organized and are detail-oriented and accurate.

  A Conventional person may choose to become an accountant, court reporter, payroll clerk, pharmacy technician, budget analyst, or construction or building inspector.

ASVAB scores may be confusing. You might not be able to tell if you did well or if your scores are mediocre. You probably have never been tested in electronics or mechanical skills, but the ASVAB is great for showing you your abilities in new areas.

The AFQT

The Armed Forces Qualification Test, or the AFQT, is used for admittance to a branch of the military. Scores rank from 1 to 99. Let's pretend you received an AFQT score of 63. This would qualify you for every branch of the military. Each branch has a different qualifying score:

- Army/National Guard/Marine Corp—31
- Navy—35
- Air Force—36
- Coast Guard—40

Does this mean that you qualify for every career choice within that branch? No. There is additional testing for some specific areas. For example, someone choosing computer programming could expect additional testing. Each branch of the service has a "line score" that must be met to qualify for some specialties. The AFQT score does not include all subtests. It places more emphasis on the academic areas (verbal skills, math skills, paragraph comprehension) and ignores many of the technical areas (mechanical comprehension, electronics information). The percentile is based on a national sample of more than 12,000 scores, male and female.

In Summary

The ASVAB, along with the ASVAB Career Exploration Guide, may be used to help undecided students find their best career option. Your school will probably offer the ASVAB and PSAT. You must take the ACT or SAT at a special center in a controlled environment. Tests are usually prerequisites to getting admitted to college.

 Quote "Do what you can, with what you have, where you are.
—Theodore Roosevelt

CHAPTER 12

How Can You Improve Your Chances of Doing Well on the ACT or SAT?

How can you improve your chances of doing well on the ACT or SAT? To answer this question, we should consider both exams together. This will show the similarities between the two.

Understand the Vocabulary

To perform well on challenging standardized tests, you must know the words used in the questions, right? Many students taking the ACT and SAT know the information addressed in the question. Because they are not sure of vocabulary, though, they are likely to select an incorrect answer. Not understanding just one word can throw the odds against you.

Note Vocabulary is critical in understanding ACT and SAT questions.

So here are some suggestions for improving your vocabulary.

Freerice.com

Memorizing definitions is rather boring. With this in mind, many schools are adding programs to make words easier to remember by incorporating creative definitions and illustrations into their instruction. Recently, a father concerned about his son's performance on the SAT came up with an idea. John Breen wanted to help his son prepare for the exam. He knew that knowing vocabulary words is key to doing well on the standardized college entrance exam. So he programmed more than 10,000 words into a site called www.freerice.com. Then, he also added a twist that would help to feed the world!

Note The site at www.freerice.com helps students learn vocabulary and feed the hungry.

In the center of the Web page is a word with four definition options. If the user clicks on the correct answer, a wooden bowl on the right side of the page fills with 10 grains of rice. This means that a total of 10 grains of rice has now been donated to feed the hungry in the world. It takes 18,000–20,000 grains of rice to feed an adult for one day. More than 65 billion grains of rice have been won for the project.

Who visits the site?

- High school students prepping for ACT and SAT tests
- Fourth grade students studying for spelling bees
- Adults wanting to improve their vocabularies
- Bored office workers during down times

Students may visit the site as many times a week as they wish to practice learning vocabulary words.

Burchers Vocabulary Method

Sam and Bryan Burchers are a father-and-son writing team. When Bryan was preparing for the SAT, it became clear that he was not well acquainted with the common words used on the exam. So his father added funny rhyming words to the definitions. Eventually, this tool became two best-selling books, *Vocabulary Cartoons: SAT Word Power* (2007) and *Vocabulary Cartoons II: SAT Word Power* (2007). *Vocabulary Cartoons* (1998) is for students in grades three through six.

> **Note** Burchers books are successful for teaching new vocabulary.

The vocabulary books use cartoons to appeal to visual-spatial and auditory-sequential learners. These books take the boring memory work out of learning vocabulary. A follow-up study indicates that three months after learning words by this method students demonstrate a 90 percent retention rate.

The majority of students no longer learn by lecture (auditory) methods. Instead, students today are visual and hands-on learners.

Take the Tests More Than Once

Plan on taking the SAT or ACT more than once. Taking the exams only once is the same as accepting the lowest score possible. Most students claim an increase of one to five points the second time. Why is this important?

> **Note** Plan on taking the ACT and SAT at least twice.

Colleges have scholarship ranges based on ACT scores. The difference between a 22 and a 25 could be thousands of dollars. While experts disagree on the need for the ACT and SAT, most colleges still rely on these exams for scholarships. Isn't taking the ACT a second or third time worth $5,000? Some students take the test as many as four times, but research shows that the biggest benefits come from taking it two or three times. In fact, there is little to no reason to take the exams more than three times.

Colleges encourage students to take the ACT more than once with the hope that scores improve. They then calculate the average of all the scores or they use the highest score from all the tests in determining the amount of the scholarship. Colleges want reasons to award funding to you. A decline in enrollment by as few as 12 students could result in the loss of a professor's job at a small college.

Practice with the Question of the Day

Prior to taking the test, students can go to the www.act.org site and find many free tutorials.

The ACT Web site offers these features at no charge:

- Online prep
- Practice test questions
- Test tips
- Test descriptions

The Question of the Day is especially interesting. As e-mails come in daily, one will contain a sample question, which will be the Question of the Day. The user selects an answer and the program instantly scores the response and identifies the correct answer. This program can be useful to you in many ways:

1. You can get used to seeing the testing format.

2. You don't have to read a thick manual of sample questions.

3. You can have instant feedback and you will know the correct answers.

By going through the questions every day for several months, you may find that your stress level is reduced at test time because you have become accustomed to the different style in testing.

 Note Subscribing to the Question of the Day is an easy way to relax and prepare for the tests.

High school tests and quizzes rarely have the type of challenging formatting that the ACT and SAT tests do. After answering a sample question each day for three or four months, the questions become less threatening. Less-threatening questions are less likely to cause test anxiety. If any tests will give students test anxieties, the ACT and SAT will! When thinking of preparation, the Internet seems to be a more palatable format than a heavy manual.

Practice Pacing

Don't get hung up while taking the test. Know how many minutes each test runs. Count the answers. Find the midpoint and stay on pace. A 30-minute test with 30 questions is easy to figure. After 15 minutes, you need to be half of the way through the test. Monitor yourself as you go along to see that you're on track.

Sign Up for Prep Courses

If you are willing to spend a substantial sum of money to have professional help as you prepare for the ACT and SAT exams, you may want to consider Sylvan and Kaplan. These agencies have a history of helping students to increase their performance on the college entrance tests. However, preparing in this way requires a large time commitment. The classes meet several times and students have homework to do between sessions. While in class, students work sample questions after being taught test-taking strategies. They learn about the "tricks" these tests contain. You might say that Kaplan and Sylvan clear the fog and let the sunshine in!

Take Rigorous Classes

Taking challenging classes in high school is the secret of success on these tests. Kaplan and Sylvan can only go so far. If the information was never in your memory bank to begin with, there is nothing to unlock. All the test-taking strategies in the world cannot make up for not taking the right high school classes. Sylvan cannot help a student who has not taken three or four credits each of math and science. ACT has been very vocal about telling students that the best way to prepare for the ACT is to take rigorous classes in high school.

 The best way to prepare for college is to take rigorous classes in high school.

While you may not know the exact questions on the ACT or SAT you are about to take, the suggestions in this chapter will lessen the stress and increase the chances for a good score.

 "If you have made mistakes, there is always another chance. You may have a fresh start any moment you choose, for this thing we call failure is not the falling down, but the staying down."
—Mary Pickford

Are Standardized Tests Fading in Importance?

M any colleges are becoming ACT and SAT optional. What is going on?

The Fair Test Movement

A growing, aggressive movement, headed by an organization called Fair Test, is against the ACT and the SAT. Robert Schaeffer of www.FairTest.org keeps a list of colleges that do not require these tests for admission. The list grows every year. It now has more than 735 schools, which are listed on the Web site by state and by alphabetical order. Of these schools, 30 are identified by *U.S. News and World Report* as being among the top 100 liberal arts colleges in America.

Note The Web site www.FairTest.org lists the colleges that are ACT/SAT optional.

The College Board strongly disagrees with Schaeffer, stating instead that ACT and SAT scores are reliable yardsticks used for predicting success in college. It is easy to understand why the College Board wants students to take the SAT tests. After all, the SAT is part of the College Board business! If students don't take the SAT, the College Board is out of business. But how valuable and accurate is the battery of SAT tests? The SAT is still recovering from a scandal that several years ago gave students incorrect scores on a grand scale. Some students were not admitted to colleges because of incorrect scores, and some were accepted into colleges above their academic level. This partly explains why the rival ACT is gaining in popularity and possibly becoming the major college entrance test.

Note The SAT scoring errors add credence to the Fair Test claims.

Schaeffer admits that the SAT tests do accomplish something. "What it measures is how well you take the SAT," he states.

And he firmly believes that the tests under-predict success for students within the following groups:

- Women
- African-Americans
- ESL students
- Poor test takers
- Right-brain learners

Abandoning the Tests

Bates College of Lewiston, Maine, accepts only 30 percent of its applicants and is considered a very prestigious school. Bates College abandoned requiring SAT and ACT tests in 1984, more than 25 years ago. Since then, it has seen an increase in applicants of 100 percent. The result? There has been absolutely no decline in the academic performance of the students. In fact, the admissions process has become more complicated because the number of applicants has more than doubled. Have the applicants been of high quality? Absolutely. Most of the students who apply to Bates College are in the top 10 percent of their graduating high school classes. The students applying without ACT/SAT scores seem to be just as successful as those who took the tests.

Note Bates College has no regrets over going ACT/SAT optional.

Drew University, a high level 2 college in New Jersey, also has decided to drop the ACT/SAT as a requirement for college admission, adopting the position of ACT/SAT optional. Drew University is in good company. In the fall of 2007, Eckerd College of Florida and Bennington College of Vermont joined the growing list of schools considering the ACT and SAT to be optional.

Drew University has seen applications rise by 19 percent since then. College of the Holy Cross has seen an increase of 41 percent. At Knox College, applications have risen 18 percent, and at Lawrence University of Appleton, Wisconsin, applications have increased by 12 percent.

 Colleges that abandon ACT and SAT requirements see applications increase.

Students who have test anxiety are greatly helped by this new policy among colleges. Many students with high grade point averages find that they do not do well on ACT and SAT tests. They are deprived of significant scholarships because of test anxiety, which is a common problem. When students are allowed to enter a college and prove what they can do, without taking the entrance exam, they perform quite well.

Approximately 30 percent of four-year universities now have the ACT and SAT listed as optional. Of course, this means that 70 percent do require these exams. While the great test takers will continue to hail the benefits of the exams, students who are not good test takers now have choices.

 Approximately 30 percent of colleges do not demand the ACT or SAT.

Applying to private colleges without taking the ACT or SAT would be ideal for the students who don't think the ACT score matches their academic record. Many students feel the tests don't reflect their academic ability accurately. These students would likely benefit the most from applying without the ACT or SAT.

"No great man ever complains of want of opportunity."
–Ralph Waldo Emerson

A few of the colleges on www.FairTest.org as ACT/SAT Optional include

- Pitzer College, Claremont, California
- Holy Apostles College and Seminary, Cromwell, Connecticut
- Saint Ambrose University, Davenport, Iowa
- McPherson College, McPherson, Kansas
- Bowdoin College, Brunswick, Maine
- Gustavus Adolphus College, St. Peter, Minnesota
- Juilliard School, New York, New York
- Sarah Lawrence College, Bronxville, New York
- Texas A & M, Texas

Implications for Right-Brain and Left-Brain Thinkers

Right-brain learners are the creative thinkers that colleges claim they want. Professors say they are tired of students who memorize for the tests, don't discuss in class, and are not creative. Colleges want the "big ideas" kids. Unfortunately, the ACT and SAT tests are left-brain tests that often confuse right-brain students. So right-brain kids don't do as well on the tests, and, as a result, more left-brain students are accepted to colleges. This, in turn, produces a higher population of students who memorize well. It's a Catch 22.

Note Left-brain individuals do better on the ACT and SAT tests.

Why do creative, right-brain students score lower on standardized tests? It's because they are creative! Left-brain students look at the four possible answers, logically eliminate the two that could not be the answer, choose the most logical answer of the two that are left, and move on to the next question. Right-brain students take a different route. They don't go directly from point A to point B. Right-brain students use their creativity to see that, under certain circumstances, each answer could be correct. So they are looking at four possible answers while the left-brain students see only one or two. By the end of the question, right brains are totally confused and more likely to choose the wrong answer even if they know the "correct" answer to the question.

The Right Brain

Right brains are honored in eastern countries. Rights don't like to read directions. Instead, they scan the page and figure out how to do the worksheet. Sometimes they are right, but often they are wrong. They think in visual, kinesthetic, and audio images and don't memorize well. Rights don't like to jump through the hoops to get something done. And they don't like to follow rules that don't make sense to them. They see the big picture quickly. What they are being asked to do in broken-down steps doesn't seem necessary, because the right brains are at the end of the process already. What's the point?

Rights are nonjudgmental and often have no opinion on many topics. They can see both sides of an issue. Rights embrace new ideas because they are future thinkers and enjoy introducing controversy. They believe that everything is possible and often don't see the pitfalls of following a particular path.

Right brains often choose the following careers:

- Entrepreneur
- Athlete
- Sales professional
- Artist
- Musician
- Craftsperson
- Dancer

The Left Brain

Left brains are honored in western cultures. They tend to be analytical, logical, and sequential. They do things in the "proper" order and, in fact, believe there is a proper order. Lefts tend to do well in reading, writing, speech, and math. Lefts naturally evaluate what's wrong and what won't work.

Left brains tend to choose among careers such as these:

- Lawyer
- Accountant
- Scientist

These careers are exacting and have many rules, directions, and regulations. So they are tailor-made for those who are left-brain. Lefts can tend to be skeptical of things that are innovative, such as an invention, a new work schedule, or a new appliance. They resist anything untried. They defend the status quo by saying, "This is how we do it here. Why change things?" or "What's wrong with how we've always done it?" Some call left brains gatekeepers to new ideas, implying that the lefts stand at the proverbial gate ensuring that none of those new ideas get past them. Lefts are not known for thinking out of the box.

It is easy to understand why left-brain people do better on ACT and SAT tests.

Formats

The ACT is more straightforward than the SAT. The SAT has more tricks, you might say. The ACT is written in random order of difficulty. The SAT is written with the easiest questions at the beginning and the most difficult at the end. The ACT does not penalize for guessing but the SAT does. The SAT deducts a small percentage for each wrong answer. The ACT is shorter than the SAT. In fact, the SAT scores declined at the same time that the test was lengthened. Many wonder if students are just simply tired by the end of the test.

Note The ACT tests knowledge. The SAT tests reasoning.

Implications for the Schools

Ned Johnson runs Prep Matters in Washington, D.C. Prep Matters trains students in the art of standardized testing. Johnson thinks that the reason so many colleges still require the ACT or SAT is to help with the blizzard of paperwork in the admissions office. When students have both a grade point average and an ACT score, the process moves more quickly and easily. When the admissions staff have to wade through documentation for classes, recommendations, grades, volunteer work, and projects they get bogged down. While the tests make the process more efficient, however, Johnson says that doesn't improve the quality of the student body at any given college.

Johnson states that the ACT is becoming more popular among his students. The ACT tests more on high school content, is shorter, incorporates fewer tricks, has fewer sections, and doesn't penalize for guessing. And, when you add in several errors in scoring that the SAT has recently experienced, the ACT just seems to be the way to go for many students. Some high schools are also using the ACT as a graduation exit exam.

Who Wins?

Students who just want to be given a chance are the winners. The creative, right-brain students and those with test anxieties are the true winners. The colleges also win. They will receive more creative, right-brain students who may have the big ideas for the future. And the logical and organized left brains will help those ideas become reality.

 Quote "Life is a grindstone; whether it grinds you down or polishes you up depends on what you're made of."

–Jacob M. Braude

CHAPTER 14

What Are Some Test-Taking Strategies?

As you consider taking the SAT or the ACT, you'll see that a few basics apply to both.

Access Practice Tests and Questions of the Day

Don't take the tests cold without some preparation. There are several no-cost ways to desensitize your brain from the testing format. Take advantage of the free practice tests. Both exams offer free questions that are sent to you daily by e-mail. All you have to do is register. One day at a time, you may answer questions and receive instant feedback. Take these practice tests seriously. They will help you to become familiar with the challenging format. Practicing will also help you to relax on the day of the exam. Sign up months in advance, not the night before the real exam!

> **Quote** "If we did all the things we are capable of doing, we would literally astound ourselves."
> –Thomas Alva Edison

Relax!

The brain reaches an unhealthy level of stress under abnormal pressure. Try to be as relaxed and positive about yourself as you can be on the day of the test. The more positive and relaxed you remain, the less you will experience the brain freeze that is all too common!

Imagine this: You're taking a test. It's harder than you anticipated. As you look around, it seems as if everyone else is ahead of you. You tense up and clench your pencil. A few students begin to turn in their tests but you still have pages to go. You start to think that you are not as smart as the others are. How will this affect your grade? What will your parents say if you don't do well? You can't remember things you memorized just last night. Why can't you remember this stuff? You know you studied this but the answer just isn't there. You stew some more, finish the test, and turn it in. The second you get back to your desk, you remember the elusive answers from just five minutes ago. What happened? You relaxed and your brain returned to the non-frozen state. The pressure is now gone and the brain works normally again. The information was there all the time but tension prevented you from accessing it.

What can you do to combat this? Tell yourself, "I know this. It will be difficult but I will do okay. Relax. Everyone is in the same boat." Know that it will be difficult—it is supposed to be. Accept it and go with it.

 "Nothing erases unpleasant thoughts more effectively than conscious concentration on pleasant ones."

–Hans Selye

Sleep and Eat Breakfast

You will be taking the tests all morning. Common sense dictates that you must get enough sleep and eat a healthful breakfast.

You will have a short break mid-morning and it might be wise to take a snack and a drink along with you. Take brain food and not a sugar snack. Note that you will not be able to carry food back into the testing room.

Prepare for the Tests

Be prepared to take four or five tests:

- The English test is 45 minutes long, contains 75 questions, and measures written English and rhetorical skills.
- The math test is 60 minutes long, contains 60 questions, and tests typical math skills for grades 9–11.
- The reading test is 35 minutes long, contains 40 questions, and measures comprehension.
- The science test is 30 minutes long, contains 40 questions, and measures reasoning, problem-solving skills, analysis, and interpretation in natural sciences.
- The optional writing test is 30 minutes long. In this, you are given one topic and you must begin to write with good writing skills. You will get a break and will be given a few minutes to sharpen pencils before taking the writing test.

As you can see, pacing is important. On the English test, for example, after 22 minutes you should be on question 37. On the math test, move right along because you must complete one problem each minute. The reading test will be more difficult to pace because you will have passages to read and you will then be asked to answer questions. (Try this: Read the questions before you read the passage. This may help you focus more while reading.) On the science test, one question needs to be answered every 45 seconds. An announcement will be made when there are only five minutes left on each test.

On the ACT you will not be penalized for guessing, but on the SAT you will suffer a penalty. So keep this in mind when quickly moving from one question to the next.

Skip Questions

As you quickly move from one question to the next, don't get hung up on a tough question or on one you don't completely understand. Mark that tough question and come back to it later. The important thing is to keep moving. When all the easier questions are completed, go back to those that were marked. Now, look at the clock and calculate how much time you have left. Five questions and six minutes left? Great! Only five!

 "It is the ultimate wisdom of the mountains that we are never so much human as when we are striving for what is beyond our grasp, and that there is no battle worth the winning save that against our own ignorance and fear."

–James Ramsey Ullman

When you return to the skipped questions and still have no idea which answer to select, look for absolutes. Do you see the words *always* or *never* in the answers? These are usually used in incorrect answers. If you have only a few seconds left and can't decide, you may want to select the longest answer. Longer answers are correct more often than short answers. Of course, this type of guessing should only be done in the very last minutes when you have no other information to go on. It is better to fill in a circle than leave it blank on the ACT, when there are only seconds left.

Remember: You will not be penalized for incorrect answers on the ACT! You will be penalized for incorrect answers on the SAT!

When the proctor says your time is up, you must stop immediately. If you do not stop, your test will not be scored.

Prepare the Day Before

Because you must be at the testing site before 8 a.m., have all materials ready to go the evening before. Only those students who have arrived prior to 8 will be allowed to take the test.

Have everything you need for the morning of the test in place the evening before.

Be sure to take these things with you on the day of the test:

- **Admission ticket.** This is a document that arrives after you have registered. Place it in an envelope and keep in a safe place. Without this document, you will not be admitted to the testing place. It is evidence that you have registered for a specific date and paid the fee.

- **Form of identification.** This must include your picture. If you don't have a driver's license, you may receive a picture ID. You may also take a picture from a newspaper clipping, as long as your name is listed below the picture.

- **Calculator.** Your calculator must be a permitted type and may be used only during the math test. You may take a backup calculator, you may not share your calculator, and you may not have memory stored in your calculator. The testing staff may ask to check your calculator.

- **#2 pencils.** Take several pencils with good erasers. You will be allowed to sharpen your pencils at break time after the first two tests. By that time you will have answered 135 questions.

Plan on arriving at the testing site 30 minutes early. There may be three people checking in students, with long lines behind each one. Be in line long before 8 a.m. This will give you time to relax and talk positively to yourself. Being rushed is stressful, and too much stress works against you. A little stress is good, as it will help you stay sharp, but being stressed out will decrease your ability to focus.

 "No one can escape stress, but you can learn to cope with it. Practice positive thinking—seize control in small ways."

–Adele Scheele

CHAPTER 15

How Can Parents Help High School Students in the College Preparation Process?

Parents, of course, play a key role in the lives of their children. Providing encouragement in high school and motivation for college are important ways in which parents influence and support their children.

Defeat Procrastination

High school students are very busy and they often think there is plenty of time to begin looking for a college. That is true for a high school freshman but that is not true for a junior! So, while students may not want to look at colleges early, that does not prevent parents from doing research on their behalf.

Parents know that each child has a unique personality, along with interests and abilities that set him or her apart from everyone else. Taking this into account, a parent can begin the process of looking for a college at any time.

> **Note** Start the college search early in the junior year or even in the sophomore year.

Waiting too long before talking about college selection can cause students to miss opportunities for scholarships and grants. Parents often assume that the high school counselor will inform them when action needs to be taken. It's true that the school will inform parents of due dates during the student's senior year. But by the time these dates are announced, massive legwork should have already been done. It's best for students to visit colleges during the junior year. In fact, if there are younger siblings who will graduate in the next few years, it might be helpful for them to go along for the college visits, as well. Getting involved in the process early does no damage!

Be Aware of Scholarship Recruiters

Don't get duped by postcards, ads, or e-mails guaranteeing scholarships for a fee. There is no such thing as a scholarship guarantee. And never pay for scholarships. While it may sound great to pay a person to find all available scholarships, the only result will be less money in the pockets of parents and students. There are credible Web sites that will search for scholarships that match the student. Fastweb.com is a good site for this. If students subscribe to the Web site and fill out the questionnaire, scholarship possibilities will begin coming in the form of e-mails. The students may look them over and see whether they want to apply for a specific scholarship. Many do require essays, but Fastweb boasts of millions of dollars in scholarships.

Note Never pay for scholarships! Scholarships are free!

Consider a College Savings Plan

Parents can save for college in many ways. There are state tuition plans, life insurance plans, savings accounts, and mutual funds. But, for families that are not earning enough money to provide for everyday living expenses, saving is nearly impossible. What then? In some cases, federal aid will assist in sending a child to college. Not only will the federal government provide funding, but state funding is also available along with college grants. All three will be part of an award package. This is all determined by the FAFSA (Free Application for Federal Student Aid) in the senior year. So, if a family thinks there is no way to pay for college, they are probably incorrect.

Kristi was a single parent receiving no child support. Her son wanted to go to a four-year private college. He had an ACT score of 20 and a GPA of 2.8. Kristi was distraught, thinking that she could not fund college for her only child. She also knew that he was not likely to get scholarships. Kristi owned a very small business and was struggling financially. She sought the advice of a college consultant and surprisingly learned that she should not look at price tags of a college. The consultant gave Kristi a list of colleges that were very financially generous in her state and at her son's academic level. Her son applied to a few colleges costing $32,000 per year. In January, Kristi and her son filed the FAFSA. When the results came back, Kristi had an EFC (Expected Family Contribution) of less than $500. Her son's favorite college honored the EFC at 100 percent, with Kristi paying $50 per month on an interest-free plan. Yes, her son had to take out loans like other students attending college, but Kristi paid for her son's education according to her ability to pay. Coincidentally, a state university with half the cost expected Kristi to pay more than $5,000. Her son graduated and went on to graduate school.

Note Federal, state, and college funds help pay for college for the truly needy.

It is sad to hear of parents who do not want to help their children attend college. The financial aid system is set up to reflect the financial responsibility of both the student and the parent. When parents refuse to take on their share, students are faced with negative options. Some students give up and drop out. Others take on $40,000–$50,000 in loans with high interest. Recently, however, private lenders have decided not to offer student loans, and this could make it very difficult for students to borrow privately.

90

Some students work two or three jobs while attending college and consequently earn lower grades to graduate. This is not a major financial hardship if the family has a low annual income and the family contribution is merely $500. But, if the family has substantial income and the family EFC is high, the student could be facing Mission Impossible.

Think About the Personality Factor

Many students are best suited to a specific college setting. Luckily, there are many options for higher education. Parents can help students think through their options and discuss what best suits their personality and situation.

A **junior college** campus is usually small and the least expensive option. However, many junior colleges have no dorms, and students are forced to live off campus. Research shows that students are more successful in college and more likely to graduate if they live in a dorm on campus. Junior colleges typically have very low graduation rates. Because they have open enrollment, students are automatically accepted if they apply, in spite of perhaps not being successful in high school. Many junior colleges have graduation rates of 35 percent. On the plus side, they are a great place save money, get a vocational education, and get a second chance in education. Of course, junior colleges are just one option.

 Note Colleges and students have personalities. The trick is to match them for success.

State universities are a fabulous choice for students seeking a wide variety of opportunities. State universities may have a student population of more than 30,000, large dorms, graduate students, professors on sabbatical, and teacher assistants conducting classes. You name it, and a large university probably has it. For students interested in engineering or veterinary science, this may be the only choice. Large universities have graduation rates in the 40–50 percent range.

Private colleges are a third option. With graduation rates in the 60–65 percent range on average, they offer a smaller atmosphere with dorms. Students attending a small private college are more likely to graduate and are more likely to get tutoring and personal attention than are students at a large university. However, small colleges have limited offerings. It does take research to find the right college with the right majors offered.

Private colleges are also most likely to offer generous financial aid. Not all private colleges are in a position to do so, but many are. It is common for students to attend an expensive private college for less out-of-pocket expense than a large university with half the tuition and dorm costs.

Of course, colleges are located among many different settings. A private college may be located anywhere: in a rural area, in a town with a population of 600 people, or in a city of 300,000. A large state university may have twice the students on campus than the total population of the town in which it's located. A junior college with 3,000 students may be set in a city of 500,000 people or in a town of 15,000. There are many opportunities to match the student with the right college.

If students find that they didn't make the right choice, often they transfer to another college.

> Jamal was a pre-med student from a small town and was attending a large university. He was struggling with one science class and had a professor who was noted for not being available to help students outside of class. Because the class was regarded as vital for someone entering the medical field, Jamal considered dropping out of college. Instead, he dropped the class. His parents encouraged him to attend a smaller college closer to home, and this is what he did. He had to take the same class at the new college and was dreading it. But to his surprise, the professor was friendly and eager to help him. With very little assistance, Jamal passed the class with flying colors and went on to medical school. He is a successful, practicing physician today. The encouragement of his parents to try getting an education somewhere else is responsible for Jamal's success today.

Consider Several Colleges

Parents should try to steer their teenager to four, five, or six colleges. Isn't this a waste of money? No. While it may seem more cost effective to focus on only one or two colleges, this can be a financial disaster, because you may pay much more than necessary. What if the top choice necessitates very high loans with no scholarships or grants? Now what? April or May of the senior year is very late to start looking for another college. Apply to several colleges and have a pool of offers to choose from. Sure, you can have favorites at the top of the list, but what if the top-choice college expects you to pay $15,000 and the second-choice college would expect only $4,000? That makes the $25 application fee and campus visit worth it, doesn't it? Keep all options open until you know the final offers.

 Note To tip the odds in your favor financially, apply to four to six colleges.

Keep in mind that taking the ACT or SAT once is not enough unless a student gets a perfect score the first time. Most students take the tests two or three times for best results. A raised score may mean $5,000 in scholarships. Just raising the score a little may be enough to put a student into a higher bracket and qualify for more funding. Take the tests at least twice and even three times.

 Note Help your student plan to take the ACT or SAT two or three times for the best results.

Be Optimistic

Colleges have different academic levels, and so do students. Students are most likely to be successful if matched with a college at the same academic level. While attending an Ivy League school may carry great prestige, success may not be possible for those students who are not among the top 50 percent in terms of academics. It is not wise to encourage a student to attend a college beyond his or her academic potential. Students should attend schools at which they can be successful. Chapter 22 explains this point in detail.

Going to college is scary. No matter how much a teenager wants to leave home and how much the parents want him or her to leave, the prospect of going out into the world alone is stressful. Many students suffer from homesickness the first semester. Teenagers may show anxiety by having second thoughts about attending college at all. Some may start arguments about college or blame parents for making them go. Others may just refuse to go as the deadline nears. These are signs of stress. Encourage and support. If college is just too much after the first year, there is a Plan B. Chances are very good that a student will make the transition successfully to college after a few months.

Quote "Be like a postage stamp—stick to one thing till you get there."
–Josh Billings

Students sometimes think that by refusing to go to college, life will not change for them. They want things to stay the same.

However, once friends all leave for college and things are not the same, these students often go on to college, after all. Keep options open for that last-minute decision to attend.

 Leaving home and going to college are both very stressful—be patient.

Freshmen return from college for the first time and find that their friends are not home. They feel like they have landed on another planet. They wanted to return to the past and have high school friends around them. Sadly, they learn that you can never come home again. Things are not the same after graduation, and they never will be. Encourage a student by saying that the best is yet to be. Don't minimize the situation by saying it's not a big deal. It is a big deal. Life has now changed forever.

 "Victory is won not in miles but in inches. Win a little now, hold your ground, and later, win a little more."

–Louis L'Amour

Starting the Search for the
Best College for You

CHAPTER 16

Who Can Be Successful in College?

M ost students fear not doing well in college. This is probably never truer than after they take the ACT or SAT exam. ACT tests are overwhelming for many students who leave the testing site feeling extremely unsuccessful. However, most of these students are pleasantly surprised to find that they fared better than they initially thought. The average ACT score, nationwide, is in the 20–21 range. Students should plan on taking the ACT twice during the junior year or during the summer before the senior year. Why? Scores quite often rise by a few points the second time. Because colleges often take the highest scores, or an average of all scores, it is worth taking the test more than once.

All colleges are not for all students. The decision about where to attend is important, and you should take as much time as necessary to make the right choice. In fact, some students may want some time off from studying before making their selection.

After-high-school options can be divided into four groups:

- Entering the world of work
- Joining the military
- Attending a community college/vocational school
- Going to a four-year college

Entering the World of Work

Some students are not cut out for postsecondary education at this time in their lives. For various reasons, they don't want to stay in school one second more than necessary. These students enter the world of work and hope to find their niche in a mall or a factory. Many of these students decide to enter college later as nontraditional students when they are more focused on what they want to do in life. In many cases, no one has seriously encouraged these students to find what they enjoy doing.

Have you given this plenty of thought? Where are your talents and abilities? What would you like to be doing in 10 years? High school counselors frequently are overwhelmed with a massive workload and just so many hours in a day. Their time is often spent with the students who do know what they want to do. Those are the students at the counselor's door. The unfocused students are the casualties of an overloaded system.

Joining the Military

For many students, the military is a calling more than a mere career choice. A job in the military can be very risky, but there are some definite educational benefits. If you explore this option, you will find that college benefits differ from one branch of the military to another, and some are far more generous than others.

Before you decide, check out the benefits associated with each branch:

- Army at www.goarmy.com
- Marines at www.marines.com
- Air Force at www.airforce.com
- Navy at www.navy.com
- National Guard at www.nationalguardbenefits.com

When you enlist, you will probably check off a payroll deduction option for the GI Bill. Then, when you leave military service, the GI Bill will pay for your college expenses. At the age of 24, you will have military experience, and you will be more likely than before to know what you want to do in life.

> **Note** The education benefits are different for each branch of the military.

The military academies are an entirely different program. In this book, academies are covered in Chapter 47.

Attending Community College

While many two-year colleges are junior colleges, they are at the same time vocational colleges. Vocational colleges offer hands-on career training for students who can't wait to get out the door to do something relevant as soon as the bell rings in high school. These students typically enjoy building things and fixing things. School is often painful for them, because it requires sitting still, reading, reading, more reading, and not using tools. While these students would not be able to find a major that would interest them at a four-year college, they can quickly find such a major at a vocational college.

Nationally, a vocation worker shortage crisis is quickly developing. As technical workers retire, few are trained to replace them. And, because these workers are vital for operating businesses, the situation is getting more serious each year. Of course, when there is a shortage of anything, the price goes up. Salaries for vocational workers are going up each year.

> **Note** Vocational college careers are on the cutting edge.

Consider the field of welding. You may have a mental picture of someone wearing a welding helmet and leather apron, with sparks flying, and making $10 an hour. This picture is changing. In 2008, the average age of a welder was 54. You can imagine that he or she will be thinking of retiring soon. By the year 2010, the United States will have a shortage of 200,000 welders. As salaries go up, in some places welders now make $100,000 per year. The American Welding Society is encouraging high school students to enter the field of welding. Information is available at www.aws.org.

Other fields that are great two-year options are opening as well. Wind energy is increasing every year, and technicians are needed for maintenance of the turbines. Alternative fuel is another field that is growing quickly. Ethanol and soybean alternative fuel production plants run 24 hours a day, needing many shifts of technicians to keep everything running smoothly. Manufacturing technology cannot find enough certified workers to fill job openings. Starting salaries for these positions are higher than many salaries for jobs requiring four-year degrees.

One- and two-year technology programs represent the wave of the future, and many students who are hands-on learners should seriously look into this education option. Those who do will see that finding jobs will not be a concern.

Community colleges also offer a liberal arts program. Instead of attending a four-year college immediately after high school, you might consider attending a community college and saving money. If the community college is in your hometown or within easy driving distance, you may choose to live at home and attend classes. This represents, perhaps, an easier transition than moving hours away from home.

However, there is a down side to attending a junior college the first two years:

- You don't get the true campus experience by commuting to a junior college. If you return home each evening, you don't get in on all the socializing in the dorms after classes.

- If you live at home, chances are good that Mom still cooks her great pot roasts and does your laundry for you. You haven't really left home and learned to do things for yourself.

- You may have trouble transferring your classes to all four-year universities. Know where you plan to attend after your first two years and get acceptance from your future college—in writing—for all your junior college classes.

- Junior colleges are often not at the same level of rigor as four-year colleges are. Adjusting to new professors and more-demanding standards are things to plan on as you transfer in your junior year.

Attending a Four-Year College

Four-year colleges represent a tradition that is here to stay. We will need teachers, lawyers, doctors, and accountants on into the future. But the college choices are so many. How do you know which school is for you?

Colleges are divided into five tiers of academic standards:

- **Level 5.** The lowest academic level among colleges is level 5. Most level 5 colleges are community colleges or junior colleges. They have open enrollment. If you have a diploma or a GED, you will be accepted.

- **Level 4.** Level 4 institutions may be private or public. The lowest ACT scores to be accepted at this level are in the 17–18 range. Many, though, prefer to see a minimum of 19.

- **Level 3.** The typical college is a level 3. Most students that receive a 20–25 ACT score are successful here. Overall, this is a very large category among colleges.

- **Level 2.** This level is considered very selective. The competition gets tougher for admission, and these schools like to see ACT scores in the 24–25 range and higher.

- **Level 1.** Colleges at this level are considered Ivy League and most selective. Some accept only 10 percent of the students who apply. ACT levels are 28–36 at these colleges. Level 1 schools have lists of students wanting to attend.

There is a spot for most students who wish to attend a four-year school and be successful. If you are a top student, there are top colleges for you. If you are an average student, there are colleges for you. If you are a struggling student, there are fewer colleges available, but they are there. Chapter 22 explains these five levels in more detail.

CHAPTER 17

What Are Colleges Looking for in a Student?

Colleges are looking for many things in the students they accept. They are looking for something a little different in the students to whom they will offer large scholarships and grants. And just to make it a little more confusing, colleges may be looking for different qualities each year.

Any student who meets the college minimum requirement will probably be accepted. However, most students want more than merely being accepted. They want good financial aid along with scholarships and grants. You probably want these things as well. How can you make it happen?

Scholastic Achievement

How well you do in high school matters to a college. Yes, grades do matter. And, for many colleges, the ACT or SAT scores really matter. Grades are very important. But they are not the only thing colleges are looking for. Colleges are also looking for character; a history of volunteerism; and athletic, musical, and theatrical achievement. Keep in mind that you have only four years of high school to show a college who you are and what you can do!

Having said that, you do not have to excel in all areas to be considered a strong candidate for a selective college. However, the more well-rounded you are, the more interesting you will look to a college. The more interesting you look, the more likely you are to be admitted. And you are also more likely to receive scholarships and grants.

Students in the top 10 percent of their high school class are certainly going to gain the attention of a college. But what about students in the top 30 percent? They are also in the winner's circle with colleges. Colleges need to fill the seats in their classrooms. A decline of as few as 15 students in enrollment at a small college could jeopardize a professor's job. So colleges are becoming very aggressive in recruiting students.

Acceptance is one thing, but getting great financial aid is another. To increase your odds of receiving a great financial aid package, plan on being diversified.

 Note Good grades are wonderful, but to look interesting to a college, go above that.

Athletic Achievement

Many athletes who do quite well in high school see themselves as recruiter magnets. Unfortunately, very few high school athletes become great college stars. While someone may be a good athlete in a small school playing against other small schools, competition is much tougher at the college level. Starters in high school often keep the bench warm in college.

Academics are an important factor when it comes to playing time in college. While you may have squeaked by in high school and remained eligible to play, college is usually more challenging. And, if you are planning to attend one of the more selective schools, you may find the academics very challenging. Colleges differ greatly in academic expectations. For example, while College A may be offering a great athletic scholarship, College B is at your academic level and you would really be better off there. Ultimately, you would probably see more playing time because you are more likely to be successful academically.

Consider Justin, who was a basketball star in a small high school. He was quick, a fabulous shooter, and 6' 7". Because of his height, Justin didn't experience many of the challenges his shorter teammates did. He signed on with a level 2 college that was known for high academic standards. Justin didn't give academics a thought, not realizing that colleges vary in expectations. In high school, teachers understood that he was important to the team and gave him extra time and assistance to ensure that he passed all his classes.

Justin realized quickly that everyone on his college team was his height. It became much tougher to handle the ball and shoot with someone guarding him who was 6'8" instead of 5'11". He was no longer the star, but just another member of the basketball team. In addition to that disappointment, his classes were much tougher than any he had taken in high school. He discovered quickly that his high school teachers were right when they tried to encourage him to take higher-level classes. And his professors didn't seem to care that he was on the basketball team. His assignments were due the same day as those from the rest of the class. Because Justin turned in some assignments late, and because the academic rigor was much greater than he expected, Justin began to fail several of his classes.

With his low grade point average, Justin found himself on probation for the second semester and in danger of losing his generous scholarship. While he did do a little better the second semester, his grades did not recover enough for him to keep the scholarship. Without that, he couldn't afford to attend the school because his parents' income level was not high.

To add to the problem, Justin's parents learned that his social life had become a top priority. Justin was rarely in his room studying when they called. In fact, they spoke more often to Justin's roommate than to Justin. They took action.

Justin's parents did some research and found a level 4 college with a strict code of behavior. Students there jokingly referred to the dorms as "the barracks." This college monitored grades, restricted social networking, required students to participate in mandatory study times in the evening and, overall, demanded adherence to a clearly defined high code of behavior. As much as he disliked it, this was exactly what Justin needed. Three years later, he graduated from the level 4 college with a solid grade point average. He played basketball all three years and felt successful. Justin's first experience was not a positive one, because the college was not at his academic level.

Being a good athlete in high school may not be enough in college.

Musical Achievement

If a college wants to improve its music program, it must recruit top musicians. If you have applied to this college as a musician, you may have lucked out. This college has a goal to focus on good musical talent. You may not have known that when you applied. Colleges don't put out ads for what they are looking for. They take a look at applicants, review the resumes, and pursue candidates who will help them to reach their goals. This is why you will want to apply to many schools. You won't know exactly what each school is looking for.

 Apply to several schools because you don't know what they are searching for.

Theatrical Achievement

A very overlooked talent is theater. Colleges have frequent musicals, dramas, and other events needing students that excel in drama. One college may react in a ho-hum manner to your talents in theater, but another college with a strong drama program may have been hoping that someone just like you would come along. And they may be willing to pay for your participation by way of scholarships.

McKinley was a bright student who believed his good looks, quick wit, and genetic ability would coast him through high school. His grade point average was—well—average. But his ACT score was a 32, which did not match his grade point average at all. His high school counselor was very frustrated with the young man and suggested he not even attend a four-year college. The counselor added that McKinley's interest in theater was a waste of time. He suggested a local junior college and the selection of a major other

(continued)

(continued)

than theater. McKinley was devastated. Theater was all he wanted to pursue.

After doing some research and consulting with others in the counseling field, McKinley and his parents began visiting suggested colleges. Lo and behold, a more selective four-year college took great interest in McKinley. Admissions counselors looked at his 32 ACT, determined he was probably bored in school, and decided to take a risk. They asked McKinley to audition for a drama scholarship. He did so and won. How much? He received $20,000 each year for four years. He received $80,000 in a major he was told was a waste of time. McKinley now had a new enthusiasm for education. This event changed his life.

 Note Remember to include theater among your extracurricular activities.

Leadership

What if a college is satisfied with its academics and sports, but campus life is listless? It looks at students who have leadership capabilities. This college will be carefully reading letters of recommendation, looking for words such as "self-starter," "motivator," "began the school newspaper," and so on. This college is looking for starters and not just joiners. If you are such a student and you apply, the college will be in hot pursuit. It needs someone to breathe life into campus activities and improve the spirit.

Colleges don't want their students going home every weekend because there is nothing to do on campus. They want student government or organizations to plan exciting and unique activities so students grow closer together. If students feel that they belong on a campus and have friends there, they are less likely to transfer to another college. Retention rates are something prospective students and parents review. Do you want to attend a college where 30 percent of the freshmen return or where 65 percent return? Exactly.

Character

Character is likely to be a deciding factor for scholarships. Doing the right thing, having honor, and going above and beyond are rated highly by scholarship committees. If you look at the college pamphlets that arrive by the truckload, you will see the words "leadership" and "character" mentioned often. If that is the main focus of the college, you want to meet those criteria.

Volunteerism

While few of us are truly altruistic, doing things for others without expecting payment in return is viewed with much respect in our society. Volunteerism ranks high on the list of what colleges want, too. You don't have to be the head of everything at your high school or plan that rebuilding trip to New Orleans three years in a row. You may quietly do many things. Being an altar boy in church for nine years speaks quietly but firmly about your character and dedication. Singing in the church choir since seventh grade commands respect. Coaching Little League for five years shows that you don't mind taking on a large project.

All these activities help to create a picture of you as an applicant. This is what colleges are looking for. Your goal is to have several activities listed on a balanced resume prior to applying. If you are a good athlete, try to mix in some speech or music with that. If you are musician, mix in some drama or cheerleading. Blend in some volunteerism, and you have a winning ticket.

A group of local counselors was visiting between workshop sessions. One counselor from a public school was complaining that the Catholic school across town always walked away with the top scholarships. Another asked why. The response was "The Confirmation program at their school demands community, church, and family volunteer projects. By the time those kids turn in their resumes, no one from another school can hold a candle to them." If two students are nearly identical but one has massive community service and the other has none, to whom would you give the scholarship? Try to blend athletics, the arts, and volunteerism for a balanced portfolio.

CHAPTER 18

What Are the Best College Choices for You?

O ne reason students hesitate to look at colleges is that they just don't know where to start. There are so many colleges! An aunt went here, an uncle went there, Dad was in the Marines, and Mom didn't go to college at all. My best friend is going here and wants me to go with her.

Family Expectations

Students pick up on family expectations. Some will pick a college to make their family happy instead of choosing what they really want—that is, if they know what they want. On the other hand, some students know where they want to go to college even before they begin elementary school.

Brenda and Jim were born into an Irish family and, since learning to walk as toddlers, they have watched every Notre Dame football game on television. During summers, the family traveled through three states to see at least one live Notre Dame game per season. That was no surprise, because Dad was a Notre Dame graduate and so were many of his siblings. It was a tradition for members of this family to graduate from Notre Dame. It doesn't take a rocket scientist to figure out where Brenda and Jim would probably want to go to college. Of course, not just anyone gets into Notre Dame. More than 90 percent of Notre Dame students are Catholic, and the college is very proud of its Catholic traditions. The academic standards at Notre Dame are very high, as well. Being a football fan and an above-average student are not enough to be admitted.

Brenda had hopes of attending a top-level college. Her ACT of 32 did help matters. She was on the wait list for Harvard, and she was accepted by Notre Dame. Two years later, here comes Jim. Jim also had an ACT of 32, but that was in the ninth grade. His score increased by several points when he took the test as a junior in high school. Harvard and Yale would have probably accepted Jim, but his dream was to attend Notre Dame. He will be a math major at Notre Dame this coming fall. The family tradition continues.

In cases like this, the students have the desire and the ability to attend a college that is part of a tradition within the family. Both Brenda and Jim applied to several colleges to play it safe but selected Notre Dame in the end.

For most students, it's not so clear where they should consider going. Many are not sure where to even begin looking.

Note Think about what you want in a college before you start looking.

Distance from Home

Do you want to see other parts of the country? The college years are a great time to explore different places. A Minnesota student may want to experience Los Angeles. A Los Angeles student may want to experience New York City. A New York City student may want to experience a small rural college surrounded by cornfields, where residents can walk safely any time of the day. While going to college may seem like getting out into that big world, you might find college life to be very sheltered. In fact, housing, meals, and utilities may be taken care of by the college. You might feel like you are on your own, but you may really be in a semi-state of independence. You will have left home, but not completely. Your parents may still be picking up the tab for many expenses. You might think you will be coming home often, but it is never really home again once your friends leave. Your new friends will be at college, and you will be at home less and less. Don't let distance keep you from attending the college of your dreams.

> **Note** Think past your backyard.

Your Major

One of the toughest things to decide on is a major. What do you want to study? What do you enjoy in school? What is your area of strength? While you might not know your major, you are probably leaning toward a career cluster that is of some interest to you. This is a place to start. Every college does not offer every major you might want. It is nice to narrow the choices down a bit so you have a general idea of where to begin looking to make sure this is a strong major at your college.

Some popular majors are

- Math
- Science
- Literature
- Computers
- Teaching
- Nursing
- Business

Colleges list majors in two different ways. A college will list all majors and minors offered. But the college guides will usually list the most popular majors in addition to all the other majors. This is something to notice. If business is a very popular major on a campus, chances are quite good that this is one of the stronger programs at that college. Strong programs attract students.

> **Quote** "First, say to yourself what you would be; and then do what you have to do."
>
> –Epictetus

There is a small college in central Kansas called McPherson College. It is located in the town of McPherson, which has a population of 15,000. The campus has approximately 550 students. It is pretty easy to not notice this college sitting in the middle of wheat country. But, when you look at the most popular majors on campus, one jumps out—auto restoration. Hmmm, that's a bit unusual, so you investigate further. The major with the most students is the car restoration program and it is the only four-year restoration program in the United States. Students fly in from all over the country to participate in this unique program. The largest building on campus is Templeton Hall, where the students learn to restore everything on a car. Jay Leno is the unofficial godfather for the college and offers scholarships and internships to students in the car restoration program. This is an example of the types of surprises you may find when you begin looking for the most popular majors on a campus.

College Size

Initially, many students think they want the large university experience. When they visit campus, it is exciting to see so many students and majestic buildings. A large university is likely to offer any major a student could want. The stadium hosts football games and major music groups. It all sounds good. Then, practicality kicks in. You have to catch a transit bus to get to your next class? It takes 20 minutes to cross campus? You have a 19-year-old teacher assistant teaching your math class? For many students, these are non-issues. But, for others, they are very important. Some students who visit a large campus become overwhelmed and ask to go home before the tour is over. They decide the small college is for them.

On a small campus, it might be possible to walk from one end to the other in 5 minutes. This may be too small for some students. Professors may be very friendly and helpful, but at the same time, there might be few instructors in a particular major field. Smaller colleges offer fewer choices for majors. A student who changes his or her major might have to transfer to another college. There are positives and negatives to both large and small campuses.

> **Note** Colleges come in various sizes and in different settings.

The size of the town or city in which a college is located may be a factor in deciding where to attend. Some colleges are set outside of towns in quiet, rural settings. For example, beautiful mountains surround Sweet Briar, an all-girls college in Virginia. Grinnell College sits outside of Grinnell, Iowa, on 120 acres of prairie grasses and flowers. St. John College and St. Benedict College are located in former monasteries in Minnesota. Bates College sits outside of Lewiston, Maine.

Centre College is located in Danville, Kentucky, population 15,000. The town offers safety yet all the essentials. Randolph College, the former Randolph-Macon Woman's College, sits in the foothills of the Blue Ridge Mountains, in the city of Lynchburg, Virginia, population 65,000. The University of Dallas is a private college located in Dallas, Texas, population more than 1,300,000. Oglethorpe University, a small private college, sits in the center of Atlanta, Georgia, with a population of more than 5 million.

Colleges are located in various-size communities, and there is something for everyone.

Teacher-to-Student Ratios

Another thing to consider is the ratio of teachers to students. Do you prefer small classes with 10–20 students or an auditorium setting with 250 students? Some colleges have 1 professor to 25 students. Other colleges have a professor for every 7 students.

The ratio of males to females is another factor. Today, campuses are female-dominated. Most colleges will have a 53–60 percent campus with males in the minority.

Most college campuses have more females than males.

Adventure!

This is a good time to explore other parts of the United States. A college campus is a nurturing environment, and this is an opportunity to visit new places and yet be in a cocoon of relative safety. Many colleges have students attending from all 50 states.

Erin grew up on a farm in Iowa. Most of her life experiences were local. As a result of her parents urging her to experience something new, she attended a small college in Virginia. Not only was the beautiful scenery of Virginia a change from the corn fields of Iowa, but Erin enjoyed weekends in Washington, D.C., and Savannah, Georgia, with her roommate as well. She had the opportunity to sing with the choir and perform at Harvard. Traveling with the volleyball team opened more of Virginia and the surrounding states to her. Erin learned so much about different customs and traditions. College can be the experience of a lifetime.

Custom fit your college to your needs and wants. College choices are plentiful.

 "Where there is an open mind, there will always be a frontier."
–Charles Kettering

How Do You Begin Selecting a College?

The best college for Mary may not be the best choice for Joe. There is no magical college for the masses. It is an individual choice—a personal fitting. When adults go shopping for a house, they often say, "This one just felt right for us." The same thing is true of students shopping for a college. That is why you must visit colleges and experience the atmosphere on campus. Students have personalities, and colleges have personalities, too. The challenge is to find the right college for you. Luckily, there are many colleges from which to choose.

> **Note** Selecting the right college is a two-year journey.

Consider Outside Pressures

When you get serious and begin looking for the perfect college, many people will enter the picture. All will mean well, but it will be confusing. Your parents may have a dream college all picked out for you. Your high school guidance counselor may have some suggestions. Friends may think you should go to College ABC because several students went there in the past. Teachers may suggest their alma mater. Your grandparents went to College BCD, and they want to help you financially. Friends may pressure you to go to the college they selected. What is the best choice?

Note Select the college that is right for you and not the one your friends are attending.

Andre has loved cars ever since he was a small boy. His eyes would light up just seeing a classic car going down the street. He was a natural with tools and fixed anything for anyone in the neighborhood. He knew he would want to get a job related to automobiles someday. He visited many colleges and liked them. However, he couldn't decide on what he would study there. Nothing interested him when he read the offerings. He thought about becoming a mechanic but that just didn't feel right. One day he hit the jackpot. He found a four-year college in car restoration! When he visited the campus, he didn't want to go back home. He applied and was accepted, and his world was good.

Then, friends began to pressure him to go to a local college with them. These were Andre's closest friends, and they meant well. He began having concerns about traveling such a distance and began giving in to the peer pressure. He visited the local college, enrolled, and struggled when he had to decide on a major. First, he selected one thing, then another, then a third. He settled for something that was rather boring compared to car restoration, but he felt pressure to select something.

The closer fall came, the more Andre became unsettled. He was having many second thoughts about the local college, but he had some anxiety about going to college eight hours away. Finally, he decided to go back to his original college choice. His biggest concern was no longer the distance but telling his friends he was not going to college with them. This kind of pressure is not unusual. Students often make poor decisions based on outside pressures.

Jessica was in love, and her boyfriend was going to a local college. Believing that love in high school lasts forever, Jessica followed her boyfriend without any thought about whether the college matched her interests. He was going so she was going. Within two months at college, the boyfriend found someone else and broke up with Jessica. There she was, at a small college and having to watch her boyfriend with someone else every day. She had expected an engagement ring at Christmas. Instead, she would be alone for the holidays. It got to be so painful for Jessica that she came home for Christmas and never went back. Jessica

(continued)

(continued)

now began her college search for the right reasons and returned the following fall to a new college. She lost a semester but found a new direction in life.

Weigh Academic Performance

The process begins with your academic performance. What is your academic level? Are you at the top, middle, or bottom of your class? Do you know your grade point average? Is it a 4.0, 3.5, or 2.6?

High schools have different grading scales, so it is confusing to match yourself to a college based on grade point average. Some schools consider 90–100 percent to be an A. Other schools regard 93–100 percent as an A. One school may have a 4.0 as the highest possible average, but other schools may have 4.25 or even higher. You may want to use your ACT score as a better gauge.

Note Know your ACT or SAT score and decide on an interest area.

Don't bother getting too serious about your college search until you take your ACT or SAT. Your scores will show how you compare to other students attending each college. The typical Harvard student has an ACT of 34. The typical student at Arizona State has an ACT of 23 or 24. Did your ACT score fall in the 30s, 20s, or teens? Once you know your ACT or SAT range, you have a good start.

Select an Area of Interest

You still don't have enough information to begin visiting colleges. You need to have an interest area. Why? Not every college offers every major. Let's pretend you want to become a teacher. Not every college has an education department. What if you are thinking about engineering? Very few colleges offer engineering. Nursing? Few colleges offer a nursing major. Music?

116

You want to find a strong music program, not just any music program. Getting the picture? At least have a general idea of what you may want to pursue. Once you pick an interest area, you have enough to begin.

Selecting a major field is something few students have under control. Students who come from small schools in small towns have not been exposed to the endless list of opportunities at a large university. Many opportunities available to students on a college campus are totally unknown to students who are still in high school. After taking some different classes, students may explore a career in a new discipline. Elective classes often open doors to new ideas that students didn't know even existed. And college advisors can lead students to opportunities that could be right for them. Colleges also lead students to job opportunities through internships. Many students who had selected majors before entering college decide to change their majors while typically staying within the same career cluster.

Note Many students change their majors after being exposed to new opportunities.

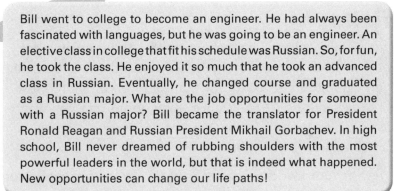

Bill went to college to become an engineer. He had always been fascinated with languages, but he was going to be an engineer. An elective class in college that fit his schedule was Russian. So, for fun, he took the class. He enjoyed it so much that he took an advanced class in Russian. Eventually, he changed course and graduated as a Russian major. What are the job opportunities for someone with a Russian major? Bill became the translator for President Ronald Reagan and Russian President Mikhail Gorbachev. In high school, Bill never dreamed of rubbing shoulders with the most powerful leaders in the world, but that is indeed what happened. New opportunities can change our life paths!

Study College Guides

Find a college guide that has all the colleges arranged by state. Your state may have 25 colleges. Look at the average ACT or SAT scores and see where you fit in. Where should you fall? In the middle or higher.

For each college that falls within your range and has your interest area, jot down the following:

- Average ACT or SAT range (for example, 21–24)
- Most popular majors
- Size of the college (for example, 1,400 students)
- Ratio of professors to students
- Size of the city
- Web site address

Determine Your Strategy

You may have a list of 20 colleges. Start visiting the colleges by researching on the Internet. Read about the college, look at a campus map, check out the social activities, consider the location, and so on. You may want to read about your top colleges in the *Fiske's Guide* or *Princeton Review*. Narrow your list to the top 10 and rank them in order of preference.

Note College guides can help you learn about colleges before visiting.

Visits

Start visiting colleges in your junior year and keeping great notes on what you saw on the visit. How did it feel to be there? Some campuses are "cold" and some are very friendly. How are the students dressed? Have a list of questions that you want answered, and ask the same questions at every college to see how they compare.

A few of your favorite colleges may also be the top choices of some of your friends. What a great coincidence! While it might be tempting to just go where your friends are going, put yourself first and stick to the college that is best for you.

Quote "With time and patience the mulberry leaf becomes a silk gown."
–Chinese proverb

What Are the Differences Among Junior Colleges, State Universities, and Private Colleges?

Junior colleges, state universities, and private colleges are all accredited institutions, but there are differences among them that make each unique. They are all quite different in what they offer to students. You could say they are the same, only different!

Junior Colleges

Junior college offerings fall into two categories: vocational track and associate track.

> **Note** Junior colleges offer a vocational and an associate track.

The vocational route, recently renamed "applied sciences," is for the student who wants to learn a trade and be out in the work force quickly. Many of these degrees are hands-on and require kinesthetic abilities:

- Auto mechanics
- Auto body
- Plumbing
- Wind farm technology
- Computer graphics

- Heating and cooling technology
- Electrical technology
- Manufacturing technology
- Carpentry
- Nursing

These degrees may be achieved in two years or less, so students can be earning salaries by the time they are 20 years old. Many of the newest and hottest jobs involve training in applied science majors. These careers are approaching a crisis, with the average age of many workers now at 55. Applied science students not only graduate in two years but have jobs waiting for them as well. In fact, many have job offers after the first year of college, with employers paying their tuition.

Note Applied science careers are hot right now.

The associate route is for students who want to attend a four-year college but prefer to attend a junior college first. They attend a junior college for two years, studying the basics, and then transfer.

Students prefer to do this for many reasons:

- Junior college may save a student's family substantial money. Junior colleges are significantly less costly than four-year public universities and private colleges. (However, many private colleges give better financial aid packages than large state universities.)
- Junior colleges have many convenient locations and students often may live at home, saving even more money.
- Junior colleges have open enrollment, which allows everyone with a high school diploma or GED to be admitted. They do not require AP (advanced placement) classes, specific ACT scores, letters of recommendation, or high academic achievement. For students who decide late in high school to get serious about their education, junior colleges may be the second chance they need to prove themselves.

- For students who have achieved high academic success in high school, the junior college may be a source of incredible financial aid—again, a great savings for students and their families.
- Junior colleges are usually small. For students who are intimidated by a large university campus, the junior college offers a less-threatening environment for the first two years.

Students selecting the AA (Associate of Arts) route prior to a four-year college need to be careful, however. Before selecting a junior college, talk to the four-year college you plan to attend eventually to make sure course work transfers at 100 percent. Get it in writing. Some four-year colleges are very selective in what they accept for credits and often snub junior college classes as inadequate. Highly selective private colleges are more likely than state universities to do this.

 Note Get approval in writing from your future college for all your junior college credits.

Some junior colleges have no dormitories. If the college is in a larger city, students commute from home, making dorms unnecessary. However, many students are not within commuting distance and must find an apartment. Apartments in a college town can be very expensive. And research has shown that students are more successful when they live in a dorm, especially in the first few years. Many junior colleges do have dorms, and some that have not had them in the past are now building apartment-like dorms to meet student needs.

State Universities

State universities are usually large colleges with 20,000–25,000 students on campus. State universities offer nearly every major and often specialize in medicine, engineering, or veterinary medicine, with state-of-the-art technology. These universities hold schools within schools, feature their own mass transit systems, and have many teaching assistants presiding over classes for professors on sabbatical. They have huge football stadiums and recruit top athletes. They also have class *close outs* that require students to attend more than four years when they can't get into the classes they need to graduate.

> **Note** State universities offer nearly all majors.

Housing is available on campus but the early bird gets the worm—or dorm room. If you apply later, rather than earlier, you may not get a room. Children of baby boomers are filling colleges in record numbers. So many universities have dorms filled to capacity that often three students end up living in a room meant for two. Many students are forced off campus for housing. Now these students are faced with finding an apartment, locating roommates to help in paying for the apartment, cooking, buying gas, and maintaining a car. If the student doesn't own a car, he or she will have to buy a mass transit pass and catch the bus to classes. It is just easier to enroll early and get a dorm room.

> **Note** At large universities, the early bird gets a dorm room.

State universities charge tuition at a discount because state taxes subsidize the real cost of education. That is why state universities charge such large out-of-state fees. Students living outside the state have not paid the taxes that subsidize the university. Large universities do not offer the generous scholarships that private colleges give because they are already offering an education at a discount rate. Families who do not qualify for much financial aid often prefer state universities.

Private Colleges

Private colleges are usually small in size. There are many colleges with 500–800 students and many with 2,000–5,000 students. But a typical size for a private college is 850–1,200.

Tuition is based on the actual cost of education at the college and is funded by parents, students, and donors. Private donors, usually successful graduates of the college, give generously to support the college into the future. In turn, the college names halls or buildings after these donors and immortalizes them on the campus. A generous donation from one donor can change the future of a college. If a private college has deep pockets, it can offer generous financial aid packages. Generous financial aid fills the classrooms. And filling classrooms gives job security to everyone at the college.

Private colleges usually receive government funding. Students receive guaranteed student loans that are funded by the Department of Education. Pell Grants are also federal funds for students who are most financially needy. Private colleges also receive tuition grants from their state. State tuition grants are in place to help offset the difference between tuition at state universities and the more expensive private colleges.

Private colleges take the strain off the public university system. For every student attending a private college, taxpayers have one less college student to support. Private donations, instead of tax money, make up the major source of financial support. However, many private colleges offer limited majors. This means that, often, if students drastically change majors, they may need to transfer to another college. Changing majors often increases the time it takes to graduate.

 Note Private colleges may offer the best financial aid packages.

Private colleges have dorms, and many require full-time students to live on campus until the first or second semester of senior year. One reason that private colleges have such high graduation rates is that they accept students who are more likely to succeed. Also, they monitor students more carefully, and the small size enables students to receive more personal attention from professors. Among junior colleges, state universities, and private colleges, private colleges have the highest graduation rates.

Note Private colleges have the highest graduation rates.

Many private colleges are also the highest academically. Harvard, Stanford, Yale, Princeton, Rice, and Dartmouth are just some examples of colleges that tower above most state universities in selectivity and academic achievement.

Each of these school types—junior colleges, state universities, and private colleges—matches specific needs of students. There is something for everyone. Selecting the right college is a big step and a major change, but it's also the beginning to a new life.

Quote "Changes are not only possible and predictable, but to deny them is to be an accomplice to one's own unnecessary vegetation."

–Gail Sheehy

CHAPTER 21

Do You Want to Attend College in Your Home State?

There are advantages, in some instances, to attending colleges in your home state. However, in some cases, there are no advantages to attending college in your state of residence. Much depends on whether you're talking about a private college or a state university. Family income also makes a difference. No wonder people get confused.

> **Note** Attending college outside your home state can be tricky.

Private Colleges

Private colleges do not charge an out-of-state fee. That's the good news. The bad news is that only in-state residents may receive the tuition grants from a particular state. Is that important? Could be. Tuition grants are state-funded grants awarded to students attending private colleges. These grants are intended to help defray the higher tuition and expenses at a private college.

> **Note** Private colleges do not have out-of-state fees.

Each state has a tuition grant program, but the amounts vary from state to state. They can be as little as $1,000 or as much as $3,000 or more. Generous out-of-state colleges often make up the difference, so a student receives the same amount of financial aid as if attending college in his or her home state. State tuition grants are based on family income. So a financially challenged student would receive a larger sum than someone from an upper-middle-class family. State tuition grants do not transfer to other states.

Let's say Jon lives in Nebraska but is thinking of going to a generous private Virginia college. His state would have given him a $3,200 tuition grant. However, his Virginia financial aid package more than made up for that. It was actually substantially less expensive for Jon to attend college in Virginia because the private school in his home state was less generous.

Note You lose your state tuition grant if you leave your home state.

State Universities

If the plan is to attend a state university in your home state, you will not pay an out-of-state fee. States want to encourage students to stay. However, the states vary greatly in what they charge for tuition and out-of-state fees. It is possible to attend a state university in another state and pay less than you would if you were to remain in your home state. Some states have low tuition as a high priority and others do not. Don't assume that all state universities cost the same. There may be significant differences in price tags from one state to another.

To make this even more interesting, consider the issue of textbooks. Northwest Missouri State University rents textbooks instead of selling them to students. That's right. You understood correctly. Students go to the bookstore, pay a $25 deposit, and take their books back to their dorms. At the end of the semester, they return the books in good condition to the bookstore and receive a $25 voucher for the following semester. They return the next week with the voucher, get their books for the second semester, and continue this cycle until the last semester. At the end of the last semester, the students return their books and receive $25. They have paid nothing for books the entire time they have attended college. That could be a savings of more than $6,000 over four years.

 Note Some universities have free books.

Consortiums

Some states have negotiated a pact and formed a consortium among state universities. The universities within the consortium agree to not charge out-of-state fees to students from participating consortium states. There is such a consortium in the Midwest. Minnesota, North Dakota, South Dakota, and Nebraska have an agreement to allow students to freely pass from one state to another to attend college without paying out-of-state fees. Iowa refuses to join the consortium, stating it would not be to the state's advantage to do so. The many Iowa students who attend Minnesota, Nebraska, North Dakota, or South Dakota state universities must pay the penalty fee.

Note Check whether your state is in a consortium allowing students to cross borders freely.

The Fees

How much does in-state tuition differ from out-of-state tuition? The difference can be massive in some cases.

It even varies from college to college within the same state, as the following list from the *U.S. News & World Report Ultimate College Guide,* 2006 Edition, shows:

California State University	in-state $2,933	out-of-state $13,103
Arizona State University	in-state $4.406	out-of-state $14,013
University of Colorado	in-state $4,341	out-of-state $21,453
Florida State University	in-state $3,175	out-of-state $16,306
University of Iowa	in-state $5,612	out-of-state $16,998
Kentucky State University	in-state $4,468	out-of-state $10,910

University of Minnesota	in-state $8,030	out-of-state $19,660
Minnesota State University	in-state $5,088	out-of-state $9,998
Northwest Missouri State University	in-state $5,325	out-of-state $9,180
Pennsylvania State University	in-state $9,822	out-of-state $19,734
South Dakota State University	in-state $4,732	out-of-state $9,719
University of South Dakota	in-state $4,452	out-of-state $9,296
Texas State University	in-state $5,252	out-of-state $13,532
University of Utah	in-state $4,298	out-of-state $13,371
University of Virginia	in-state $7,180	out-of-state $24,100
Virginia Tech	in-state $6,378	out-of-state $17,717

The obvious lesson is to check out the out-of-state tuition fees before you decide where you are going to attend college. You can attend a four-year university in one state for the same price as a junior college in another state, even after you pay the out-of-state fees. If you are attending a generous out-of-state private college, you will probably do well with financial aid despite losing the home-state tuition grant. However, crossing the border to attend a state university could be tricky. It depends on what border you are crossing. But don't be afraid to cross that border.

 Quote

"Whatever you do, you need courage. Whatever course you decide upon, there is always someone to tell you that you are wrong. There are always difficulties arising which tempt you to believe that your critics are right."

–Ralph Waldo Emerson

CHAPTER 22

What Are the Levels of Colleges?

If you take a look around any classroom, you see students of assorted shapes and sizes. It is also easy to spot different abilities and talents. You can quickly call out the name of the smart one, the musician, the actor, Mr. Fix-It, the one who is nice to everyone, the athlete, and the artist. The great news is that colleges come in assorted sizes and specialties, too. Colleges come in various levels of academics as well. The student who has a 4.0 is headed for a college on a higher tier than the student with a 2.8. The good news is that they are both going somewhere—and at a level at which they can be successful.

Five Different Levels

Colleges are ranked on five levels: level 1 through level 5. Colleges vary greatly in what they expect from students, and these rankings reflect that. Some colleges accept 100 percent of applicants and others accept only 11 percent of those who apply. Explore where you rank as a student prior to visiting and applying to a college. If you don't, you will be wasting not only time but money as well.

Typically, college visits require parents to take time off from work and to spend money for gas, food, and often lodging. Who wants to do that when the college is not for you? Why visit a college that is not likely to accept you and that won't give you any scholarships? Visiting a college above your level of academics is a total waste of time, effort, and money. Let's check out the five levels and see where you belong.

Level 1

Level 1 schools, identified as "most selective," make up the top-ranked tier of colleges. The phrase *most selective* means that these colleges accept only a few of the students who apply. Colleges at the top are considered Ivy League, and these accept only the best of the best. Many people think of them as schools for the rich, but they are not. In fact, Ivy League schools are beginning to offer a tuition-free education to students who come from families with incomes of approximately $60,000 a year. If you have the academic requirements for an Ivy League school but your family income is low, it is possible that it may cost you nothing or little to attend. These schools do not want to be seen as elite. Instead, they want diversity on campus, and they try to attract students from all over the country and from various socioeconomic groups.

Level 1 schools like to see ACT scores in the range of 30–36. As 36 is the highest score possible, you have to be a very strong student to be considered by a level 1 school.

Some level 1 schools are as follows:

- Amherst College
- California Institute of Technology
- Columbia University
- Duke University
- Georgetown University
- Harvard University
- Johns Hopkins University
- Princeton University
- Stanford University
- University of Virginia
- Washington and Lee University
- Yale University

Level 2

Level 2 schools are labeled "more selective" and are good choices for academically strong students. These colleges have excellent reputations and usually offer generous financial aid because they have successful graduates who donate generously. These colleges often offer academically challenging majors. Level 2 schools like to see the ACT range of 24–29.

Some level 2 schools include these:

- Brigham Young University
- DePaul University
- Drew University
- Eckerd College
- George Washington University
- Gustavus Adolphus College
- James Madison University
- Knox College
- Occidental College
- Pepperdine University
- Rutgers University
- Sarah Lawrence College
- United States Naval Academy
- Vanderbilt University
- Villanova University

Level 3

A large number of colleges fall under the category of level 3, which is known as "selective." Most solid college-bound students will be accepted at a level 3 college and stand a good chance of graduating. There are higher level 3 and lower level 3 schools.

These schools prefer an ACT range of 21–25. There is often an overlap between level 3 and level 2 schools.

- Buena Vista University
- Coe College

- Dominican University of California
- Dowling College
- George Mason University
- Kent State University
- McPherson College
- Merrimack College
- Niagara University
- Old Dominion University
- Rider University
- St. John's University
- University of Iowa
- University of Minnesota

Level 4

Level 4 colleges, referred to as "less selective," offer a solid education for students who may fall into the lower ACT range. These colleges accept students in the ACT range of 18–23. Students that fall above this range find that they can receive a great education with generous scholarships. Because these schools have lower ACT scores on campus, the graduation rates tend to be lower. However, students who want to succeed usually do well.

Here are some level 4 colleges:

- Bluefield College
- College of St. Joseph
- Fisk University
- Florida A & M
- Greensboro College
- Liberty University
- Lincoln University
- Memphis College of Art
- Morningside College
- Pfeiffer University

- Piedmont College
- Regis College
- Texas College
- William Penn University

Level 5

Level 5 colleges are "least selective." These schools accept students with ACT scores below 18. Many level 5 schools are junior colleges with open enrollment. These colleges are indeed a second chance for students who have not focused on hitting the books while in high school. For many students, this is a great opportunity to make up for unsuccessful high school years.

Some level 5 schools are listed below:

- Benedict College
- Bennett College
- California Institute of the Arts
- Cheyney University of Pennsylvania
- Florida Memorial University
- Jarvis Christian College
- Kentucky State University
- Lamar University
- Manhattan School of Music
- Regent University
- Shaw University
- St. Paul's College
- Virginia State University

Most high school students fall between level 2 and level 4. Only students at the very top of the class fall into level 1. Often, in fact, the valedictorian does not qualify for level 1.

Academic Expections

Prior to visiting a college, you should explore what the academic level of expectation is at the school. Where do you fall among the applicants there? You want to fall mid-range. If you have an ACT of 23, you are a level 3 student. You want to fall in the top half. So you will be looking for colleges that have 50 percent of the students falling in the 21–25 range.

Let me explain the ACT range. If the ACT range at a college is 21–25, that means that 50 percent of the students fall within that range. It also means that 25 percent of the students have an ACT above 25 and 25 percent have an ACT below 21. You want to fall in the top half. Definitely avoid the bottom 25 percent range. If you fall in the top 50 percent range, not only will you be academically above half the students at the college, you will be in the scholarship range. And who doesn't want to be in the scholarship range? The higher you are among the average campus population, the more likely you are to get a scholarship.

So your homework assignment is to research colleges in your academic range and then begin studying which majors are offered. What you truly want to find is a list of colleges that are a custom fit for you. Compile a list of 6 to 10 and then place them in order of preference. Start visiting the top choices. And you're off!

CHAPTER 23

What Is the Timeline for a College Search?

A timeline is what everyone wants to have. What are we supposed to do and when are we supposed to do it? Well, here it is. It's very simple.

Forget about your high school telling you what to do. Your counselors are far too busy for that. The responsibility falls on each family to do its own research.

Freshman and Sophomore Years

Take solid classes and maintain a grade point average that is interesting to colleges. What would that be? Colleges like to see an average of 3.0 or higher. What if you have a 2.8? You are still interesting, but you'll have to find just the right college. Work to raise your average so you will inspire greater interest.

Junior Year Is "the" Year

Your junior year is the big year for finding a college. Thought it was your senior year? Wrong! By the time the senior year rolls around, you should have things rolling toward the finish line. Students who begin visiting colleges in the senior year are very late and will not be as successful as those who began the year before.

"Counting time is not so important as making time count."

–James J. Walker

You can follow a timeline as listed in the following sections.

August

Take the ACT or SAT at the beginning of your junior year. Plan on taking it a second time in the spring. You may want to take it a third time right away in the fall of your senior year. You need to know what your ACT score is so that you know which colleges are your best prospects. Not having your ACT score in your hand is like shopping for furniture when you don't know which house you will buy. It makes no sense at all.

September

Talk with your school counselor about your plans. She or he may be able to steer you toward some specific colleges. Double-check your classes to make sure you are taking those that are necessary for college. In many schools, counselors are too busy to schedule appointments with students. So you may have to take the responsibility of making an appointment.

If you are a strong student, register for the PSAT/NMSQT, which is used to determine National Merit Scholars.

Go on www.fastweb.com and register for scholarships. Fill out the questionnaire so scholarship information comes directly to you.

October

Once you know your ACT score, think about what you would like to do in the future. What are your strong subjects in school? Are you creative and artistic? Are you just naturally gifted at knowing how to fix things? Are you a star in science? Is math easy for you—and you don't understand why others find it hard? Can you just pick up a piece of music and sight read it when others find that difficult? There is some area that must interest you more than any other. Whatever that interest is, it could be a place to start as you consider a college major. It can be general right now. You will get more specific later.

Begin researching colleges by your ACT level and major. As you go through the various college guide books (*U.S. News & World Report Ultimate College Guide* or *College Board College Handbook*, for example), list colleges that are in your ACT range and that identify your major as a strong or popular one. This is a good place to start.

E-mail colleges for brochures and start comparing schools. Make a folder for each college and keep information together so you don't get confused or lose things. Don't be afraid to select colleges from other states. If you are thinking of attending a private college, there is no penalty for "crossing the border." Attending a state university that is out-of-state is a different matter. Check out the out-of-state tuition rate before you get too excited about attending.

November

Start planning visits to colleges that are at the top of your list. Try to schedule the visits on a day your school may have a break or in-service while the college is in session. Make a list of questions to ask at each college. Be sure to ask the same questions at each college you visit so you can compare apples to apples.

December

Go to a college night for juniors if your school offers it.

January

Register for your next ACT or SAT test in the spring.

Update your resume if you have already compiled one. If you haven't, now is the time to get it together. Chapters 43 and 44 explain resumes in detail. Continue to visit colleges.

February

Check with your counselor about taking classes for college credit next year.

March

Check out any college fairs in the area. This is a good way to get information. Many colleges have short videos of the campus and programs.

April

Take a look at the application forms the colleges have sent you. At the end of each one there is likely to be an essay question. Start writing several essays and have them ready by fall.

May

Update your resume with any awards you've received or any recent volunteer work.

Summer

Save money for college if you have a job. Look for volunteer work. Keep writing those essays!

 "I wish I could stand on a busy corner, hat in hand, and beg people to throw me all their wasted hours."

–Bernard Berenson

Senior Year Countdown

August

Sit down with your parents and discuss your top college choices. Narrow down the choices to six colleges. Check priority deadlines and put the date on each folder cover.

 Don't miss any priority dates or financial aid deadlines!

Make a list of the teachers from whom you would ask for a letter of recommendation in a few months.

Start checking the counselor's bulletin board often for scholarship applications.

Register for the ACT or SAT if you need to take it a third time.

September

Ask your teachers and principals if they will write letters of recommendation for you.

 Apply to colleges in the fall.

October

Take the ACT or SAT.

Make a last visit to a college if you have unanswered questions.

Have teachers check over the essays you have been writing over the summer. You want the essays polished by Halloween.

 "To be courageous means to be afraid but to go a little step forward anyway."

–Beverly Smith

November

Start applying to your top four, five, or six college choices. Include your updated resume with each application. Watch deadlines carefully. Some colleges may have a November 15 priority deadline. Make a copy of everything you send to colleges and keep the copies in the appropriate college folders.

December

Print a FAFSA form from the www.fafsa.ed.gov site and begin penciling in information for January. You and your parents will both need a PIN number.

Submit the FAFSA as soon as possible after January 1.

January

File the FAFSA (Free Application for Federal Student Aid), if possible. Check the financial aid deadlines at all your college choices. Don't miss these deadlines. Some may be as early as February 15.

February

File the FAFSA if you couldn't file in January. Put in information from last year, if necessary. You can always update later. Don't miss the deadline!

You may be getting scholarship applications from the colleges that have accepted you. Look through your pool of essays to see if they can be a good start for you.

Attend scholarship weekends if invited.

 "Don't put off for tomorrow what you can do today, because if you enjoy it today you can do it again tomorrow."

–James A. Michener

March

Colleges may ask for a copy of your tax forms. Don't be alarmed—this is a routine request.

Keep those grades up. Colleges may rescind your acceptance if your grades slip.

April

Compare your financial aid packages. Which college is giving you the best offer? Involve your parents in the discussion as you compare and narrow your options.

May

Make your final decision based on the best package and on the best environment for you. Don't be afraid to ask a college for more funding.

Enjoy your graduation.

Overall Considerations

The three most important things to remember in this timeline are

- Apply to colleges in the fall.
- File the FAFSA as soon as possible.
- Don't miss any deadlines.

"To exist is to change, to change is to mature, to mature is to go on creating oneself endlessly."

–Henri Bergson

CHAPTER 24

What Can You Learn from College Guides?

College guides have so much valuable information about schools on those tissue paper pages. I'll go through the information and tell you why those 2½-inch-thick manuals that resemble an old family Bible can be a great aid.

You can find several college manuals in high school libraries, guidance offices, and public libraries. Below are just a few titles:

- *U.S. News & World Report Ultimate College Guide*
- *College Handbook* by the College Board
- *The Right College* by Arco

These manuals are similar to one another, and they all contain pretty much the same information. Once you have selected your top colleges (10 or so), do a little research. Jot down information on a large index card for future use. You will very quickly get good information from the guides, and then you can be off and running.

Note the college Web site and go exploring. Some Web sites are better than others, but you can learn so much about a college by reading the history and "about us."

The following information explains the sections of college guides and how to best use the sections.

Location

One important thing to check out is the location of the college:

- How large is the city? Do you want to be in a city that large?
- Where is the college located within the city? This information can be found on a map of the city or state. Is the college in a safe area?
- Is the college out in the country? Do you want to be out in a wooded area or on a prairie?

Staying overnight is an option at some colleges. Potential students may stay overnight in the dorms and get a feel for what it would be like to be a student on this campus. They attend some classes, get in on the campus social life, and visit the city.

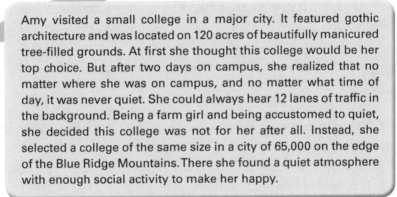

Amy visited a small college in a major city. It featured gothic architecture and was located on 120 acres of beautifully manicured tree-filled grounds. At first she thought this college would be her top choice. But after two days on campus, she realized that no matter where she was on campus, and no matter what time of day, it was never quiet. She could always hear 12 lanes of traffic in the background. Being a farm girl and being accustomed to quiet, she decided this college was not for her after all. Instead, she selected a college of the same size in a city of 65,000 on the edge of the Blue Ridge Mountains. There she found a quiet atmosphere with enough social activity to make her happy.

Average ACT Score

The average ACT scores of students is one of the most important statistics you will learn about a college. The average ACT scores show you how you compare to the other students on campus. For example, Colorado State University has the following ACT stats:

25%	50%	25%
Below ACT of 21	ACT of 22–26	ACT of 27 or higher

The above numbers show that half of the students attending this college have an ACT score between 22 and 26. 25 percent are below this range, and 25 percent are higher. If you are planning to attend Colorado State University in Fort Collins, you should have a minimum ACT score of 22 or preferably 24. Why? You absolutely do not want to be in the bottom 25 percent. Who wants to be in the bottom 25 percent of every class? Right, no one—especially you.

> **Note** Your goal should be to place in the top 50 percent academically.

Being in the top 50 percent increases your chances of receiving a scholarship, especially at a private college. By being in the top 50, you also increase your chances of being successful at that college.

> **Note** Know where you fall compared to other students on campus.

The acceptance rate at Fort Collins is 83 percent. The acceptance rate at Harvard is 11 percent. If you fall into the top 75 percent of ACT scores at Fort Collins, you are likely to be accepted. In fact, it is probably a sure thing.

Faculty-to-Student Ratio

How accessible would you prefer your professors to be? Students often seek out a professor if they are struggling in class. It is interesting to watch the professor-to-student ratios shrink as the colleges get more exclusive. There is one professor for every 18 students at Fort Collins. That is quite good, considering there are more than 20,000 students on campus. However, there is one professor for every 7 students at Harvard, and one professor for every 3 students at the California Institute of Technology.

Note For individualized assistance, choose a low professor-to-student ratio.

Average Debt

Debt information could be very useful if guaranteed student loans are a concern to you. The typical Fort Collins student graduates with a debt of around $17,000, while the average student at Iowa State University graduates with a debt of more than $27,000. This could mean that one college is more generous with financial aid, or it could mean that students attending Iowa State University often have to attend school for five years to get all their classes because of class close-outs.

Students at the Ivy League school of Amherst in Massachusetts have an average debt of $10,000. It could be that the school is generous, or it could mean that parents are paying the complete bill and the students don't have to borrow very much, if anything at all. This would be a question to ask on your college visit.

Admissions Information

Admissions information is more than just the phone number to the admissions office. This section also includes deadlines. What deadlines? Deadline for admission, application for financial aid, early action, and early decision. Chapter 48 explains these terms in detail.

This section includes the application fee and whether the college accepts a "common application." Some colleges accept the generic common application, but many colleges prefer that you use their own application.

There is a way to defer paying the application fee. Some schools let you apply with no fee if you send your application by a certain date. Other colleges will waive the fee if you apply on a college visit. Some colleges will waive the fee if you apply online, and others will waive it if your family income is below a certain level. If you plan on applying at six colleges (and you probably should), fees ranging from $25 to $50 can add up.

Academics

Here is where you find out about the offerings at a college. Not only will the guide list every major and minor, it will also list the most popular majors. A college may offer a business major, but if it is a popular major and 16 percent of the students are enrolled in business, this is likely to be a strong program. After all, if you have 20,000 students on campus and 16 percent are in the business program, that means 3,200 students are business majors.

The guides will also list information about the following:

- Preprofessional programs
- Special academic programs
- Reserve Officers Training Corps
- Faculty members and demographics
- Advanced placement and international baccalaureate credit information
- Student body statistics
- Freshman returning for sophomore year
- Graduation rates

Returning Students

The number of students returning to college for the sophomore year could be significant as well. Fort Collins students return for their sophomore year at a rate of 82 percent. Grinnell College in Grinnell, Iowa, has a return rate of 92 percent. Harvard has a return rate of 97 percent.

Graduation Rate

The graduation rate is also something to consider. At one college, 53 percent of the students might graduate. At another college the rate might be 75 percent, and at another it might be 95 percent. Obviously, one college is much more successful at something. Level 1 colleges accept very successful students. The expectation is that these students will succeed, but this expectation is not always the case. Quite often, smaller colleges monitor grades, have mandatory study sessions, provide free tutoring, and offer mid-term check-ins with an advisor. These colleges are very proactive at retaining students.

Campus Life

This section will tell you whether the college has dorms and, if so, whether they include coed dorms, women's dorms, men's dorms, sorority housing, fraternity housing, apartments for single students, special housing for disabled students, or special housing for international students. This section will list the campus organizations, the percentage of students in sororities and fraternities, and the percentage of students who stay on campus on weekends. It will include NCAA or NAIA data and information about campus safety, technology resources, counseling services, basic services, and intercollegiate varsity sports.

In terms of the campus size, where is your comfort level? 1,000 students, 4,000 students, or 25,000 students? Bigger is not always better, and smaller is not always better. Jot down the phone number and e-mail address of the college to learn up-to-date information.

In a Nutshell

In just a few minutes, you can learn many things about a college. Review the information, take notes, and move on to the next college. After researching 10 or more colleges, a few will look more interesting than others will. Arrange them in order of your preference. Try to select a pool of six that you may want to visit.

CHAPTER 25

What Are Some Important Details to Learn About a College?

While the college guides give valuable information about a college, certain facts not mentioned in the guides are important to know.

Average ACT and SAT Scores

As outlined in Chapter 24, one of the most important facts to learn about a college is the average ACT and SAT scores of students who attend there. What's the big deal about ACT and SAT scores?

Keep in mind that many scholarships are based on ACT and SAT scores. Just a few points could make the difference between a $2,000 scholarship and a $5,000 scholarship. Colleges will list the scholarship requirements in the literature that's sent to your home. Check it out. This is another good reason to take the ACT or SAT at least twice and perhaps three times. And, if you maintain the required grade point average at the college, the scholarships are renewable each year. Isn't it worth taking the ACT or SAT a third time for $20,000?

Note ACT or SAT scores qualify you for scholarships.

Average Percentage of Need Met

The college guides will also list the average percentage of need met. What does this mean? When you file the FAFSA online in

January or early February, you will receive the SAR, Student Aid Report, in two or three weeks. This will take longer, four to six weeks, if you file on paper. On the Student Aid Report, look at the top right-hand corner. There you will find "EFC," along with some numbers. The letters EFC stand for Expected Family Contribution. The numbers stand for dollars. Colleges will not address the EFC or tell you what the numbers mean. But the information here tells how much your family is expected to contribute to your education. Aside from this, you will have your own financial responsibility with loans and books.

 Note How generous a college may be is very important.

The college guides will list how generous colleges are. Here are some examples:

- Vanderbilt University—99 percent
- Drew University—83 percent
- University of Michigan—Ann Arbor—90 percent
- University of Virginia—100 percent
- Iowa State University—82 percent
- Stanford University—100 percent
- University of South Florida—32 percent

How can you use this information? Once you know your EFC, you know what the best offer will probably be.

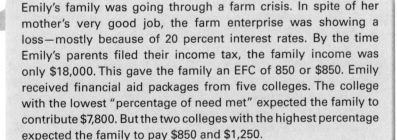

Emily's family was going through a farm crisis. In spite of her mother's very good job, the farm enterprise was showing a loss—mostly because of 20 percent interest rates. By the time Emily's parents filed their income tax, the family income was only $18,000. This gave the family an EFC of 850 or $850. Emily received financial aid packages from five colleges. The college with the lowest "percentage of need met" expected the family to contribute $7,800. But the two colleges with the highest percentage expected the family to pay $850 and $1,250.

While there are no guarantees, the odds are in your favor that you will receive a better financial aid package from a college that posts a higher percentage of need met.

Having said that, there are exceptions. If a college wants an exceptional musician, mathematician, soccer player, or academic student, it is likely to offer a generous package even if the percentage of need met is low overall.

The bottom line is that you just never know what a college will offer until the offer is in writing. Coaches may promise offers and admissions counselors may promise offers, but until you see it in writing, you shouldn't take it to the bank. That is why you should apply to at least four or five colleges—or even six—and wait for the offers to come in the spring. Spring of your senior year is very late to start looking for another college if you don't receive a good offer.

Foreign Language Requirement

The language requirement at colleges and high schools varies greatly. Some high schools require two years of a foreign language and others require none. Some colleges require two years of a foreign language in high school and some require none. But there may be some glitches at the college level, and you may be very unpleasantly surprised. Inquire about this while visiting a college. What are the foreign language requirements for graduation? Admission and graduation requirements may vary.

Jason had taken two years of Spanish in high school, as his counselor suggested. He was accepted at a large university that required no foreign language for admission. Jason thought he was set. But here is where the surprise came in. His major was law, and Jason was surprised to learn that, in order to graduate, he had to have four years of a foreign language in high school to be exempt from taking a language in college. Because the college required four years total, Jason ended up taking two years of Spanish at the college level, which was much more difficult and time consuming than the high school classes would have been.

He and his parents did not know that entrance requirements can be different than graduation requirements.

Computers and Repair

A new trend among many colleges is to issue a laptop or laptop notebook to each student on campus. Before you get too excited about this, note that these computers are usually not completely free. Students pay a fee for them, but it is lower than the market price of the computer. Dell or Apple often gives the colleges a large discount with the mass purchase. At the end of three years, students may turn the computer in for a new one or purchase the used laptop for a nominal fee. Many college students give the older computer to a younger sibling in high school.

You will want to be careful about giving your computer away. You may think you deleted all information but many computer experts know how to get information from an "empty" computer. The history of every Web site you visited will still be there somewhere. Credit card numbers, business transactions, and PIN numbers could all be on your computer. You could be giving away information you don't want others to have even after the computer has been cleared of data.

Note Personal information may stay on a computer forever.

What about computer repairs? Some colleges will repair computers at no cost only if the computers were issued by the college. Other colleges that don't even issue computers will repair your computer at no charge. Computer-savvy students often earn their work-study hours by fixing laptops for other students. A computer not working properly is a major issue when you use your laptop to take notes, send papers electronically to professors, and communicate with the world. Just a few days without a computer can be a major inconvenience. And computer repairs can get very expensive. On your college visits, ask if computer repairs are free or if there is a charge for them.

Food

Food can become an issue of student protests if it's not very good. Now, we all know that no one cooks a pot roast like Grandma. We don't expect a college cafeteria to equal Grandma's cooking. But the food should be reasonably tasty.

As part of the college visit, eat in the cafeteria. Ask how the students like the food, or ask the students, themselves. If students spend time and money driving to a fast-food restaurant off campus or are ordering pizza delivered to the dorms, your food budget is going to explode.

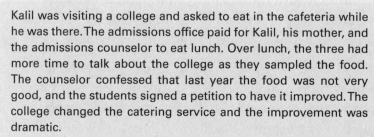

Kalil was visiting a college and asked to eat in the cafeteria while he was there. The admissions office paid for Kalil, his mother, and the admissions counselor to eat lunch. Over lunch, the three had more time to talk about the college as they sampled the food. The counselor confessed that last year the food was not very good, and the students signed a petition to have it improved. The college changed the catering service and the improvement was dramatic.

Kalil also learned that pizza, hamburgers, and Mexican entrees are served daily, but the other offerings vary each day. He also learned that a sandwich bar is open between and after the three meals each day. Students make themselves sandwiches at the refrigerated deli bar. No reason to go hungry at that college! Other colleges have access to fruit and fruit juices 24/7 in the entryway of the cafeteria. If students get caught not having time to eat a meal, they know there is food after hours. Find out whether the colleges at the top of your list have food available after hours.

 Quote "Never eat more than you can lift."

–Miss Piggy

Free Tutoring

While this may not seem like a big deal, if you find yourself struggling in an English, math, or science class, it will become a big deal quickly. Paying for daily tutoring can destroy a budget faster than eating out. You can talk yourself out of eating out, but if you need the tutoring assistance to avoid failing a class, that is a tougher choice. Some colleges allow students to charge a fee for tutoring. Other colleges have free tutoring as a way for students to earn work-study hours. The tutors will be in the Success Center two or three hours each day to help other students. Find out which kinds of tutoring your college choices offer.

 Quote "What does not destroy me, makes me strong."
–Friedrich Nietzsche

There is more to selecting a college than the cost of tuition. This is why you want to start early and apply to several colleges.

CHAPTER 26

What Are Seven Reasons to Not Pick a College?

There are many good reasons to select a college—and many good reasons not to. The following are poor reasons for selecting a college.

Your Boyfriend or Girlfriend Goes There

Sorry to announce the bad news: Many high school romances do not survive in college. High school relationships often are based on convenience. A special person was there, conveniently, when you wanted to begin dating, and you had a few things in common. There are 89 students in your class; half are girls, and half are boys. You have 45 potential dates. Suddenly, you arrive on a college campus and that number may increase to 200.

Keep in mind that personalities continue to form until approximately age 25 or 26. When you get to college, you will continue to change—and so will everyone else. In college, you will have the opportunity to meet someone with whom you have many things in common. Pretty soon, the old relationship may break apart or you and your partner may simply grow apart. But you will be on the same campus and, perhaps, even have classes together. Seeing your former boyfriend or girlfriend with someone else can be very painful. Many students want to leave college when this happens.

Note Don't select a college based on a high school romance.

You Like the Football or Basketball Team

You've been watching this team play for years. You've even put up posters of the team in your bedroom. It's been your dream to watch the games live, so you are going to go to this college. This way, you can get cheaper tickets and get them for your friends. What wrong with this? For one thing, the school may not be at your academic level. Does the school offer a strong program in your major? You may continue to be a great fan of this football team for many years, but that does not mean you need to attend this college.

They Offered You a Scholarship

Colleges often send scholarships to academically strong students before these students apply or visit the campus. This can be very flattering and tempting, but is this the right college for you? Would it be in your top five choices if the college had not sent you a scholarship? Have you visited the campus yet? Does it seem to be the perfect fit for you? Go and visit to find out. But, if it doesn't seem to be right, attending this college because of a scholarship may not be the best way to go.

Quote "Money doesn't always bring happiness. People with ten million dollars are no happier than people with nine million dollars."
–Hobart Brown

It's Close to Home

You've never been far from home and have doubts about being on your own. You think you want to come home every weekend because you will miss everyone. (Of course, you don't realize that no one else will be home when you get there.) There is a college 20 miles away, so you decide this is the best way to go.

This could be the right college for you, but visit several other schools also. Visiting five or six schools is a good rule of thumb. You may just fall in love with a school 100 miles from home that is the perfect fit for you. Spread your wings and explore new situations.

Note Don't be afraid to venture out of your comfort zone for college.

Doug was the oldest of five siblings. He was a very good student and looked forward to college, but he just couldn't see himself going very far away from home. So he decided to go to the college that was located in the town in which he had spent his entire life. Living on campus instead of commuting would be perfect, he thought.

The first year, Doug lacked confidence. After a year, he realized that all his friends were not coming home for weekends. They were in a new environment and meeting new friends while he was in the same place he had always been. He seemed to be in a rut, and he wanted to experience something totally different. Doug decided to try a different atmosphere and moved eight hours away to attend a small private college in Chicago. Wow— was that ever a change!

Everyone Goes There

Some high schools have a popular college for their graduates. It seems like everyone just goes to this college. No one is really sure why, but it has always been this way. The college rep loves this high school. One visit is guaranteed several applicants. But one size does not fit all.

Remember that it's a good idea to visit five or six colleges. If you do this and find that this "chosen" college is still the one you want, you may decide to attend. But apply to several and see where the best award letters are. Sometimes students are afraid to go off into the unknown, and having a group from high school may seem comforting. However, it is easier to grow into the person you really are if you go without high school friends.

That popular college for everyone else may not be the one for you.

Your Parents Want You to Go There

Some families have a tradition established. "Everyone in our family has graduated from College ABC," it is announced with pride. Some families go as far as to pay for only one college. "If you go to another one, you are on your own. There will be no financial aid from us."

In this case, students must just hope that the college matches their interests. The major that would be the best career choice for a student may not be offered at the parents' chosen college. Financially, the student may have no choice but to go along with the parents' choice—or not go to college. Ending up with a career that you don't enjoy is a sad way to live.

 "Never underestimate your power to change yourself; never overestimate your power to change others."
–H. Jackson Brown, Jr.

Brenda was college bound. Her parents were fortunate to have a very good income. Brenda's parents had selected one and only one college that she and all her sisters would attend. While it was a good college, it was a very small, conservative Lutheran college in a rural area. When Brenda decided to rebel and attend a larger college, her parents informed her it was either the school they had chosen for her or no school at all. With her parents' income, Brenda would get no financial aid and could not afford to go to another college. Brenda chose to go to the college her parents selected.

It's the Cheapest College

College fees run on a sliding scale. Most students and families do not pay the full price for tuition and room and board. Unless you do not qualify for financial aid, looking at price tags doesn't really make sense. A family with a low EFC (Expected Financial Contribution) will get a discount at nearly every college regardless of tuition rates.

To find out what your family's expected contribution would be today, go to http://testdev.act.org/finaid/packages.html. Click "Financial Aid Resources" and then "Financial Aid Need Estimator." This calculates the EFC and what you would expect to pay for college per year at a generous college.

Note Don't look at college price tags. College is on a sliding scale.

Select a college based on personal reasons and not because of someone else's opinion.

CHAPTER 27

What Is the Role of the Counselor?

Y ou need to put your best foot forward at all times in high school. Your performance in high school becomes part of your permanent record that is a reference now and into the future. In addition to classes, grades, attendance, test scores, and class rank, the opinions of a select few individuals carry much influence.

At the High School Level

Counselors and principals are two very influential individuals in the college entry process. Counselors are vital because they assist students in scheduling the classes necessary for college admission.

> **Note** Always be in good standing with your counselor and principal.

Academic Study

The classes necessary for high school graduation are not the same classes necessary for college success. There are actually three levels of academic study in high school:

- Level one is taking minimal classes with a goal to graduate from high school. *If it's easy, sign me up.* This level of academics does not ensure entry into or success in college. ACT tests are based on the difficulty of classes. By meeting bare-minimum graduation requirements and getting a low ACT score, you are less likely to be admitted to college or to be successful there. Graduating from high school and doing well in college are two separate issues.

- Level two is selecting the minimal college entry requirements, which are slightly above the high school graduation requirements. *Okay, okay. I'll take a few college prep classes but I'm not going to knock myself out.* Students in this category take the bare-bones version of college prep classes. If the suggested years of math are three, four, or five, these students take three and not five.

- Level three is selecting the maximum high academic classes available. This often means that students must forego many electives and fluff classes. These students try to take AP classes, dual-credit classes, five math classes, and four years of classes in other important academic areas.

Transcripts

Counselors submit your transcripts to colleges. Transcripts contain not only a list of classes and grades, but also the grading system used to achieve the grades. Some schools have a liberal grading scale with 90–100 percent required for an A. However, many private schools require 93 percent or even 94 percent for an A. One student could receive an A for a score of 92 percent in a biology class, while a student in another school could receive a B for the same 92 percent score. This can greatly alter a GPA, so the grading scales are sent with transcripts to ensure that colleges know this vital information. Colleges know that a student holding a 3.4 GPA could easily have a 3.8 GPA in another high school. This is often taken into account in considering admission and scholarships.

Note Your entire high school academic record is sent to colleges.

Letters of Recommendation

Counselors, principals, and teachers are asked to write letters of recommendation to colleges. Sometimes, parents and community leaders are asked as well. Admission office staff state that counselors' letters are exceptionally influential in the acceptance and scholarship process. This is particularly true at private colleges where there are more opportunities for scholarships.

If there is any doubt about the potential success of a student, the counselor's opinion carries much weight. Letters from the counselor and principal become critical pieces of information used to help create a profile of the student. The data in a transcript is only a partial picture. A good letter from a counselor can put all the pieces together.

Note Letters of recommendation from a counselor are very influential.

Character is a popular word in college admission. If you look at the college literature, you will see that character is mentioned frequently. Colleges are looking for diversified students who possess good character with leadership qualities. Principals address issues of discipline, attendance, and character. The administrator has contact with the student during all four high school years and usually has a good grasp of the student's total image.

The principal's letter gives an overall view from an administrative perspective, and this can be a critical component in the college process. Give the principal some evidence of your character so he or she can highlight it in the letter.

Note Colleges frequently request a letter from the principal.

At the College Level

While having good references on your side at the high school level is a great thing, the heavy hitters are at the college level.

When you enter a college admissions office, you see many individuals at work. There might be work-study students, secretaries, admissions counselors, and, of course, the director. All letters of inquiry come into the office, and the director assigns each student to a counselor.

While the director may seem like the most important person at the college, the counselor will be your contact. The director is a traffic coordinator in charge of making sure everything gets done. Directors do not personally contact students on a regular basis after the initial contact. Instead, the counselors are in charge of all contacts. It is their job to visit high schools in their area and generate interest for the college they represent.

Counselors usually serve a specific territory. If you are from a certain region, you will be assigned to the counselor who recruits in that region, and you will become a client of that counselor. The counselor will become very important in your life. Arrange a campus visit with your counselor. When planning your visit, be sure to select a day when he or she will be there.

A counselor's job includes

- Sending out mailings
- Making phone calls
- Making personal visits
- Giving campus tours
- Doing interviews
- Calling parents
- Having parents call prospective parents
- Having coaches call the student
- Having professors call the student
- Following up with any students that seem to express strong interest

If you inquire once and don't call or inquire again, a busy counselor will assume you are no longer interested in admittance to the college and will move on to a student who makes regular inquiries.

Your Best Friend

If you show strong interest in a college, the counselor may be your best friend. What can the counselor do for you that is so vital?

In January or February of your senior year, counselors, the admissions director, and financial aid personnel will sit around a big table and discuss how and where to administer scholarships and grants. When this happens, you will want to have built a personal relationship with the admissions counselor. This person will go to bat for you and ask for a generous package because you have convinced him or her that you deserve it. This will not be possible if you are a stranger.

Note Your admissions counselor is a key person.

Building a Relationship

How can you build a relationship? Showing interest is very important.

Visit the campus. A visit shows great interest. You can also show interest by calling the counselor and asking questions before and after the visit. Colleges have toll-free telephone numbers, and you should call with prepared questions during free time. Ask pertinent questions that have come to mind. You will not be bothering the counselor. Remember that it is the job of the admissions counselor to take questions from interested students. This is especially true at private colleges.

Every time a phone call comes in, a college logs the inquiry. The larger the number of inquiries, the more interested a student appears to be. Parents can also call with questions or concerns. A busy admissions counselor will focus on the interested students and support them in preference to the students who have made only one or two inquiries or no more than initial requests for information.

In the competition for scholarships and grants, you cannot afford the luxury of waiting and hoping a college will eventually notice you and your assets and qualifications.

You also need to be aware of the college's interest in you. If a college calls frequently or writes a handwritten letter, you have caught someone's eye. Don't just have one college in mind. Be open to see what comes to fruition from several colleges. College selection can be very competitive, and you may be surprised by the college you choose in the end.

 Note Pay close attention to any handwritten notes.

The Financial Aid Package

It is quite common for one college to offer a substantially better financial aid package than other schools. Be open to the experience and the risk involved in being recruited. Save your decision until April when all the cards are on the table. Admission is in the hands of the counselor, and this is the person to impress at a college.

The college counselor evaluates all data and letters from the principal and the counselor at your high school to make a decision about you. If the counselor is impressed with you, he or she will do everything possible to get you the best offer in the hope that you will attend the college. Making a positive impression on the counselor is a critical step in the process of making college affordable.

So you need to impress three major people during high school: the high school principal, the high school counselor, and your personal college admissions counselor. Put your best foot forward during high school.

Quote "If you're climbing the ladder of life, you go rung by rung, one step at a time...Sometimes you don't think you're progressing until you step back and see how high you've really gone."
–Donny Osmond

CHAPTER 28

What Are Some Trends in College Admissions?

The colleges of the 1970s are not the colleges of the late 2000s. Parents who rely on things being the same as when they went to college are very disappointed. Many things have changed over the past 30 or 40 years.

Increasing Number of Students

Thirty years ago, more high school graduates were able to find successful jobs without a college degree or a certificate. Today, that is getting more difficult. Employers want some evidence that workers know how to do what they say they know how to do. In the 1970s only 50 percent of graduating seniors went on to college. Today, that figure is closer to 65 percent. The shrinking college classrooms that so many feared were coming never became reality.

Society is changing. And many adults in their 30s and 40s are going back to college to train for a new career. This was much less common 30 years ago. Once out in the real world, adults learn that getting that promotion often hinges on a college diploma.

Note A diploma or certificate is more important today.

More Women Students

In the 1960s, men were expected to be the breadwinners, and many women were the support system, not bothering to get an education beyond high school. In the 1970s, the ratio of men-to-women getting a college education was 3:2, or three men for every two women. In the 1990s, it was even, with the same number of men as women enrolled in college. However, by the year 2000, women surpassed men in the race for getting a college degree, with a ratio of six men to seven women, 6:7. Fewer women are getting married at a young age, and many want a career before marriage and family. With the divorce rate rising, women see the importance of a solid career for the future. It is projected that by the year 2013 the ratio will be seven men to nine women in college.

 Note Women make up the majority at most college campuses today.

More Minorities

Not only is the ratio of men to women changing on campuses, but the ethnic diversity is changing, as well. In the late 1990s, whites made up 81 percent of the population on a college campus. In 2003, whites were 76 percent. The percentage of black students has decreased from 11 percent to 10 percent. For Asians, the percentage has increased from 5 percent to 9 percent, and for Hispanics the increase is from 4 percent to 7 percent.

Note More Asians and Hispanics are attending college.

Less Religious Orientation

Campuses are also becoming less religious. While some regions of the country are seeing an increase in religious preference, overall, the number of students stating they have no religious preferences is growing. In the last 20 years, these numbers have increased from 8 percent to 18 percent. Parents who want their family to maintain religious beliefs may feel pressured to send their children to colleges where a high percentage of students share that belief. For example, it is still true that the majority of students attending Notre Dame are Catholic. At many other religiously affiliated schools, the majority of students do not profess the belief system of the college.

Note Religious identity is becoming less important among college students.

Changing Philosophical Outlook

A statistic of some concern is how students set their theoretical goals. In the 1970s the ratio was 2:1 for having a meaningful philosophy of life over making money. In other words, twice as many college students thought being happy, being a good person, and making a difference were top priorities. Today, half as many students think this way, and instead the top goal is to be well off financially rather than to have a meaningful life.

Note Earning money is becoming more important than having a meaningful life.

Changing Political Views

The far left seems to be shrinking on the college campuses. Some campuses are politically quite liberal, and others quite conservative; overall, the trend is toward less liberalism. In 1970, more than 36 percent of students saw themselves as far left or liberal, with less than half in the "middle of the road" category. Today, only 27 percent see themselves as far left or liberal, and those in the middle of the road have increased to 50 percent. At the same time, the conservative category, which was represented by only 15 percent of students in the 1970s, is now at 23 percent. The far left professors who have enjoyed so much support on campuses in the past are now finding more students complaining about their views.

> **Note** Students are becoming more conservative.

The Role of Parents

In the past, parents have been rather passive while colleges actively recruited their children. This, too, is changing. Education costs are rising faster than inflation and parents are contributing more to their children's college costs. The process is not as simple as it once was, and a growing number of parents are seeking assistance from private college consultants to fill out the FAFSA and to help with essays, applications, and resume writing.

Colleges Coming to High Schools

While you may have attended a college day in your high school, college night is something different. The typical college night involves college representatives telling about the colleges and handing out brochures. But some colleges have a different twist. Students might come prepared with application forms and resumes in hand. After meeting with a college rep, they are either accepted or declined on the spot. Some students who are declined may be accepted on the condition that they take remedial classes.

Why would colleges do this? Some students have parents who cannot take time off work to go on a college visit. They simply can't afford to miss work. Other parents are intimidated by college personnel because they never attended college themselves. To make it easier on the students and families, some colleges are coming to the students.

Greater Number of Smaller Scholarships

In the past, the class valedictorian would win a full-ride scholarship, leaving classmates with few scholarships to be distributed among them. Today, more students get scholarships in the $3,000–$7,000 range, and fewer are winning the full rides.

The rationale is to help the greater number of students instead of a chosen few.

Options for ACT and SAT

In the past, students took the ACT or SAT once, sent in a transcript with an application blank, and the process was complete. Today, colleges want to see students take the ACT or SAT Writing Tests, subject tests, Advanced Placement classes, International Baccalaureate classes, college-credit classes, and dual-credit classes. The demands upon high school students are higher and more stressful today than 30 years ago!

The group at www.FairTest.org opposes the ACT and SAT testing altogether and wants to see the exams eliminated. They have a good start. The Fair Test Web site lists all colleges in the United States that accept but do not demand the ACT or SAT. Approximately one third of colleges are ACT- and SAT-optional schools. Each year, Fair Test adds more colleges, and each year the testing corporations state how valuable their tests are. Colleges claim that the quality of students has not declined, but, rather, improved. The number of applicants to colleges has also increased.

Note At one-third of colleges, ACT and SAT tests are optional.

Quote "To keep our faces toward change and behave like free spirits in the presence of fate is strength undefeatable."

–Helen Keller

The changes have been many. History will tell whether they were for the better.

How Can You Get a Good Letter of Recommendation?

Having a weak letter of recommendation is like having no letter at all. What can you do to improve your chances of receiving a good letter?

First of all, you have to give someone something to write about. Are you holding a solid grade point average? Are you involved in school activities? Are you developing your natural talents? Have you been doing volunteer work at the school, at your church, or in the community?

If you have done your part so far, there are several ways to increase your chances of getting a great letter instead of a ho-hum letter.

Contact the Right Person

Trying to get a great letter from someone who is not capable of writing a great letter is useless. It's probably not going to happen.

 Note Pick the right teacher to write a letter.

Select a teacher who has seen you do something well or who has seen you at your best. If you are active in music—vocals, strings, or band—your music teacher would be the logical choice. If you have overcome a physical difficulty with the assistance of a teacher, select that person. Who is the teacher with whom you have the best relationship? Which one is most likely to be complimentary about you and perhaps be most eloquent?

Find the Right Time

Students are very busy in high school. Unfortunately, so are teachers. You need to leave two or three weeks, or even more, for a teacher to write a good letter and mail it off to a college for admission or scholarships.

Ask teachers for the letter when they have a minute of free time. Approaching them in the hall as the tardy bell is ringing probably won't get you much of anything. For one thing, the teacher is not likely to remember who asked for the letter an hour later. Too, they won't know where you want it sent. And they won't know when it is due. Three strikes and you may be out if you are counting on a good letter appearing soon.

Note Wait until the time is right.

Let's try this method instead. Prepare a resume of your high school years. (I think I heard groaning!) Chapter 45 explains resumes in detail. Students who want to give a professional look to their request will include a resume. Teachers may know you, but they don't have you memorized and will not be able to construct a laundry list of your accomplishments. Your resume may refresh your teachers' memories of you.

Watch for Nonverbal Cues

Look at the teacher when you are making a request. If you get a wince or roll of the eyes, move on. The wince may mean many things. It could mean that your teacher is planning to be gone for a week or two and won't have enough time to write a good letter. The roll of the eyes could mean that this teacher might not hold you in high regard. If you have been accused of bullying, if you have gotten into some fights after school, or if you have been caught cheating on tests, this teacher may write a very vague letter, which is exactly what you don't want. Vague and generic letters may leave the college wondering what is not being said or what is being hidden.

But if a teacher seems honored to be asked, if he or she smiles and says, "I would love to write a letter for you," you have a winner. Please ask the teacher to save the letter on a computer because you may be applying to several colleges. Teachers appreciate the heads up.

 "Of all the things you wear, your expression is the most important."

–Janet Lane

Write a Cover Letter

What? You have to write a cover letter? Well, yes. You want to include an explanation of the letter's purpose. Is it for admission into college or admission into the school of music? Is it for an athletic scholarship or a drama scholarship? Identifying the purpose will help your admissions counselors as they evaluate your letter and your qualifications.

The cover letter should also state the admissions counselor's name and the deadline for submission. Submitting a request without stating the deadline could mean a late letter. Keep track of all deadlines on each college folder and place the deadlines on your main family calendar, also.

One more thing—include an addressed, stamped envelope. Paper clip the cover letter, resume, and envelope together, and you will have a polished request to hand over to your teacher. This way, the teacher will know the purpose of the letter along with the deadline for submission. He or she will also have a thumbnail sketch of you over the past four years. With all this at hand, the teacher will can easily write the letter and drop it in the mail when completed. Mission accomplished.

"Kindness is a language the dumb can speak and the deaf can hear and understand."

–Christian Nestel Bovee

On the folder, jot down the date you gave the request packet to your teacher. If the teacher is late and the college calls saying they have not received the information, you may say, "Gosh, I'm sorry. I requested the letter three weeks ago. I'll check on it and get back to you." Colleges understand that teachers are busy and forget things. They probably won't hold it against you.

 Have teachers save each letter they write for you.

Ask for Other Letters

In addition to the standard letter or two from teachers, colleges often ask the principal to write a letter. The principal may be able to give insight into a student that the teacher cannot. While an instructor may teach you in a specific academic area, the principal is able to give an overall picture of your four years in high school.

Counselors often are asked for letters of recommendation, as well. A counselor's letter usually carries much weight. If a student is on the edge of an admission decision, an influential letter from the counselor may sway the college.

Should you ask for a copy of a letter of recommendation? Absolutely not. There are several reasons for this. One reason is that these letters are to be honest statements directly from the teacher, principal, or counselor to the college. A second reason is that students may not be able to resist showing other students the letter. So much for confidentiality, right? What if your teacher considers you her top math student and says so in the letter. Another student reads this and is surprised, because he thought he was the top student. The letter has just created a problem for the teacher.

"Be nice to people on your way up because you'll meet them on your way down."

–Wilson Mizner

Express Gratitude

If a teacher, counselor, or principal writes you a letter of recommendation, some form of gratitude is in order. The bare minimum is a thank-you card. While these individuals may write a letter only once and save it, you might be asking them to send that letter out to six colleges. They will have to change the date and the admission counselor's name and perhaps tweak the letter to fit the purpose. After they have done this four, five, or six times, a thank you from you is definitely in order.

 "Feeling gratitude and not expressing it is like wrapping a present and not giving it."

–William Arthur Ward

Students in the past have given a variety of tokens of appreciation:

- Homemade cookies
- Movie passes
- An original painting
- Gift certificate to the local coffee shop
- Scented candle
- Gift certificate to a local store
- Gift certificate to a local restaurant

A good letter may take several hours to write, rewrite, and proof. Showing gratitude is a sign of good manners—something to keep in mind always.

Maintain Documentation and Meet Deadlines

Again, keep track of all requests by a college. A folder for each college is a good way to organize everything. When you request a letter from Mrs. Smith, write that on the folder with the date requested. That way, you will always remember who you asked to send the letter and where it is going. You may ask several teachers to write letters to different colleges. While you think you will remember everything, you probably won't.

Note Taking time to be organized will save time in the end.

Don't miss a deadline! If a scholarship competition deadline is February 15, it is February 15. The college will receive plenty of applications on time. They won't have to consider yours if it's late.

State universities are less likely to require letters of recommendation. But, then, they are also less likely to give large scholarships and notice your unique qualities.

Quote "Always bear in mind that your own resolution to succeed is more important than any other one thing."

–Abraham Lincoln

CHAPTER 30

What Are the Most Popular College Majors?

Colleges in the United States fall into two categories: two-year and four-year institutions. The major fields of study, of course, are different in each group.

Two-Year Institutions

The hottest majors at the junior college level are those in the field of applied science and technology, once known as vocational technology. However, not everyone attending a junior college is an applied science and technology major. Some students take prerequisite classes for a four-year program and then transfer.

When polled, most parents indicate that they want their children to attend a four-year college. However, the majority of new careers require a two-year degree. At a four-year institution, students take two years of general requirements and approximately two years of classes in a major field. At a junior, or two-year, college, students take classes in their career field and skip all the general requirements. So the two-year program is intense training in a field of choice. Junior colleges are very quick to react to the needs of society. If an industry needs new technology and new workers, the junior colleges react quickly to provide them.

Filling the Need for Workers

For a while, junior colleges were eliminating some vocational majors. This action has created a developing crisis in the supply of necessary workers. Baby Boomers aged 41–62 are retiring in record numbers. Many are the mechanics, welders, machinists, contractors, plumbers, and electricians who learned their trade through military service and the GI Bill. Unfortunately, as these workers retire, few skilled workers are available fill their shoes.

Junior colleges are attempting to meet the needs of society. However, once a program is eliminated from a college's curriculum, it is costly and time-consuming to reinstate. There are now waiting lists for many junior college majors. In the meantime, a factory may need five skilled workers in a specific field and get only two applicants for those positions.

As with any shortage, wages go up as demand increases. Nurses were once underpaid and now enjoy higher wages and plentiful jobs as the nursing shortage intensifies. It is common for certified mechanics to be paid from $50,000 to more than $100,000 a year, as qualified mechanics become harder to find. Some pipe welders earn more than $100,000 a year. Blue-collar jobs are no longer underpaid jobs.

Career Fields

Some of the popular two-year careers fields include the following:

- Agriculture Technology
- Automotive Collision Technology
- Automotive Technology
- Biofuels Technology (ethanol and biodiesel)
- Biotechnology
- Broadcasting
- CAD (computer-aided design)
- Carpentry
- Computer Networking Technology
- Computer Repair
- Culinary Arts
- Dental Hygiene (three years)
- Diesel Technology

- Emergency Medical Services
- Graphics Technology
- Hospitality Management
- Industrial Electrician
- Industrial Mechanics
- Logistics and Transportation Management
- Maintenance Electrician
- Manufacturing Technology
- Medical Lab Technician
- Medical Transcription/Records
- Nursing
- Radiologic Technology
- Turf Management
- Wind Energy Technology

Many of these fields are in a critical state of shortage with agencies unable to fill current openings. Job placement for graduates of junior colleges is extremely high. Employers have stepped up their recruiting efforts to find qualified employees.

 "The shoe that fits one person pinches another; there is no recipe for living that suits all cases."
 –Carl Jung

Although junior colleges offer excellent career choices, many students choose to go on for more education and move into more traditional fields.

Four-Year Institutions

While junior college students must select a vocational field when they begin classes, students on the four-year plan have much more time to decide.

Choosing a Major

A place to start when choosing a major is to consider your favorite classes. Your favorite classes are probably those in which you get the best grades. And they probably are areas in which you have talent and strength in those areas. Choosing a major in your strength area makes sense. It is going with the grain instead of going against the grain.

 Quote "Everyone excels in something in which another fails."
–Latin proverb

Encarta, the online education guide, recently announced the 10 most popular college majors. Unfortunately, there is absolutely no guarantee that selecting one of the most popular fields will have anything to do with getting a job after graduation. No one can predict the future or the economic implications that arise from events such as a war on terror, gas prices, or an epidemic. But, there is a popular trend in 10 fields, as described in the next section.

Career Fields

Business. For a major in business, you should have an interest in accounting, management, finance, marketing, or human resources. While receiving a business degree is good, receiving a Master of Business Administration (MBA) degree may be even better. An advanced degree gives you more chance for promotion.

Quote "In the end, all business operations can be reduced to three words: people, product, and profits. People come first."
–Lee Iacocca

Psychology. Studying people and their behaviors is always fascinating, and psychology is a popular subject. If human behavior is fascinating to you, you may want to consider studying this further. But this degree is not very profitable unless you go on to get a master's degree or a PhD.

Elementary education. There is a shortage in some teaching areas, but elementary education is not one of them. Instead of choosing a general field such as elementary education, you would be better advised to select certification in a field such as Resource (Special Education) or Reading Specialist.

> **Quote** "If you think education is expensive, try ignorance."
>
> –Derek Bok

Biology. Whether you are interested in trees, microbes, marine life, or medicine, this field is wide open. Genetics, biotechnology, and medical research are areas to consider if you have an interest in biology. Many biologists move on to become biochemists, environmentalists, optometrists, or veterinarians.

Nursing. Our population is growing and aging. Many people thought there would soon be a nursing surplus, but that is not the case. Jobs exist in hospitals, schools, corporations, the military, nursing homes, and clinics. And because nurses are necessary 24 hours a day, the need is for three shifts each day rather than one. Nursing is not for everyone. Not only can it be physically demanding, but the academics are challenging as well. Nurses may elect to get a two-year degree, a four-year degree, or a master's degree. Many go on to become nurse practitioners.

> **Note** Nursing comes in two-year, four-year, and master's degree options.

Education. High school education is reaching a crisis in many regions of the country. Shortage areas are math, sciences, foreign language, music, and industrial arts. It is common for schools to hire a foreign teacher to teach a foreign language. Other career fields to consider in education are speech pathology, guidance counseling, and administration.

"It is the studying that you do after your school days that really counts. Otherwise, you know only that which everyone else knows."

–Henry L. Doherty

English. English is a field with unlimited options. English majors often enter journalism, reporting, advertising, public relations, writing, speech writing, teaching, or even law. If it is connected to communication, English majors may apply.

Communications. Influencing human behavior is communication. Whether it is through advertising, government, or media, it is communication. Public relations, human resources, and business are but a few areas for communications.

"Communication is depositing a part of yourself in another person."

–Anonymous

Computer science. Who would have thought that a high school student would be taking a school-issued computer home for completing assignments? In addition to school work, computers are needed in robotics, language recognition programs, business applications, medicine, and outer space. Those computers require networking and repairs.

Political science. This broad major requires an area of concentration. Some choices include voting behavior, public policy, statistics, campaigns, diplomatic service, and lobbying.

While deciding which college to attend, see if the area of interest you select is listed as a popular major at the college. Popular majors at a college or university usually result in more professors and more opportunities for students in that field.

Whether you select a one-year track, a two-year track, or a four-year track or more, you will need to select a track. In today's progressive and fast-paced world, employers want to see that piece of paper that tells them what you are certified or qualified to do.

CHAPTER 31

What If You Have a Learning Disability?

The good news is that there are colleges specifically for students with disabilities. In fact, there is one college to which you can't be admitted without a disability. The bad news is that few colleges are like this. However, colleges are becoming more knowledgeable about making modifications, and students are becoming more successful.

> **Note** Colleges are now making modifications for the learning disabled.

Specialized Programs

A few colleges are beginning to have specialized programs to help students with learning disabilities—and not only the physical disabilities aided by automatic doors and elevators. In the past, colleges offered a learning center or tutoring services but did not address learning disabilities specifically. Colleges often monitored students, but this was not enough. Now things are changing.

In the past, many very capable and often far-above-average disabled students did not dare enter college. Dyslexic students, students with nonverbal learning disabilities, and severe ADHD (attention deficit hyperactivity disorder) students are now demanding equality under the Americans with Disabilities Act. It is now law that students with these disabilities must have modifications and accommodations made for them. It is not an option. Sadly, some colleges that would not expect a student to get an education without a wheelchair deny learning-disabled students what they need to succeed.

Many colleges state that they assist students with learning disabilities. This is often not enough for a learning disabled student who could be more successful in a different environment. Students who do not see themselves as equal to their peers have learned to blend in and not ask questions. They are not very proactive in having their educational needs met, and they often fail because of this.

Note Finding the right college to meet your needs may not be easy.

Some resource teachers are on the cutting edge of research and are able to teach students how to succeed despite a disability. But many students are not fortunate enough to have teachers like this. To succeed in college, an LD (learning disabled) student must have specific strategies taught and used with some monitoring from college staff.

A learning disability does not always mean lower ability. The reverse is often true. Many learning-disabled students fall above average in ability, and many are considered gifted. Quite often, these students simply need to be taught differently. The mystery is in discovering how they learn and finding what works.

Assistance: Three Categories

Assistance to students with learning disabilities at the college level falls into three categories. In the first category is the college that offers some tutoring and a learning center with assistants but not specialists in learning disabilities. The second category includes the college that offers a specialist in learning disabilities closely monitoring the student and teaching strategies for success. In the third category is the college that has a mission statement to help learning-disabled students succeed at the college level.

Category One

Category one is appropriate for students who are proactive and who have learned strategies in high school to overcome their learning disabilities. For students who have already met the challenge of their disability and succeeded, a college that has assistance available when needed could work well. Colleges at this level do little to help students succeed, and the responsibility falls primarily on the student. Most colleges can assist at this level. In many cases it isn't a matter of the college refusing to help students. Instead, the institution simply may not know how.

Category Two

Category two is for students who are still working far below their potential despite a high ability and for those who have not mastered learning strategies. A new pool of colleges is targeting small groups of learning-disabled students and working with them on a one-on-one basis. These colleges often have a learning specialist in an office for disabilities or a learning disabilities program on campus, not merely a success center providing occasional tutoring. A handful of colleges per state may assist at this level.

Category Three

Category three is for students who want to attend an accredited college specifically made for them. Landmark College in Putnam, Vermont, is custom-made for students with learning disabilities. Landmark College offers a two-year associate degree. Students receive such a personalized education that Landmark boasts of the nation's lowest professor-to-student ratios. You must have an official diagnosis to attend this college. Landmark will admit you only if you have average-to-above-average ability and dyslexia, attention deficit hyperactivity disorder, or another specific learning disability. After two years at Landmark, students will have learned strategies to help them achieve success and move on to a four-year college.

While Landmark provides a great learning experience for a few students, it is not a college for everyone.

Applying for Assistance

If you know a student with a disability or if you are one of these students, what needs to be in place prior to applying to college and asking for learning assistance?

- The student must have a diagnosis made within the past three years. The diagnosis must be from a professional in the medical field or from a psychologist.

- The student must list his or her disability.

- The student must have a developmental history. School records would show problem-solving meetings, testing scores, or interventions.

- The limitations of the student must be listed: For example, the student has poor motor skills and cannot do key-boarding. Or the student's dyslexia is so severe that he or she can learn only by verbal methods.

- Accommodations must also be listed. If the student has poor motor skills and cannot do keyboarding, it is reasonable to expect a computer program will be made available that operates on verbal cues from the student. If the student is so severely dyslexic that reading is not possible, it is reasonable that a Kurzweil computer program be made available to read textbooks and worksheets for the student.

- The student must currently have an IEP (Individualized Education Program) and must be receiving accommodations. A 504 plan, which outlines educational services, may not be considered sufficient. Some colleges will accept a 504 plan, but others will accept only an IEP.

When these items are in place, a student may approach a college and ask for the same modifications at the college level that he or she had in high school. Some colleges are open to making accommodations quickly, while others procrastinate. Procrastination may be a subtle way of saying it just isn't going to happen.

According to the Rehabilitation Act of 1974, colleges may not discriminate against students with disabilities by refusing to provide modifications and accommodations in an IEP. Any institution accepting federal funding must comply with this law. The only exception is when the student has no evidence of having a disability or has not let the college know that there is a disability.

Note Instructors can't help you unless you speak up and say you need modifications.

Monica was a college student with Scotopic Sensitivity Syndrome, a form of dyslexia. But Monica did not know she had SSS. For some reason, she could not read but she understood and retained information perfectly if someone read to her. Her mother had dedicated her life to reading every textbook every evening throughout Monica's school years. While a sophomore in college taking an evening class, Monica had a professor who suspected something was wrong. Monica used a piece of paper to keep her writing on the line, a symptom of SSS. The professor screened Monica for SSS, and the results were amazing. By merely placing a dark blue overlay on a book page, Monica could see the words clearly as never before.

She went to the Irlen Clinic in Kansas City and got fitted with eyeglasses in her specific color. Monica is now a resource room teacher and is helping other students with the same disability. Throughout her school years, she was in the resource room and referred to as "a slow student." All that time, Monica was a bright and frustrated student who was unable to see the printed page like other students.

Antonio was diagnosed with dyslexia in fifth grade. At his small rural school, Antonio's parents asked for a meeting to explain the diagnosis to the administration and to ask for modifications. What modifications did the school make? Antonio was asked to sit in the back of the room and not cause problems. Then he would be passed on to the next grade.

Luckily, Antonio learned quite well by listening. In college, he was taking a class from the same professor that Monica had. Monica was passing the colored overlays to students while explaining SSS. When Antonio placed the orange overlay on his textbook, he stood up, looked at the class, and said, "Is this what the rest of you see?" The print was clear for the first time in his life.

Antonio explained that what he usually saw looked like a text that had been sent through the copier about 20 times, with the letters barely legible. No wonder he was a slow reader. Antonio did not have a vision problem. He had a perception problem with an easy fix.

With some effort, most students will be able to find a college in category two that has a disability specialist on staff and a modified Landmark program that is available to a small group of students.

Apply early, because a small college might accept only 20 students per year. There is usually an extra fee for this program, but vocational rehabilitation funds often will cover the extra expense. When selecting colleges to visit, ask whether they have an office of disabilities or a learning disabilities program.

 Note While researching a college, ask whether they have an office of disabilities or a learning disabilities program.

When the law is not followed after reasonable requests, students may file a protest with state agencies, the Office for Civil Rights in Washington, D.C., at 202-205-9645, or the Department of Justice at 800-524-0301.

The Rehabilitation Act of 1974 attempts to level the playing field in education. This act works in the same way as the law demanding accessible doors, curbs, and elevators for individuals in wheelchairs. Those with learning disabilities, as well as physical disabilities, deserve to have modifications made.

It may be easier to find an existing program at a college than to force a resistant college to meet your needs. You may waste much time and energy pushing a wall that will not move.

PART III

College Visits: A Key Step in Finding the Best School for You

When Should You Visit Colleges?

When should you start college visits? This question is not asked soon enough. Forget visiting colleges in your senior year. That is old misinformation. Junior year is for visiting.

Classes in Session

Visiting a campus void of students does not let you have a feel for the campus atmosphere. Many college selections are made by how prospective students feel about being on campus. Note that many homes are purchased because of how the buyers feel as they tour the home; cars are often purchased based on how the driver feels behind the wheel. The same is true of colleges. Some feel like the perfect choice once you visit. But many things must be in place for you to get the true feel for the college.

> **Note** Visit a campus when classes are in session.

Visiting a campus while classes are in session also gives you the opportunity to visit the dorms and see how students live. Touring an empty dorm room is not the same as visiting when students are there. Eating in the cafeteria lets you experience the quality of the food and observe students. Visiting in the summer allows you to see gutted dorms undergoing remodeling, a closed cafeteria, and empty classrooms.

Admissions Counselor

You should always visit a college when your admission counselor is there to greet you. Make an appointment to visit the college, and make sure your counselor will be there. This may be the only time for the two of you to meet, and your counselor is a very important person in the college selection process. It is nice to have a face associated with the name, and it will give the counselor a chance to get to know you better. That is always a good thing.

 Note Don't visit a campus if your personal admissions counselor is not going to be there that day.

In-Service Days

Your high school is likely to have several in-service days and breaks throughout the year. Try to visit a college on a day that your high school is not in session. Colleges are likely to have breaks at different times than high schools do. When you know the dates that your high school is not in session, call a college and see whether the college is in session and if your counselor will be available.

Your admissions counselors are visiting high schools, recruiting students on a regular basis. If they have made an appointment to be at a school on a certain date, you will have to select a different day to visit. As you schedule your visit, you will learn that colleges have different schedules and different breaks. What doesn't work for one college may work for another.

Note Try to visit a college when your high school is not in session.

Parents

Try to visit when your parents can accompany you. Yes, it will be your college and not theirs, but your parents are making a financial investment in your college education. They may think to ask questions that you don't. These questions could be critical to your decision about where to attend. Parents may also see safety issues, crowded classrooms, and poor maintenance.

Let's face it: You want to leave home and every college looks pretty good because of the freedom factor. Parents help put your feet back on the ground, and they help you to be realistic.

Note Go with a parent on a college visit.

Lili's first college visit was to a smaller university that was sprawled all over the town. The highways leading to the college were narrow and in poor condition. It didn't even look like a college campus. There was a building here and a building there, with residential homes between. The signs were faded and there seemed to be no landscaping. You couldn't see where it began or ended. The athletic center was on the other side of town, and the buildings were poorly maintained. The admissions counselor was quite rude and seemed more interested in telling Lili how she wouldn't qualify for scholarships than in helping her to feel comfortable. Despite this, Lili was in love with this college and with the guys on campus. She was sure she had found her spot.

Her mother insisted that Lili visit other colleges. Lili visited five more colleges and could not believe she ever saw anything of value in the first one. After visits to other schools, she could see why her mother had insisted on other trips. The admissions staff members at the other colleges were friendly, the buildings were amazing, professional landscaping beautified each campus, and the colleges were entities in themselves. Some even had gates for entrance and safety. Had Lili's mother not accompanied her on the first college visit, Lili might not have visited other schools.

You almost have to be desensitized to see past the glamour and glitz. Visiting several colleges will do that.

Note Visit several colleges so you can compare and contrast.

Have a Plan

The time to begin thinking about college is your sophomore year in high school. Some students begin visiting in the sophomore year, but this is too early for many. The best way to begin the process is to take the ACT or SAT early in the junior year or prior to that year. Of course, a good way to prepare for these tests is to take challenging classes in high school.

Why begin so early? You may not like your scores when you take the ACT or SAT the first time. Many students do much better on the second try. Consider the first time a trial run. Since the ACT and SAT exams are given only a few times during the year, you will need time to get the second test registered, taken, and scored before you know which colleges to visit.

Match Scores

Colleges have a mid-range of ACT or SAT scores based on the scores of the students attending. Avoid falling in the bottom 25 percent. If you receive an 18 or 19 on your first try on the ACT, take the test again before you rule out any colleges. Students often receive a 21 or 22 on the second try.

If your scores fall into the middle range or higher, you can safely visit this college without it being a waste of time and money. Your scores are a match.

 Note Match your scores to the scores at the college.

As soon as you know your school calendar and ACT or SAT scores in your junior year, you may begin scheduling visits. Don't start visiting randomly. This is a waste of time and money.

Visiting with friends is better than not visiting at all, but getting a personal tour will let you think about what you like and don't like instead of focusing on the opinions of your friends.

CHAPTER 33

Which Colleges Should You Visit First?

As you begin to research colleges, some will seem to be better matches than others. The more a college has what you are looking for, the better it will seem as a prospect.

Find Your Best Match

Create a list of things you would prefer in your college.

Large College or Small?

Take an honest look at your personality. While many of us would like to think we are the assertive and outgoing type, many really are not. Extroverts gain energy by being with people—the more the better. After a long day of classes, extroverts rush to the student center or commons to be with people. An introvert regenerates by being alone and finding a quiet place. Big crowds drain the energy out of an introvert, and he or she often spends evenings alone, trying to recharge for the next day.

> **Note** The size of the college is a personal choice based on personality.

If big crowds are not for you, you may not be material for a university of 25,000 students and auditorium lecture halls that seat 300. A small college with small classrooms may be a better match for you.

Large City or Rural Setting

Does the size of the city matter to you? Are you used to the metropolitan setting, or do you want to experience it for the first time? Do you prefer the quiet setting of a town of 10,000? How about a rural setting in the mountains or a prairie? It is up to you.

Religious Preference

Most students do not give religious preference much weight. Many parents do. Parents know that college romances often end in marriage. Many prefer that their children have a one-religion relationship. Others simply want their children to attend a college that reflects their beliefs.

College guides will tell you the religions of students attending, in most cases. Buena Vista University in Storm Lake, Iowa, is a small, selective college that wants to maintain a strong enrollment. BVU is a Presbyterian college, but only 5 percent of its students are Presbyterian. The University of Notre Dame is a Catholic university in Notre Dame, Indiana. There, 84 percent of the students are Catholic. Notre Dame is a highly selective college and wants to maintain its Catholic identity.

Jamie "majored in social life" at his first college. It was a very liberal private college with very few dorm or campus restrictions. During the second semester, Jamie's parents were horrified to learn about the lifestyle their son selected and transferred him to an ultraconservative Baptist college. The campus rules were very rigid, and Jamie had to follow them or go home and stay there. Jamie decided to conform to the rules and was successful as a student.

 Quote "If matters go badly now, they will not always do so."

–Horace

ACT and SAT Scores

The colleges you select should match your ACT or SAT scores. No one wants to be at the bottom of each class. If the middle range of students falls between 21 and 25 at a particular college, and you have an 18, you probably don't belong there. These scores mean that 50 percent of the students have scores between 21 and 25; 25 percent have scores above 25, and 25 percent have scores below 21. Just picture being in classes with students who have taken tougher classes in high school, earned higher grade point averages, and outscored you by a wide margin on the ACT. Does that sound like fun? Pick a college that falls in your range. They are out there.

 Colleges should match your academic achievements.

Majors

Check whether the colleges you want to visit have your interest area as a popular major. Then, check to see whether they have your major at all. If it is not a popular major, find out how many students have selected that subject area as a major. For example, you are interested in biology, and it isn't listed as a popular major. The college has more than 5,000 students, and you learn that 8 are biology majors. You may prefer to attend a college that has 150 students as biology majors.

Note Make sure your college choices offer the major you chose.

Professor-to-Student Ratios

Some state universities have very low professor-to-student ratios, but many have high ratios. Many private colleges have very low professor-to-student ratios, but many do not. Your research will enable you to find the data and then decide how important it is to you.

The lower the ratio, the more assistance you can expect as a student when you need to talk to the instructor. Some colleges have a 1:25 ratio. Good luck in finding the instructor free there.

Costs and Financial Aid

Colleges give figures for costs, but college costs are on a sliding scale. The less you have, the less you pay. If your family income is on the lower end, you will not pay the full cost. You don't want to pay close attention to college costs. What you do want to pay attention to is the generosity of the colleges. In the guides under Costs and Financial Aid, the average percentage of need met is listed. This tells you how generous the college has been in the past. If a college states that it meets 50 percent of the percentage of need, don't expect anything spectacular at this college. But if a college states it meets 95 or 100 percent of need, you stand a better chance of receiving a generous package. Remember, every student is different, and every college is different.

 "It is good to have things that money can buy, but it is also good to check up once in a while and be sure we have the things money can't buy."

—Unknown

Campus Life and Extracurricular Activities

If you are a student who has dreamed of joining a sorority or a fraternity, make sure your college choices offer this. Some do not. Some colleges may have the sorority/fraternity population at 45 percent of the campus population. At these colleges, the sororities and fraternities may control social life, with not much left over for everyone else. Other campuses have a very small percentage of students—or none—joining the Greeks.

"Almost every man wastes part of his life in attempts to display qualities which he does not possess, and to gain applause which he cannot keep."

–Samuel Johnson

Services and Facilities

If you want to know if a school has counseling services, computer services, provisions for campus safety, or assistance for a learning disability, you should look to services and facilities. If something is unclear, call the admissions office for clarification. Read Chapter 31 for information on learning disabilities.

Rate Colleges

Get a large index card for each college of interest and gather the facts. Assign a number range to each fact—1, 2, or 3. For example, if the size of a college is important, give the size of the college a range of 1–3. If a college is the wrong size, give it a 1. If it is the perfect size, give it a 3. Move on to the size of the city and the rest of the data. Arrange the colleges in order of scores and start at the top. Visit the college with the highest number of points first and continue. After you visit several, a few colleges will begin to rise to the top. Your number one choice may not stay in first place after you visit.

On the other hand, you may change your mind about how important some of the factors are. You may not have chosen a large city, but once you visited you found that you liked it. Or you wanted a large city, but once you visited you decided it was definitely not for you. You get to decide where you want to live. That's part of the fun.

 "Nothing is more difficult, and therefore more precious, than to be able to decide."

–Napoleon Bonaparte

CHAPTER 34

What Should You Look for on a College Visit?

You've researched college choices and found several that are good matches. Now you are actually going to visit the colleges. Because you want to visit once and not get confused, you need a plan of what to ask each college. After all, college visits can be costly in terms of time from work or school and expenses for gas, food, lodging, and even airplane tickets.

Meet the Counselor

Don't make plans to visit a college unless your personal admissions counselor will be there. Make sure the counselor can make time to speak with you and possibly give you a tour. If the counselor will not be available that day, consider visiting on another day.

While visiting, show interest in the college. This is not the time to discuss negatives. You can do that on your way home in private. After all, if you don't act interested in the college, the admissions counselor will not act very interested in you. Not all students who visit a campus will attend. The counselor will focus on students who are most likely to attend.

> **Note** Act very interested while on the campus tour.

Show you have done some research on the college and talk about what you are specifically interested in. It could be the athletic program or the science program. It could be the reputation of the music or nursing program. Let the counselor know that you are there for a reason and didn't just walk in off the street to look at the campus.

Be sure to ask these questions:

- What is the preferred application date?
- What is the financial aid deadline?
- By what date are the dormitories likely to be filled?

Keep information together for future reference. It is easy to get confused after visiting several colleges.

Take a Campus Tour

On the day of the campus visit, go directly to the admissions office. This is the key office for visitors.

As you get out of the car, it is difficult not to be impressed. Many colleges have amazing architecture and landscaping—Gothic spires, Greek columns, blooming flowers, breathtaking building interiors, brick sidewalks, and bell towers. The atmosphere can be almost regal, and most families are in awe of their surroundings. However, remember that each college must fill the desks to stay open. Colleges want and need you as much as you want and need a college. You should interview the college just as the college interviews you.

 Note Shop around for a college. Look for details that match your likes and dislikes.

Student Life

By the time you walk onto a campus, you should already know the ratios of males-to-females and professors-to-students, the number of undergraduates, the school's academic ranking, the average ACT or SAT scores, the graduation rate, and majors of interest to you. There are still many things to watch for and to ask about.

Clothes

How students dress is something to observe. Is everyone in jeans and T-shirts, or are they dressed in khakis and polo shirts? Will you be comfortable dressing this way? And speaking of clothes, how much closet and dresser space are you going to have in each dorm? Are there formal events you should bring clothes for?

Cars

Here are some questions to ask if you're considering a car on campus:

- Are freshmen allowed to have cars?
- Where are the parking spaces located?
- Is parking free?
- Is parking secured or fenced?
- How often are cars vandalized or burglarized? If cars are being trashed in a parking lot not far from campus, you may be better off not having a car.

Student Center

Here are some things to look for and some questions to ask when you visit the student center:

- How many students are there?
- What is posted on the bulletin boards? Are students asking for used books and rides home? Are there many activities for weekends?
- What do the students have to say? Talk to some of them if you feel comfortable doing so. Do they like their instructors? Does the computer lab work most of the time and is it accessible? Is the food in the cafeteria good?
- How many students stay on weekends?
- Is tutoring free?

Classes

- Do you see smaller classrooms with 15–20 chairs or auditoriums seating 300?
- Are the students and instructors friendly and happy?
- Do the classrooms have high-end technology?
- What would it be like to take classes in your field of interest? Attend a class and perhaps talk to the instructor afterward.
- Do teaching assistants teach, or are all the instructors seasoned?
- Ask how many teaching assistants will be teaching you.

Computers

Investigate these computer questions:

- Does the school issue laptops? Every two or three years?
- If they do, what are the charges?
- Is the campus wireless?
- Is the computer lab working properly?
- Is someone present to troubleshoot?
- Is the computer lab accessible when you need it?
- Are computers repaired at no charge?

Campus Features

Notice these campus features:

- Is the campus gated?
- Is it well maintained?
- How long does it take to cross campus? Is it 5 minutes or 20?

Campus Convenience and Safety

Ask these questions about the campus:

- How far is the nearest shopping area?
- Is the neighborhood around the college safe?
- How is the safety/crime record?

- Is campus security available?
- Are city police or the college student council called in to settle disputes?

Follow Up

Now that you are home, write a short note within two or three days, thanking your counselor for the tour. Let him or her know that you enjoyed your meeting. Then list a few of the best moments you experienced.

What impressed you? Was it the instructor who took time to talk for 10 minutes? Was it the warm atmosphere of the campus? Friendly students? The way the campus is designed? Technology?

A short handwritten note to the admissions counselor is in order. E-mail is good, but a handwritten note is better. Gratitude is always impressive.

 Note A thank-you note to the admissions counselor is a must after a college visit.

Compare and Contrast

Give yourself a day to decompress. Then sit down with your family and discuss the pros and cons of your college visit. Compare this college with any others you have visited. Rank them in order as of that day. Does this most recent college rank as first out of three, or is it dead last? Does this college bump any others you have visited? How does it meet your needs?

After visiting four, five, six, or even seven colleges, rank them in order of best to worst. This will help in the confusion of selecting a college in the spring when the award letters begin arriving.

CHAPTER 35

What Should You Look for in Housing and the Cafeteria?

The housing and cafeteria can become very important if they are inferior. Check both carefully.

Dorms

Carefully check out the dorms. Dorms can be in frightening shape or in excellent condition. They may be brand new or 100 years old. Don't shrug your shoulders and pick any dorm. This is where you will spend a great deal of time.

It may be tempting, but do not live off campus. Student success in college drops for freshmen and sophomores when they live off campus. Statistics show that students do better living in dorms. This is why so many colleges demand students live on campus all four years or at least until they are seniors.

Ask these questions about dorms:

- Are the dorms air-conditioned?
- Is wireless service available?
- How far are the dorms from freshman classes?
- How far are they from the parking lot? (This is important if you plan to take a car.)
- Is there a fee for parking?
- What is the distance to the cafeteria?
- Are the dorms gender-specific?

- Are there co-ed dorms? Co-ed by floor or mixed floors?
- Do the dorms have elevators?
- How many students share a room?
- How much storage space is available, including desks, dressers, and closet space per student? Is there storage under beds?
- Are the floors carpeted and well-maintained?
- Is there a kitchen on every floor?
- Is there a fee for laundry facilities? What is the cost per load?
- Is there room for a personal fridge and furniture?
- How accessible are the dorms to the general public?
- Is security available 24/7?

Jot down your first, second, and third dorm choices while still on campus. This is a question that will be asked on the application form. Chances are very good that you will not remember which dorms were impressive a few days after you leave the campus.

Cafeteria

Some cafeterias are located right in the dorms, but most are not. My son and I recently visited his dream college. As we toured the cafeteria, the student tour guide stated, "Last year the food service was terrible. No one ate here unless they were starving. The students wrote letters to the president protesting the food. We have a new food service this year and it is fabulous. This place is packed." That is what you want to hear. Poor quality food raises out-of-pocket college expenses when you buy food at other places.

Cafeterias can vary greatly from campus to campus. The more colleges you visit, the more you will notice the differences. Students at some colleges have a chef preparing the menus with themes. Other colleges have a chow line with few choices. Some colleges give students the choice of six to eight cuisine entrees daily. It would be a good idea to eat at the cafeteria while visiting, if possible, just to sample how good the meals are.

Ask these questions about the cafeteria:

- What is the cost per semester?
- What are the meal plans? How many meals per week?
- Are you billed by the meal or by the food item based on points?
- Are students limited to a specific cafeteria?
- What are the cafeteria hours?
- Are students allowed to get sandwiches, fruit, or juice after hours?

The cost for food will probably not vary too much from college to college. However, the meal plans and quality will. A meal plan consisting of 20 meals may mean no Sunday evening meal, or it could mean that Sunday meals include a brunch with an evening meal. You don't want to return on Sunday afternoon and have to cook your own meal. If you are planning on staying on campus most weekends, you will appreciate the Sunday evening meal.

The point system for meals can really hurt large, hearty eaters. Hungry students can quickly use up points by Halloween or Thanksgiving. That means extra expenses.

Larger colleges often assign students to eat meals at one cafeteria. They can estimate how many students will eat meals there. The problem with this is that students can be on the other side of campus working on a project when it is time to eat. To cross campus for a meal and return could take 45 minutes. This could be precious time wasted on a tight schedule. So students skip the meal—not good.

Some colleges have short cafeteria hours. Breakfast can be over by 8:30 a.m. Snooze, you lose. Other colleges have expanded hours. There is something available most of the time. Some schools offer a deli bar at all hours, which reduces the need for junk food. It's like the fridge at home.

CHAPTER 36

What Should You Do at a College Interview?

So you are being interviewed by a college and you're nervous. Calm down. Remember that, in most cases, the college wants you to attend as much as you want to attend. It's a two-way street.

In-Person Interview

If you are meeting with a college admissions counselor for the first time, you may see the interview process as a quiz. It really isn't. The counselor is not looking for you to mess up. What he or she is looking for is your true personality, interests, and character. You probably have already submitted ACT scores, your high school transcript, and letters of recommendation. Now your counselor wants to learn more about you as a person.

> **Note** The college just wants to know you a little better.

The counselors realize that high school students have little experience in going through personal interviews. They understand that many students are not prepared and have little idea of what questions will be asked. With some preparation, you can be ready.

Here are some tips:

- Have good eye contact.
- Enter the room looking at the counselor.
- Maintain good posture when entering the room.
- Show confidence.
- Smile.
- Give a great handshake.
- Let the counselor begin the conversation.

Note Practice entering a room with confidence and giving a good handshake.

Dress Correctly

You want to be remembered for who you are and not for some bizarre outfit or hairstyle. Avoid anything that would take the focus away from what you are saying. A screaming orange top, a short mini-skirt, a Mohawk haircut, green hair, eight pairs of earrings, jeans with holes, or a nose ring would definitely distract the counselor while talking to you. Although your look may be the latest in fashion, you want to be remembered for what you say and not how outrageous you are. Tone it down a notch. Be a little conservative.

Note To be safe, dress on the conservative side.

Show Enthusiasm and Interest

Be excited to be there. Show interest in the college. Have questions prepared to ask about the college. Remember that this isn't just about your counselor interviewing you. Show interest in the college by interviewing your counselor. If you seem excited about what you see on campus, the counselor will be more excited about going to bat for you when it comes to financial aid and grants. If you act bored or not very interested, the counselor will be very gracious but may focus on other students who seem to want to be there. After all, each college hopes that students are excited about being on their campus.

Have something unique to share without being shocking. Use a little humor—but not at someone else's expense. Be animated by varying the tone of your voice. Stay focused on the counselor. Avoid topics on race, religion, and politics. Be gracious when speaking about any political or religious candidates, if they are mentioned. You may wrongly assume that everyone is a liberal or a conservative like you. In fact, the counselor across the desk or table may be your exact opposite. This is the person who is going to help you get accepted into college and negotiate a good financial aid package, remember?

Answer the Questions

Just like in any interview, some questions may throw you. But you should expect certain questions during a college or job interview.

If you're not prepared, these questions can leave you stuttering:

- Tell me about yourself. (Here is one of the most dreaded questions. Focus on your interests, education, and future.)
- What is your greatest fault? (Make this into a positive.)
- What is your favorite subject in school, and why?
- What is your favorite book? (Have one ready.)
- Do you have a major in mind? (Have a general idea. It can be very broad.)
- What would you like to be involved in on campus? (Have ideas ready.)
- Tell me about your favorite teacher. (Have one in mind and talk about his or her best qualities.)

Note Be prepared with answers to some typical interview questions.

Talk About Yourself

You want to be able to talk about yourself without being boastful and without put-downs. Putting yourself down is a sign of low self-esteem. On the other hand, being too pleased with yourself doesn't send the right signal and might cause you to be seen as rather obnoxious.

Your greatest fault could be not wanting to stop working until a job is done. It could be being very friendly in a group situation. Pick something negative that could be seen in a positive light.

Your favorite subject in school could be based on your natural ability, or it could be a subject you like because of a great teacher. It could be biology, government, or art. If you are asked why this is your favorite class, have an answer ready. Perhaps the class is very easy for you. Or maybe it is a class that is a challenge, and you don't mind working hard to do well. Are you the top student in this class?

Do you have a favorite book? Don't try to bluff your way through this one. Be sure you have read the book you mention. Why? The counselor may have just finished reading the book and may want to chat about your favorite characters or the best part of the book. It can be just about anything—a Harry Potter book or a mystery. Be prepared to state why it is your favorite. Do you like everything this author writes?

A likely major for you is one in the area in which you are finding success. We usually do well in what we like. If biology is your favorite subject, you probably do well in it. If music is your favorite area, you probably have talent and do very well. At least have a general idea of what you would like to study if you were to attend this college.

Campus involvement is what colleges want to see. A college wants students to be involved in the radio station, student government, sports, music, drama, and social activities. Have an answer ready of what would appeal to you.

A favorite teacher could be someone you would want to be like someday—that teacher who can magically get students to understand a difficult concept without their losing dignity. A fair teacher, a gifted teacher, or a kind teacher is one worth mentioning.

 "You cannot teach a man anything; you can only help him to find it within himself."

–Galileo

Share Your Portfolio

Some colleges like to see a collection of what you have accomplished in high school. If you have a portfolio, feel free to take it to the interview. Most colleges will not expect you to be carrying a portfolio of your accomplishments. Note, however, that it is a nice touch to have a resume along with your application or inquiry. A portfolio would only be evidence of what you entered on your resume.

Long-Distance Interview

If your college is several states away, the interview may be performed by a graduate of the school who lives in your area. If you are living in Nebraska and are interested in a college in Ohio, an interview may be arranged for you in Omaha for your convenience.

Think of an interview as a getting-to-know-you session. It is nothing to lose sleep over unless you have applied to Harvard, Stanford, or Yale, which accept less than 15 percent of students who apply. Most of the time, this is not the case. Put your best foot forward and be yourself.

 "You are only what you are when no one is looking."

–Robert C. Edwards

CHAPTER 37

What Are Some Recent Changes on Campus?

Colleges are constantly evolving and reflecting society. What are some changes that have been occurring?

Campus Life

The changes in the past 20–30 years on college campuses are many. Your parents' college is not necessarily your college.

Open Dorms

A generation ago, students had to check out and in when they left the dorm and returned. At many colleges, students had to list with whom they were going and where they were going. Doors locked at 10 or 11 p.m., and students had to beat that deadline. If they were late, the students were locked out and had to ring the doorbell and explain to the housemother why they were late. Sometimes they faced a punishment.

Permission in writing was necessary to have a male on the floor in the women's dorm. Typically, this happened only on special occasions such as homecoming. But on these occasions, the girl's door had to remain open, and the time for visiting was limited to specific hours such as 2–4 p.m. Males usually were allowed only in the building's lounge area, where they could contact the girls by telephone. Then, when they received a guest, the girls went downstairs to visit.

Today at most colleges students are coming and going without restrictions. Co-ed dorms are common, with shared floors and even shared bathrooms.

> **Note** Dorms have few visiting restrictions.

Baylor University in Texas, Notre Dame in Indiana, and Liberty University in Virginia are exceptions to the few-restrictions trend. Baylor has curfews and standards for behavior. Catholic values are upheld at Notre Dame. Liberty University has standards set by the late Jerry Falwell, and students have curfews. Visits from the opposite sex are not often permitted. The dorms are jokingly called barracks by the students because of the rigorous regulations.

But these colleges make up a minority of all colleges. You may safely assume that in most cases few limitations will be in place.

> **Note** Some colleges enforce a strong code of behavior.

Dress Codes

In the past, students were told what to wear and when. Boys were required to wear shirts and ties to Sunday dinner, and girls wore skirts or dresses. If students showed up in jeans and a sweatshirt, they were denied food until they dressed appropriately. Jeans were considered dorm attire and not suitable for classes. If the weather report stated that wind chill would be –10 or –20 degrees, the campus radio would announce permission for the girls to wear slacks to class on that day only. Colleges became pseudo-parents in exchange for tuition and room and board.

Today, students are not denied meals for improper attire. In fact, most colleges don't bother with dress codes. Students are free to express themselves as they choose. Unfortunately, some become labeled in a negative way very quickly because of what they wear on campus.

> **Note** Clothes are a personal choice, but you may be labeled quickly.

Partying

Alcohol is a major problem in college. The mix of college and alcohol has always been a concern, but in the past, college students usually limited their drinking to weekends. Today, students are binge drinking and unfortunately dying at a higher rate than ever. Universities are getting tougher on this out-of-control behavior. In addition to the tragic loss of human life, alcohol deaths are causing insurance premiums to rise. Some colleges are decreasing the number of fraternity houses because of these climbing rates, and fraternity parties and hazing are being addressed more often.

College officials no longer consider this "students will be students" behavior. Date rape and sexual harassment are increasing as the two genders spend more time together outside of class. Some universities are canceling celebrations that have been a tradition for more 50 years because of alcohol-related problems.

> **Note** Colleges are cracking down on drinking.

> **Quote** "The best way to haze freshmen is to make them study."
> –Anonymous

Academics

Changes have occurred on the academic side as well.

More Remedial Classes

Colleges are overwhelmed with students needing remedial classes in math. The problem is becoming so large that colleges are seeing the need to rewrite textbooks, do more reteaching, and force students to take remedial courses without credit.

The American College Testing organization, ACT, stated in its spring 2007 newsletter, *ACTIVITY,* that the gap between the type of education that high schools are delivering and the type of education that colleges need to see is widening.

High schools offer general information in many areas, while colleges prefer in-depth information in fewer areas.

Note Colleges complain that students are not prepared.

In Japan, students may spend an entire year mastering four math concepts. In the United States, students cover more than four concepts during the first quarter of school. Schools are told by state departments of education what to teach. The disconnect is that these education departments are not speaking to the colleges before they dictate what should be taught.

College Credits

A generation ago, all freshmen were arriving in September without college credit classes. Today, students are entering college with 30 college hours or more. These students have taken classes at the local junior college, the local four-year college, online, or at the high school with teachers holding at least a master's degree. Many students take AP classes and dual-credit classes prior to enrolling in college classes.

Quote "If you fear change, leave it here."
                                                    –Sign on a restaurant tip jar

CHAPTER 38

What Can You Learn from Viewbooks, Brochures, and Magazines?

Y ou will probably receive *viewbooks* when you inquire at a college. You will receive many other informational pieces as well, including catalogs and brochures, that offer information about the college.

The Viewbook

A viewbook is different from the other information pieces produced by a college. It is a beautiful commercial between two covers. Just as Saturday morning commercials were so enticing that they made you want to buy that toy, a viewbook is meant to entice you to attend this college.

> **Note** Viewbooks are college commercials on paper.

The front cover of the viewbook might show students sitting on the grass with a beautifully manicured campus in the background. The students will be smiling, socializing, and studying. The hope is that you can picture yourself having fun while attending this college.

On the back cover you are likely to find telephone numbers, Web site addresses, and fax numbers, making it easy for you to contact the college at any time.

Brochures

Every few weeks, you might receive a new brochure on any number of topics. One could be about campus living, showing you the floor plans and dimensions of dorm rooms. The dining hall rules may be listed with sample menus. There might be a list of items not to bring (such as space heaters, microwaves, pets, illegal drugs, halogen lamps, candles) and what to do in case things don't go as planned. Of course, you will see many pictures of students cooking meals, studying, working on computers, or watching television—and everyone is smiling.

You might receive a brochure about the performing arts program showing, in vivid color, students having so much fun performing in choral music, with the jazz band, in theatre, or on the dance line. The athletic brochure will show students playing soccer, softball, volleyball, basketball, or football, or participating in rodeo, cheerleading, or wrestling. There might be a perforated postcard for you to fill out and mail to the college for more information.

Magazines

Some colleges produce monthly magazines to keep you abreast of what is happening on campus. In the 14 or so pages, you will learn what students on campus are doing in their majors, why they selected this college, jobs that graduates have landed, and contact information. You might learn that some students were undecided when they arrived but that they have a direction now. Of course, you see that *you* could be successful at that college as well.

 Note College magazines keep you updated on activities, awards, and job opportunities.

Small colleges tend to stress small class sizes and a family atmosphere. Large colleges are less likely than smaller schools to send promotional brochures but, when they do, they often emphasize the large selection of classes and activities. The brochures you receive will allow you to make mini-visits to the college without getting in your car.

Promotional Materials

As a junior, you will begin receiving promotional materials monthly or more often. The mail carrier will wonder what is up at your house. You've suddenly become very popular. Colleges you have not contacted will send you promotional brochures because they have purchased your address. Don't pitch these brochures. They contain important information such as special days to visit campus, scholarship information, and ACT or SAT testing dates. File them in your various folders. The brochures might just contain the information you will need to make a final decision on your college.

While the college campuses may seem quite full today, the future is not looking very comfortable. High schools are shrinking, and the boom on college campuses will reach a peak in the next year or two. After that, college sizes will be declining, and the competition for college students will become tougher. Recruiting may become even more aggressive in a few years.

Note Be prepared for an avalanche of mailings from colleges.

What Is a College Catalog and How Should You Best Use It?

After receiving viewbooks, you will be very disappointed in catalogs. Catalogs are not commercials but informational manuals. If there are any pictures, they are likely to be in black and white. Boring is the word to describe catalogs as compared to viewbooks. There is no need to ask for a catalog unless you are very serious about attending a college. Many colleges now offer catalogs online only.

> **Note** Catalogs are filled with important but rather boring information.

General Information

If those colorful automobile pamphlets could be compared to college viewbooks, the owner's manuals are comparable to college catalogs. You may pick up a colorful flyer to review, but not too many people get excited about reading an owner's manual. However, at times the information they contain is necessary to know.

In the catalog you will find the college mission statement, a description of the campus, information about accreditation, and the disability policy.

The catalog contains detailed information organized by category:

- Campus life: Details of living on campus, student regulations, health services, computer access, athletics, the library, and mail.

- Admissions: The admissions process, including information for transfer and international students, and methods for admissions appeal.

- Financial information: Information about financial aid, scholarships and loans, employment, the financial aid calendar, student expenses, the academic calendar, and refund policies.

- Academic program and policies: Attendance, academic integrity, credits and grade point average, honor roll, commencement, major requirements, minors, course load, special courses, and the student records policy.

Note Catalogs hold all the rules and regulations in a college.

The rest of the catalog lists classes offered under the majors with detailed descriptions, administration, faculty, and trustees. Look at the college catalog when you need to know information but don't know who to ask. Because the college catalog could choke you with information you may not want to know initially, it is best to leave the catalog request for when you have given the college serious consideration.

Note Catalogs list all the classes you need to take to graduate.

When you begin taking classes, make sure you never lose the catalog for that year. If there is any confusion or disagreement about which classes to take for your major, you will have the catalog to use for reference. It may not hurt to have a second catalog as well, tucked safely away at home in a drawer. The catalog will list all the classes you need to take to earn a degree at this college.

Practical Information

The catalog also contains practical information about student life and academic issues. When you have questions, try looking in the catalog for answers.

For example, if you are a transfer student, you want to make sure all classes transfer from one school to another. In a transfer situation, it is important to be sure that the classes required at the new college are the same as those required at the original college. Even the wording of the class descriptions is important.

If you want to change majors, you want to compare your newly required classes to the classes you took under your former major. Are most of the required classes the same? If not, you could be looking at an additional semester—or even an additional year—of school.

 "To find out what one is fitted to do and to secure an opportunity to do it is the key to happiness."

–John Dewey

If you earned a scholarship and have not maintained the grade point average necessary to keep it, you may want to read the specifics on scholarships.

If your instructor considers your behavior in class a problem and threatens you with permanent removal from the classroom, does he or she have the right to do this? The catalog would explain your rights to you. (Unfortunately, the professor probably has the right to remove you.)

 Professors have the right to cut you from the roster for bad behavior or being excessively absent.

If you have a disability and you do not feel you are being treated fairly, what would you do? The catalog will list the office to which to voice your complaint.

If you are a smoker, you want to know whether you can smoke outside your dorm room or if you have to totally step off campus.

If you have allergies and use an inhaler on a regular basis, you might wonder if the college has a full-time or part-time nurse. Would someone take you to the hospital as needed? The catalog is where you find out this information.

The catalog is your rule book to everything on campus. If there is ever a question about regulations, how things are done, or who needs to be contacted, look in the catalog. The answer is probably there.

 "If I wanted to become a failure, I would seek advice from men who have never succeeded. If I wanted to succeed in all things, I would look around me for those who are succeeding, and do as they have done."

–Joseph Marshall Wade

Applying to the Best Colleges for You

CHAPTER 40

How and When Do You Choose a Major?

Very few students have decided on a major when they begin college. If they do have a major, many change. It is common for college sophomores to not be clear on their choice of a major.

But, if you are leaning toward a career such as nursing, engineering, or computer science, colleges may expect you to declare a major as a freshman because your classes will be sequential. If you delay, you will be out of sequence, and it could be very difficult to catch up.

Finding what you want to do in life is not an easy task. When working adults are surveyed about their job satisfaction, approximately 30–40 percent are happy with their work and feel it is what they were meant to do. That leaves 60–70 percent of workers unhappy, or at least not working at their dream career.

So how do you discover your best career? This chapter and Chapter 41 offer suggestions.

Your Childhood

When thinking about a career, you may find answers if you look back into your childhood.

Eileen grew up on a farm and was always caring for the cats that lived on the acreage. She went into the house on a regular basis looking for supplies to wrap damaged limbs. On one occasion, Eileen found gauze and wrapped the frostbitten tip of a cat's tail. Another time, Eileen used Popsicle sticks to form a splint for a suspected sprained leg.

When Eileen was 13 years old, a baby brother became her project and she was by choice his "second mother." It was no surprise to her mother that Eileen decided on a career in nursing. Eileen now holds a B.S.N. in obstetrics and is giving some thought to becoming a nurse practitioner.

Raul had great interest in maps and airplanes. That's a pretty good combination, because few people would want to fly with a pilot who couldn't read maps. Raul also had a talent for working with engines and for fixing just about anything. In seventh grade, Raul represented his county in the state geography bee. He also attended Concordia Language Village, learned Japanese, and returned with a great appreciation for other cultures and the environment.

As a high school senior, Raul decided to become a Marine and selected the field of avionics. Raul graduated at the top of his class and worked on experimental Boeing aircraft, making sure the planes were in perfect condition prior to being placed on aircraft carriers. He was triple trained in electronics, body, and engine. After five years, Raul enrolled in a university with two years of avionics college hours from the Marine Corps and a double major in geography and environmental science. He also earned a pilot's license.

Barbara used to play school in her free time. Her students were her younger sister and stuffed animals. She passed out worksheets, supervised recess, and arranged chairs in rows as desks.

In middle school she tutored struggling students during recess. In high school she was fascinated with outstanding teachers and how they could explain something so much better than the other teachers could. Barbara became a teacher herself and later became a school counselor.

Lisa was a very creative child and was always planning plays. By the seventh grade, she was writing scripts and creating costumes for her younger siblings and cousins. She was a detail-oriented person, and the drama events were flawless. Her family was provided with years of entertainment. Lisa majored in communications and now has her own business planning corporate and social events with precision and perfection.

Note Childhood interests often lead to adult careers.

While childhood interests are not always a predictor of adult careers, interests do give some possible clues.

Hobbies

Do you like to study the stars, fix and build mechanical gear, write computer code, or care for animals in your free time? Look to your hobbies and personal interests for possible direction on a college major.

Favorite School Subjects

What are your favorite subjects? What subjects do you do well in? As you consider choices for the future, be sure to research your many options. Start by going online at http://www.bls.gov/k12/index.htm. Several books are listed in the next chapter.

Help from Teachers and Counselors

Keep in mind that your teachers and your counselor are available for help in your career exploration. You may be able to take a career interest assessment.

CHAPTER 41

What Are Some Sources to Help You Decide on a Major?

I f you experienced career discovery at the elementary school, middle school, or high school levels, you are truly fortunate. Many students are not that lucky.

If you are a high school senior or a college freshman and still don't know which way to go with a major, in some cases that is okay. You have time. However, as mentioned in Chapter 40, some majors need to be declared when you are a freshman so that you can take classes in sequential order.

> **Note** Some majors demand you make a selection in your freshman year.

This chapter lists some excellent sources to help in your major decision.

10 Best College Majors for Your Personality

Laurence Shatkin, Ph.D., has written a book based on John Holland's personality types titled *10 Best College Majors for Your Personality*. The book lists the six major personality categories and the jobs related to these categories.

Realistic. These individuals like work activities that are practical and hands-on, and they enjoy finding solutions. Don't give them paperwork. They would rather use tools, wood, and machinery. Give them a job outdoors.

Investigative. People in this category would rather think than be physical. They enjoy researching facts and figures.

Artistic. These personalities enjoy working with design, form, and patterns. They would prefer self-expression and few rules at work.

Social. These individuals want close contact with other workers. They enjoy assisting others, promoting learning, and enhancing personal development. They would rather be of service to others than work with objects, machines, or data.

Enterprising. People in this category like projects. They like starting them and carrying them out. They enjoy taking a risk and making business profits. They like action.

Conventional. These personalities want preset activities and routines. Don't give them concepts—give them data and details. They like working with precise rules and a particular way of doing things.

Note Holland's personality categories have stood the test of time.

Each category has a partner. For example, a Realistic personality is likely to be similar to Conventional. On the other hand, some combinations are not compatible:

- Realistic is not a match with Social.
- Investigative is not a match with Enterprising.
- Artistic is not a match with Conventional.

Shatkin has a 180-question assessment that will determine each category. Then the book outlines career choices with specific information on each career.

90-Minute College Major Matcher

Laurence Shatkin's second book on college majors uses Holland's six personalities as a basis for finding a major. However, this book does not include the 180-question inventory. It does have careers divided by RE, RC, IER, IC, I RIE, and so on, to match the personality types listed in the preceding section. The *90-Minute College Major Matcher* provides information about average earnings, job growth statistics, and job openings. You may select a major and see if it matches you, or you may select a Holland personality type and see what careers are listed there.

> **Note** The *90-Minute College Major Matcher* highlights 120 majors.

Shatkin lists the following:

- 120 majors
- Specializations in the majors
- Typical sequence of college courses
- Typical sequence of high school courses
- Career snapshot
- Related jobs
- Characteristics of the related jobs

This book is likely to be successful in connecting you to a major and career if you are in college and still undecided.

College Majors Handbook with Real Career Paths and Payoffs

Neeta P. Fogg, Paul E. Harrington, and Thomas F. Harrington combine efforts to focus on 60 college majors. This trio divides the 60 majors into 7 categories:

- Behavioral and Medical Sciences
- Business and Administration
- Education
- Engineering
- Humanities and Social Sciences
- Natural Sciences
- Technology

> **Note** 150,000 college graduates discuss 60 majors.

The findings and analyses in this book are not based on the opinions of the three writers. The data is based on the results of a survey given to 150,000 college graduates across the nation. This National Survey of College Graduates represents the largest study of college graduates ever conducted.

Part One contains several short assessments to assist you in narrowing down the choices and encouraging you to do self-exploration.

Parts Two through Eight go into detail with each career in the following areas:

- Workplace
- Occupations
- Activities on the job
- Salaries
- Postgraduate activities
- Employment outlook

This manual is a good resource for those who want to know more details about fewer careers.

Professors

Don't forget about that wonderful resource on campus—your professors. There are probably a few professors who teach classes that interest you. Stop by their office during office hours and throw out some interests of yours. See what they have to say about opportunities in various fields. Colleges are very assertive in finding jobs for graduates, and an instructor may see you as a perfect fit for a new and hot career in a particular area.

> **Note** Professors may give you great insight into yourself.

Favorite Classes

Each semester you take boring classes, not-too-bad classes, and downright interesting classes. Which classes interest you the most? Investigate this field and see which careers would be of most interest to you, have the best outlook into the future, and pay the best. A good online source is the Occupational Outlook Handbook, available at the library and online at http://www.bls.gov/oco/home.htm.

Finding the career just right for you is not an easy task. Of the U.S. population, 70 percent have not succeeded in doing this. There is more help available now, so take advantage of it.

 "Either control your own destiny, or someone else will!"
                                                                          –John F. Welch, Jr.

CHAPTER 42

Why Should You Apply Early and Often?

There is no magic number when it comes to college application numbers. Having said that, I'll point out that it would be a big mistake to apply to only one college.

Financial Aid

The biggest reason to apply at several colleges is the financial aid package. Colleges vary greatly in what they offer in financial aid, and you will not have all the information you need until April of your senior year. If your dream college does not come through for you, it is too late then to begin visiting and applying at other colleges. Why?

Note Fall: Apply to colleges.

After Christmas, many colleges begin earmarking funds for grants and scholarships. If you have not applied, you are missing that opportunity.

The college admission year is divided into three informal stages:

Fall: Application

Winter: Grant/scholarship designation

Spring: Award letters and commitment

You want to fit into that sequence. You are at an advantage if you apply in the fall. The latest priority date would be before Christmas.

Scholarship Competitions

January is often the beginning of the scholarship competitions. If you have applied in the fall, your acceptance letter should arrive by the Christmas holiday or shortly after. Then in January the scholarship competition forms begin arriving from the colleges. Many of these are in the form of a scholarship essay, but some colleges will invite students on campus for a weekend scholarship competition. If this competition occurs in February and you have not applied or been accepted, say goodbye to that opportunity. Scholarship weekends often award scholarships in the range of $1,500 to $10,000.

 Note Winter: Apply for scholarships.
Spring: Accept the best financial aid offer.

Housing

State universities do not often give out large scholarships like private colleges do, so there is not as much lost with a late application. But dorm rooms are often gone by late fall for the following academic year. Upper classmen reserve their spots in the dorms in the spring, leaving incoming freshmen without rooms if they apply late. Studies show that living on campus is a better formula for success than living off campus. This has not been a big problem in the past, but it is today.

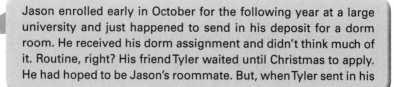

Jason enrolled early in October for the following year at a large university and just happened to send in his deposit for a dorm room. He received his dorm assignment and didn't think much of it. Routine, right? His friend Tyler waited until Christmas to apply. He had hoped to be Jason's roommate. But, when Tyler sent in his dorm selection and deposit, he was told the dorms were already full. He would have to get an apartment. Unknown to Jason, he had received one of the last available dorm rooms in October.

Many universities are experiencing a boom of students, with the end of the baby-boomer children entering college. This will end in a few years with colleges scrambling to fill the spots in the classrooms and dorms. But, for the next few years, competition will be tough for space at large universities. What we see in our high schools as the largest classes graduate with small kindergarten populations entering is what colleges see, as well.

Note Campus housing may be tight for several more years.

Thomas had always wanted to attend a major state university for engineering. He had the scores for engineering. His ACT was 32, and his score on the math test was 33. His mother was a single parent and physically unable to find a better job. The family EFC was zero, and the family fell below the legally designated poverty level. Thomas qualified for Pell grants, work-study, and subsidized student loans. According to federal guidelines, Thomas's mother should have paid nothing toward his college expenses. Unfortunately, Thomas applied to only one college, and colleges are not forced to honor EFC figures.

When the financial aid package arrived very late in June, instead of April, the family was horrified to see what the university expected. The college expected the mother to pay $12,500 toward her son's college. This was nearly the amount this parent made in a year. In addition, Thomas was given no work-study and was granted unsubsidized loans instead of subsidized. A phone call was made to the college asking if there had been a mistake, and the answer was, "No mistake was made. We have a very large freshman class, and we just can't afford to meet everyone's needs."

Meanwhile, a local private college was contacted. That college not only expected Thomas and his family to pay nothing, they offered to give Thomas a stipend for living expenses based on the low family income and high ACT score. Thomas also received an offer of work-study and subsidized loans.

(continues)

(continued)

> Ultimately, Thomas refused the offer when an uncle offered to pay the outrageous family fee to the large university. Of course, not everyone is that lucky, and, for most people, the options will be limited. This is a perfect example of why you want to shop around.

Award Letters

Award letters are a major reason to apply to five or six colleges. Apply to a combination of private and public universities. You may think this will get expensive if you apply to so many schools. No, not really. Many colleges will waive the fee if you apply on a campus visit or prior to an early deadline in the fall. Many also waive the fee if you apply online.

Some colleges do not charge an application fee at all. They are confident that they can beat out the competition with their generous financial aid. They waive the fee hoping you will apply and be impressed with what they offer in the spring.

 Note Don't let application fees stop you from applying to five or more colleges.

Award letters can be almost shocking in terms of their differences from college to college. Let's look at a family that has an EFC of $1,200. *EFC* is the Expected Family Contribution that is the result of the FAFSA financial aid application filed in January or February. This student has applied to seven colleges. The bottom-line figure appears in the award letter. Each college tells the family what it will have to pay for the child to attend:

- State university, $8,500
- Private 1, $7,200
- Private 2, $5,800
- Private 3, $3,500
- Private 4, $2,300

- Private 5, $1,800
- Private 6, $1,200

You don't need to study these figures too long to see which college is the best choice financially. In most families, money talks. Now, take a look at the two or three top choices and see which one is truly best. Keep in mind that the best package may or may not be from the college that is perfect for you. In this case, college 5 just might be worth paying a little more. This is why you do not want to select your college before you see the financial aid package. You just don't know which college is going to offer you what.

Why did private college 6 offer such a tremendous award letter and meet the family EFC at 100 percent? There could be many reasons:

- The college probably has deep pockets and large endowments allowing them to be very generous.
- The student probably had exactly what the college was looking for. If the college was weak in drama and this student was outstanding in theater, that could be the reason.
- If the college wanted to raise the average ACT scores and this student had impressive ACT scores, that could be the reason.
- Perhaps the student was a member of a minority group or from out of the region, and the college wanted to diversify the population on campus.
- Maybe the college decided to increase the enrollment by 50 students to fill the dorms and was willing to pay for it.

 Quote "Know what you want to do, hold the thought firmly, and do every day what should be done, and every sunset will see you that much nearer the goal."

–Elbert Hubbard

You just never know from year to year what makes one student more impressive than another at a particular college. So, by applying to several colleges, the odds increase in finding the right college that wants you.

So do you have to apply early in the fall? No. Do you have to apply to five or six colleges? No. But it is very easy to understand why the students who do apply early and apply to several colleges are more likely to receive affordable packages.

 "Perseverance is a great element of success. If you knock long enough and loud enough at the gate, you are sure to wake up somebody."

–Henry Wadsworth Longfellow

CHAPTER 43

How Can You Increase Your Chances of Acceptance?

Applying to a college is not the lottery. You can predict whether you are likely to be admitted. If you do your homework, admission will be automatic at the majority of colleges to which you apply.

Colleges are looking at certain items for admission. There are many ways to tip the odds in your favor for not only being accepted but for receiving scholarships, as well. You will be assured that you will be accepted; you can predict where you would probably get a better scholarship.

There are many pieces to the college admissions puzzle. You want to cover your bases with all of them. Try to do your best in all categories.

Find Your Best Academic Match

First on the list is selecting a college at your academic level.

Where do you fall among other students looking for colleges? That is a key piece of information to learn. If a college has ACT scores that average in the range of 21–24, 50 percent of the students will fall here. Of the entire student body, 25 percent will score 25 or higher and 25 percent will score 19 or 20. (See Chapter 22 for more on this.)

Four-year colleges don't really want to accept students who score below 19 on the ACT. Statistics show that many of these students struggle so much that they end up dropping out. This is not good for the student and doesn't help the college graduation rate, either.

On the other hand, students who are much better academically than the test scores indicate should take the ACT or SAT twice or even three times to boost that score. ACT or SAT scores could weigh in at 25–40 percent of the admission decision.

Note Be an academic match with the college.

Look at Your High School Record

The most important information you can submit to your prospective college is your high school record. It isn't all about the grade point average, even though many students think it is. Actually, it is about the classes taken, as well as the grade point average you earned. Colleges want to see that a student has taken challenging classes.

While it is great to have a 3.5 GPA, colleges will be looking to see if a student took four years of English; four or five years of math; three or four years of science; three or four years of social studies; and two, three, or four years of a foreign language to achieve that 3.5 GPA. If the student took three years of English, two years of math, three years of science, two years of social studies, and no foreign language to achieve a 3.5 GPA, the college will not be very impressed with the 3.5. ACT scores are also likely to be lower with the weaker class list. At many colleges, the high school record could be 50 percent of the decision to accept.

Note The classes you take in high school do matter.

While many high school students think they can coast through and then really kick into gear in college, colleges think the opposite. Colleges are of the opinion that you will perform the same in college as you have done in high school.

Write a Good Essay

Your essay could be as much as 10–20 percent of the admission decision at a private college and as little as 0 percent at a state university. The 20 percent amount is substantial and could make a big difference when considering scholarships. Essays are too important to be thrown together at the last minute.

Obtain Letters of Recommendation

Letters may also fall into the 5–15 percent range. State universities don't usually require them, but private schools do. Again, essays and letters of recommendation could count for as much as 15–35 percent in determining admission and scholarships.

Plan for Interviews

The interview process can also enter into the picture. If a student interviews well, speaking ability and personality can make up for a less-than-stellar essay, letter of recommendation, test score, or overall high school record. Some interviews are given on scholarship weekends at which there is competition for large scholarships. The weekend can produce a scholarship in the range of $2,000 to $10,000 or more.

 "One of the things I learned the hard way was that it doesn't pay to get discouraged. Keeping busy and making optimism a way of life can restore your faith in yourself."

–Lucille Ball

Do Volunteer Work

One critical factor that is often overlooked by students is volunteer work. Colleges, especially private colleges, are looking for character and leadership. Having a long list of volunteer experiences when applying to a college could boost a student's assessment rating by 15 or even 20 percent. If a college's promotional campaign is building leaders, that means they want leaders on campus. A student who can show leadership in helping others and the community is likely to be favored above those who do not have that on their side.

Miscellaneous Factors

Other factors contribute to the acceptance and scholarships process:

- Are you the third generation to attend this college?
- Do you have a sibling already attending?
- Are you a Dutch Reform Lutheran applying to a Dutch Reform Lutheran college?
- You are from New York City and applying to a small college in Nebraska. Diversity could be a factor in your favor.
- You are a great golfer, and the golf team may need one more top player to be in competition for a record-breaking season.

These factors could count for as much as 30 percent or as little as 0 percent in the admission process. It isn't about just grades or the ACT or SAT score. Colleges are looking for a package. The more items you have that look good in the package, the more you increase your chances of being accepted and getting scholarships.

Of course, you can't get all this accomplished at the last minute of your senior year. Good planning and consistent efforts throughout high school make this all possible. Apply to colleges with confidence because you have done your homework. Plan ahead and be prepared.

CHAPTER 44

When Would You Use a Resume?

A resume is a thumbnail sketch of your four years in high school. The details should fit on one page that can be easily scanned by the eye. (See Chapter 45 on how to construct a resume.) The uses for a resume are many, and you will find it well worth the time it takes to construct one. And it is just a good practice to update a resume periodically throughout your lifetime. Opportunities may pop up unexpectedly, and it is the person who is ready at that very moment who will take advantage of them.

Applying to a College

Every private college application should include the following:

- Cover letter
- Resume
- Application
- Essay

In fact, the items should be arranged in this order in the envelope:

- The **cover letter** is a professional way to greet your personal admissions counselor, letting him or her know your intent and identifying the contents of your application package.
- The **resume** continues the professional look by giving the counselor a quick overview of who you are.
- The **application form** provides the college with all the information requested.

- The **essay** shows your writing ability and lets the staff at the college know something about you in addition to what appears on your resume or on the application form.

The resume is also a great time-saver. On the college application form, you will be asked to list all honors and high school activities. Space is tight, and you will risk typos or not having enough room to express yourself as you would like. By using a resume, you will have much more flexibility in how you craft your responses. In fact, you can include your resume and then leave a portion of the application blank, stating "see resume." This may be done for each application.

 "He who seizes the right moment, is the right man."

–Johann Goethe

Letters of Recommendation

A big part of applying to a college is asking teachers and administrators for a letter of recommendation. To give the teachers and administrators everything they need to write a good letter, you should include your resume and a cover letter indicating the deadline, where the letter should be sent, what you are applying for, and a stamped envelope.

You might think your teachers know you quite well. However, teachers may easily see 150 students a day. If you had a class with this teacher last year, that may be 300–400 students ago. Do the teachers a favor and refresh their memories. A resume can help them recall things they might otherwise have forgotten.

 "It is character which builds an existence out of circumstance. From the same materials one man builds palaces, another hovels. Bricks and mortar are mortar and bricks until the architect can make them something else."

–Thomas Carlyle

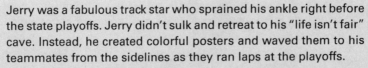

Jerry was a fabulous track star who sprained his ankle right before the state playoffs. Jerry didn't sulk and retreat to his "life isn't fair" cave. Instead, he created colorful posters and waved them to his teammates from the sidelines as they ran laps at the playoffs.

Jerry's attitude about life's unfair moments may be more important than his running talents. The teacher may be reminded of this when she sees "track" on his resume. The letter may take a totally different direction than Jerry thought it would, and it will probably impress the college much more than a letter about a track star because it gives insight into Jerry's character.

Scholarships

Competition for scholarships is tight. It is possible that 300 students may apply for one scholarship. Something has to set you apart from the other 299, right? It is one thing to state what you have achieved, but the more important thing might be how you state it.

Quote "The people who get on in this world are the people who get up and look for the circumstances they want, and, if they can't find them, make them."

–George Bernard Shaw

Student One fills out the college application form and attaches an essay. She has fulfilled the request on a minimal level.

Student Two fills out the application form and attaches the required essay but also attaches a resume and takes the time to write a cover letter. The cover letter thanks the scholarship committee for considering her submission and reviewing her resume. Those two items have set a professional tone and show that this student is serious about her application.

The majority of students are not likely to submit a resume and cover letter because these items were not requested. If you do, you are showing that you are willing to do above and beyond what is expected.

Applying for a Job

You are applying for a job. You go to the place of business and pick up the form and take it home to fill out. When you return it, attach your professional-looking resume. Why? Because very few applicants will. You have the resume anyway, right? Just print it off and attach it. This will get the attention of the employer. Employers want employees to put their best foot forward with customers and with colleagues. Including a resume tells the employer that you probably know how to be professional. It also shows extra effort, which could translate into "I really want this job." If you really want the job, you are more likely to come on time, work hard, follow directions, and stay for a reasonable length of time.

It isn't a guarantee that you will get the job, but you may have eliminated someone who has the same credentials as you— someone who did not attach a resume. You have also greatly reduced any chance for errors in dates or misspellings that might show up on your application form.

Begin keeping documentation of awards, achievements, and volunteer work in your freshman year of high school. You may be able to use a resume for other reasons before you begin the college process. It may help you get a job before you apply to a college. Let your resume speak for you.

Sample resumes are available on the CD-ROM included with this book.

CHAPTER 45

How Should You Organize Your Resume?

Your resume should be a showcase of your accomplishments in high school. It should be easily scanned on one sheet of paper. How do you organize and showcase your accomplishments?

Contact Information

First, at the top of the page, will be your name and information explaining how to contact you.

This portion of the resume is bold. You want your name to pop, so make it larger than the rest of the text. The mailing address beneath your name could be much smaller.

What is the easiest way to contact you? Home phone? E-mail? Cell phone? If you don't check your e-mail often, start checking it daily if you place this contact information on your resume. Someone may be waiting for a very important reply. If your best option is a cell phone, make sure your music and message are appropriate and not offensive.

List of Activities

High schools offer so many opportunities to participate in activities: speech, football, mock trial, jazz band, swing choir, yearbook, marching band, and so much more.

Find large index cards and place a category heading at the top of each one. For example: Band. Under that category arrange your entire list of band activities and honors.

Band

Jazz Band 20XX–20XX

Saxophone First Chair 20XX–20XX

All-State 20XX–20XX

Woody Herman Award 20XX

Concert Band 20XX–20XX

Marching Band 20XX–20XX

Do the same for every category. Arrange the index cards in order of importance and begin composing your resume.

Note Place each category on a large index card and compile information.

The dates should be in descending order, with the most recent dates first. This gets a little tricky at times, but you get the point.

Don't abbreviate titles or awards if they are not well known. Not everyone knows that CYO stands for "Catholic Youth Organization." While you may know that Silver Steppers is the drill team, others may not. So this could be better stated as "Silver Steppers Drill Team."

Take a look at your categories. Which categories shine more than others? Place your most successful activity first, then the next, and the next. Why? While you hope that everyone will read every entry on your resume, the reality is that they probably won't. Admissions staff, scholarship committees, and employers are all very busy. They are looking at many application forms, essays, and resumes. They will scan your resume quickly and perhaps not read to the end. This is why you load a resume from top to bottom. It is great that you played basketball all four years, but it is better that you received multiple awards in jazz band and were in All-State. The band category should take top billing over basketball.

> **Note** Place your more dazzling accomplishments first.

Academics

If you are a very successful student academically, you may want to place this category at the top of your entries. But all the data below your contact information (including academics) should be in a small font, 12 point or even 10, depending on how everything fits. You may need to shrink the print to get it all on one page.

> Justin was an active and gifted student. He played baseball all four years in high school but was not a star. He also played basketball all four years but again was not a star. He participated in speech, mock trial, and track, but his real strength was in academics. As a freshman in high school, he scored 28 on his ACT. And his score increased each year. So Justin would probably choose Academics as his top category when putting together his resume. Grade Point Average 4.0, National Honor Society, and ACT 34 would be in the spotlight. The other categories would be included as well but farther down the page.

But what if you blend in with the average college students? You may not want to put academics on your resume; instead, focus on other eye-catching achievements.

> **Quote** "People become really quite remarkable when they start thinking that they can do things. When they believe in themselves they have the first secret of success."
>
> –Norman Vincent Peale

A Variety of Activities

Your goal is to give a balanced look to your resume. It is wonderful to be a great musician, but show that you are versatile. Include some athletic events. What if you are not really great with any activities involving that round thing called a ball? How about drill team or cheerleading?

> Lucas had a balanced resume. He was a football player, he participated in track and speech, he was active in photography, and he sang in the concert choir.

Like Lucas, you might try a variety of activities.

Volunteerism

One area that is very important is community service. This is a tiebreaker category for scholarships and admission to a highly selective college. A balanced resume must have some volunteerism on it.

Think of the group of high school counselors who were meeting at a seminar a few years ago. They were venting frustrations because their students always lost the top community scholarships to the Catholic school across town. In the discussion, the point was made that a part of the Catholic Confirmation process included many community service projects. Students must serve family, community, and church over the course of several years. Of course, the students placed these activities on their resumes. The list of volunteer jobs included adult choir member, altar server cantor, lector, teacher in the religious education program, church usher, participant in community clean-up day, builder for Habitat for Humanity, Little League coach, and so on. The lists went on forever. When there was a tie between two students being considered for a scholarship, the one with the long list of volunteer work usually received the scholarship.

If you were on the selection committee, you would probably make your selection the same way. It just looks impressive for a student to be involved with volunteer organizations like these.

Volunteer work is the most likely category to be forgotten. Keep dated newspaper clippings in a special place for later. You may be doing more volunteer work than you think.

Presentation

You want the recipients of your resume to be able to read it completely. They won't if the paper hurts their eyes. While fluorescent-colored stationery may catch your eye, it is also blinding and difficult to read for any length of time. And this is not the time to buy stationery with hearts, rainbows, angels, or kittens that distract from the words on the page.

You want to be remembered for your accomplishments and not for an unprofessional choice of stationery. Attention-seeking stationery shows a lack of judgment—not the impression you want to give.

Select white, off-white, tan, light gray, or cream-colored stationery. Yes, it's a little boring, but that is the point. You want the stationery to be the vessel to deliver your information, not the focus of your reader's attention.

Sources of Information

Have a resume completed by the end of the junior year in high school. Add to it as long as you are applying for college admission and for scholarships. Resumes are worth the effort.

What if you don't remember all the activities you were involved in? Ask to see your transcript. Many activities will be listed on a transcript. Moms keep scrapbooks, or there may be a drawer at your house that holds all those newspaper clippings. While it is ideal to begin compiling a resume in your freshman year, very few students do. At least keep newspaper clippings in a special place and jot down your volunteer work as a reference for later use. After all, you want to receive credit for work done.

CHAPTER 46

Where Are You Most Likely to Get a Scholarship?

There is a way to predict where you are more likely to get a scholarship.

Sources of Scholarships

Scholarships come from two major sources: from local groups and from colleges.

Local Scholarships

You are more likely to receive a local scholarship if you apply for it. No, I'm not trying to be funny.

A few years ago, a local scholarship was offered for $500 to the student who would write the best essay on a patriotic topic. The scholarship was offered by the local chapter of the VFW, Veterans of Foreign Wars. Scholarship applications were posted on the high school counselor's bulletin board for weeks. No one applied for the scholarship, so no one received it. If just one student had applied for it with a patriotic essay, he or she would have received the $500.

> **Quote** "Work is effort applied toward some end. The most satisfying work involves directing our efforts toward achieving ends that we ourselves endorse as worthy expressions of our talent and character."
>
> –William J. Bennett

College Scholarships

Where you apply to college greatly affects your chances for scholarships. It is all about your academic position at the college. Where you place among other students makes all the difference in the college's decision to give a scholarship to you or to someone else.

Quote "Sometimes it is more important to discover what one cannot do, than what one can do."

–Lin Yutang

Strategy

There is a strategy to increase your odds for a scholarship. This is how it works:

- Take your ACT or SAT. After you've taken the test once or twice, you will know where you fall.
- Begin searching for colleges and research data on ACT or SAT scores.
- Make sure you fall within the top 50 percent. That is the scholarship range.

Note Don't just start randomly looking at college. Have a strategy.

Quote "Let us not be content to wait and see what will happen, but give us the determination to make the right things happen."

–Peter Marshall

Amanda was quite gifted in math. Her ACT in math was 30. She didn't have a dream college in mind but did want to go to college on a large scholarship. She began searching for colleges. While she could be accepted at any college in the state, she began selecting colleges that had good reputations but ACT averages in the 20–25 range. By doing so, she placed herself in the top 10 percent and increased her odds of getting a large scholarship.

(continued)

(continued)

In the end, a level 4 college with mid-range ACT scores of 19–23 gave her a full-tuition scholarship for four years. All Amanda had for expenses was money for room and board.

 Quote "Far and away the best prize that life offers is the chance to work hard at work worth doing."

–Theodore Roosevelt

Interesting Resume

You are also more likely to be noticed if you include a resume with your scholarship application. A resume will not make up for a poor academic record or a lack of volunteerism. But, when the scholarship committee is looking at the top applicants and they all look fairly equal, a professional-looking resume with a well-written cover letter could be a small factor. In a tie situation, a small factor may be all you need.

Have a wide variety of categories on your resume. Try to be well rounded. Don't settle for being a good student. Branch out into drama, music, or sports. And do not forget to do volunteer work in the community.

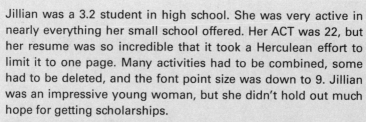

Jillian was a 3.2 student in high school. She was very active in nearly everything her small school offered. Her ACT was 22, but her resume was so incredible that it took a Herculean effort to limit it to one page. Many activities had to be combined, some had to be deleted, and the font point size was down to 9. Jillian was an impressive young woman, but she didn't hold out much hope for getting scholarships.

Jillian selected schools in her ACT range and applied to six colleges. The scholarships were astounding. She received leadership scholarships and character awards. Jillian received the Bar Award in high school and held multiple leadership roles. She was fortunate that several of her colleges were looking for leaders on campus. They were willing to pay Jillian generously to get her on campus as a leader. Jillian received more scholarships than some of the higher-placed students in her high school. Unfortunately,

Jillian's success was greeted with jealousy from her friends with higher ACT scores and higher grade point averages. They didn't have a strategy like Jillian did.

Research

By doing advanced research and planning a strategy, you will have a much better chance of getting scholarships. If you don't do the research and planning, the price could be giving up your dream college.

 "There is always something about your success that displeases even your best friends."

–Oscar Wilde

CHAPTER 47

What Are Some Common Mistakes Made in Searching for a College?

Some common mistakes can be avoided by starting early, looking for a college that fits you, and applying to several schools.

Starting Late

The most common mistake is beginning the entire process late. You can make up for many mistakes, but once you lose time, you can't create more of it. The college process is sequential. To prevent missing deadlines, begin the process early. Is the sophomore year too early? Actually, no. As a sophomore, you can be thinking about careers, high school classes to take, size and location of colleges, and building a solid grade point average. If a senior brother or sister is making a late college visit, you might want to go along to experience being on the campus.

Quote "It is too late to come with the water when the house is burned down."

–Italian proverb

Lindsey had dreamed about going to college at a prestigious university on the East Coast. She had the grades and she had the ACT score. But her school counselor was acquainted only with local colleges. When Lindsey talked to her repeatedly about contacting the college she wanted, she was told there was no hurry—she had plenty of time.

The clock ticked away and it was senior year. The counselor continued to say Lindsey had plenty of time. Lindsey and her parents bought tickets to visit the college in early November. When Lindsey called to make her first contact and schedule a campus tour, she was told that the college had stopped taking applications for the following year. The family had three plane tickets and no longer a need to fly halfway across the country.

 "Who rises late must trot all day."

–French proverb

Don't wait for your counselor to get the ball rolling. The responsibility is yours.

 "Better late than never, but better never late."

–Anonymous

Not Knowing Your ACT

Another common mistake is visiting a college before you know your academic status. Colleges vary greatly in admission expectations. If you have a GPA of 2.9 and an ACT of 19, you may be college bound, but you are not bound for a level 2 college. Visiting a level 2 college would be a complete waste of your time and money. Your strategy should be to visit level 4 colleges that offer majors that interest you.

 "Don't undermine your worth by comparing yourself with others. It is because we are different that each of us is special."

–Brian Dyson

James had a great time in his junior year in high school. Every time a friend went to visit a college, James went along. He had an awesome collection of college T-shirts and souvenirs from numerous colleges. Unfortunately, after James took his ACT late in his junior year, he learned that he had not visited a college at which he would likely be accepted. It was now May of his junior year and James was starting over—except now it was very late to begin finding the right college.

Following Friends

Going where your friends are going is probably one of the weakest reasons for attending a college. The right college should be custom fit to the interests and abilities of each student. It is doubtful that your friends have the same needs, academic levels, and career in mind that you do. Leaving home to attend college can be scary, but keep in mind that everyone is in the same boat. You may get a little homesick at the beginning, but almost everyone who goes off to college is away from home for the first time. You will probably get homesick whether you go with friends or by yourself.

 "Your vision will become clear only when you can look into your own heart. Who looks outside, dreams; who looks inside, awakes."

–Carl Jung

Shelby wanted to go to a four-year college but all her friends were going to a local junior college and planning to live in an off-campus apartment. Shelby would not know anyone at the four-year college and decided to give in and go with her friends. They no sooner moved in than the arguments began. One girl wasn't paying her share of the rent on time, and the landlord didn't care who owed what. He wanted his money. Food was disappearing from the refrigerator, and there was little money to buy more because the rent had to be covered. Cable was disconnected due to a late payment. Having one bathroom and four girls getting ready in the morning only led to more arguments.

By Halloween the girls were no longer friendly with one another. By the end of the semester, they had moved out of the apartment and into dorms. Shelby decided to transfer to her original college choice. Now she was beginning at a new college in January, but everyone in the dorm had already established friendships and she was alone for a while. Shelby eventually made the transition, but it would have been easier had she gone for orientation and become acquainted with others during that time.

Picking the Closest College

Attending the closest college so you can go home every weekend is not the best reason to select a college. While the closest college to you may indeed be the best one for you, be independent and stay on campus on weekends.

Weekends on campus typically are filled with events that will help you make friends and feel part of the college. Yes, Mom may do your laundry when you go home, and you may also bring back great care packages, but keep trips home to a minimum. You are in college and now home will never be the same. Your friends won't be there. They will be away at other colleges.

Charlie picked a college only 35 miles away from his home. He either went home every weekend or his parents came to visit. When they visited, Charlie and his dad went to football or basketball games while Mom cleaned Charlie's room and washed his clothes. When he went home on weekends, Charlie's mom did his laundry and waited on him hand and foot. While Charlie may have thought he had it made; he was being set up to have problems in relationships.

Charlie found a girlfriend his second year in college. Mom and Dad were not coming as often and Charlie was staying on campus because of Cheryl. You can imagine Cheryl's reaction when Charlie asked her to clean his room and do his laundry. By his sophomore year, Charlie was learning how to do his own laundry and clean his own room.

Ella was so excited to go home for the first time after two months. She was attending college in another state, and it took major connections to arrange a ride home. Her parents knew she was coming, but her boyfriend, Mike, didn't.

It was Halloween weekend and she couldn't wait to surprise Mike. However, the surprise was on Ella when she called him and a girl answered. Unknown to Ella, Mike had arranged a date with another girl for Halloween. Mike offered to break the date and go get Ella, but she was too upset.

They broke off the relationship that Ella thought was exclusive. She began calling her high school friends, and all of them were at college. Ella spent the weekend with her parents watching television. Life changes after high school graduation. Home is never quite the same again.

Take the risk of staying on campus. Don't let fear keep you from becoming independent.

Following a Boyfriend or Girlfriend

High school relationships rarely last in college. Following the love of your life to college to be with him or her often ends painfully. Dating in college is different. There are so many new people to meet and get to know. And here you are, unable to explore other relationships because of that person next to you. It is better to select the best college for you and go your separate ways. If the relationship is meant to last, it will.

Following Football

While football is a great sport, the college still has to be a good match for anyone attending.

Amy and her parents went to many football games at the nearest university. Amy was a great fan of the team, and she saw college as an opportunity to attend all the games. Amy was introverted and not someone to be assertive in making friends or approaching professors. The college was filled with sororities and fraternities that controlled many social events on campus.

After the first semester, Amy was miserable. She felt lost at this large university and made few friends, because many students went home on the weekends. When the holiday season arrived, Amy went home for Christmas and refused to return. Instead, she transferred to the local junior college in January and lived at home.

Looking at Tuition Costs

Many people assume that because they don't have a generous family income, they can't afford a private college. Don't look at price tags. Look at how generous the college is, instead. Many state universities give poor financial aid, and some are very generous. Many of the most expensive private colleges give the best financial aid.

It is common to see students attend a private college for much less out-of-pocket money than they would spend for a large state university. The only way to find out which college offers the best package is to express interest in several and apply to four or five schools. Then, in the spring, decide where you can afford to go.

 "There is enough in the world for everyone's need, but not enough for everyone's greed."

–Frank Buchman

Feeling Intimidated by a School's Size

Many students are very intimidated by a large university. However, many majors are offered only at larger universities. What can you do? You can try attending a smaller school until you feel you have the confidence to attend a large university. Once you get the hang of college, the large setting may not be as scary. Some of the anxiety is the idea of college itself.

 "Worry does not empty tomorrow of its sorrow, it empties today of its joy."

–Anonymous

Applying to Only One College

Setting your heart on one college is a dangerous thing to do. Especially if the college is out of state. You can cross the state line and attend a private college with no penalty. But the out-of-state tuition penalty at some public universities is outrageous.

Your family might find that while you could afford a private college, an out-of-state public university is totally out of the picture. And, if this is the only college you visited or applied to, you will be starting over in the spring of your senior year.

Time to push the panic button! You can forget about having any leverage or negotiating power now. You will have to settle for leftovers at most colleges.

 "Mistakes are often the best teachers. The shortest mistakes are always the best."

–French proverb

CHAPTER 48

Are You a Candidate for a Military Academy?

Military academies are something to consider only after long thought. Academies are rigorous, not only physically, but also academically. A military career is for those who truly know what they want, not for the undecided.

The Procedure

Military academies provide a tremendous opportunity for students who are very strong academically and for those who are well rounded and athletically successful. A student who is considering a military academy should begin the process no later than fall of the junior year in high school. However, it would be better to start the ball rolling before that.

> **Note** Start very early if you are interested in a military academy.

Can you just apply? Well, no. A member of the U.S. Congress must nominate you to a service academy based on your qualifications. Each member may nominate just one individual per service academy. The decision of whom to nominate is based on an applicant's outstanding moral behavior, extracurricular activities, community activities, and ACT/SAT scores. It is not a simple process, so applicants should start early and put forth effort to build a positive record.

If you are an applicant, note that your character and behavior will need to be verified. This can be done through letters of recommendation from several individuals who know you well. In addition, your file should be void of any harassment issues, theft, assault, or malicious acts, because they disqualify you from a nomination. Many people think that being accepted at an academy is as difficult as getting into Harvard and other top Ivy League colleges.

Note Squeaky-clean history is a must.

Why are extracurricular activities so important? They show that an applicant has the ability to multitask, along with an interest in learning new things. Time management is necessary if a student wants to participate in many activities and continue to have top grades. Community activities, which are often known as volunteer work, show a gratitude for what has been received and then an effort to give back to the community.

How do the academies compare to other colleges? Academies are in a class by themselves.

United States Air Force Academy

The Air Force Academy in Colorado Springs, Colorado, is ranked fourth in the nation for academic experience, according to the *Princeton Review*. It is ranked sixth as a top science and engineering school by the *U.S. News & World Report*. The current grade point average for students at Colorado Springs is 4.0, and average ACT scores fall in the 27–32 range. This means that 25 percent of the students have an ACT score of 33 or higher. The professor-to-student ratio is 1:8.

What does tuition cost? Nothing. There is no tuition because once a student is accepted, tuition, room and board, medical care, and monthly pay are provided.

U.S. Air Force Academy data:

- 4,272 enrolled
- 82 percent male
- 12,430 total applicants
- Most popular majors: engineering, business, social sciences, and biological and biomedical sciences

Learn more at www.usafa.edu.

United States Military Academy at West Point

West Point is 50 miles north of New York City and is ranked fourth among engineering schools by *U.S. News and World Report*.

West Point also has no tuition fees because tuition, room and board, and medical and dental care are provided to all those admitted. A four-year education at West Point is valued at approximately $300,000. ACT scores for incoming students should be in the 27–30 range or higher.

Students at West Point receive a salary while attending school. The faculty-to-student ratio is 1:9.

West Point data:

- 4,183 enrolled
- 85 percent male
- 11,881 total applicants
- Most popular majors: economics, political science and government, aeronautical/aerospace engineering, systems engineering, and civil engineering

Learn more at www.usma.edu.

United States Naval Academy

The Naval Academy at Annapolis, Maryland, is first in the nation for accessibility of professors, seventh nationally for tough admittance standards, and twentieth for the best overall academic experience.

Full tuition, room and board, and medical and dental care are provided to students. Regular active duty benefits include commercial transportation and lodging discounts plus the ability to fly space-available on military aircraft around the world.

Approximately 1,500 applicants are accepted annually out of a pool of 13,000–14,000 applicants. The professor-to-student ratio is 1:7.

Note Annapolis is ranked #7 for toughest admission.

U.S. Naval Academy data:

- 4,349 enrolled
- 83 percent male
- 14,426 total applicants
- Most popular majors: political science and government, economics, systems engineering, chemical and physical oceanography, and history

Learn more at www.usna.edu.

Fine Print

Four years of education are provided at no cost unless a cadet drops out. If a student leaves an academy during the freshman or sophomore year, there is usually no charge for the education. However, if a student leaves in the junior or senior year, he or she is expected to pay the academy for the education received. The annual cost can be $75,000 per year.

If you're interested in the military, attending an academy can be a great opportunity. But changing your mind once admitted can be a serious error with overwhelming consequences.

Note Five years of military service are repayment for an academy education.

Some branches of the military require service first. Then, through a GI Bill, military personnel receive their education after their tour of duty. Academies provide an education first and ask for repayment with five years of military service.

United States Merchant Marine Academy

This academy is different from the others. Located in Kings Point, New York, the Merchant Marine Academy is a college with a Navy ROTC (Reserve Officers Training Corps) program.

For students here, the average high school grade point average is 3.6. Of all freshmen, 89 percent return for the sophomore year. Tuition is under $7,000 with no out-of-state fee, and there is a 75 percent graduation rate. The average ACT range is 25–31. The professor-to-student ratio is 1:11.

U.S. Merchant Marine Academy data:

- 962 enrolled
- 86 percent male
- 1,791 total applicants
- Most popular majors: marine science/merchant marine officer, naval architecture and marine engineering, and systems engineering

Learn more at www.usmma.edu.

Academies are not for everyone, but they represent a great opportunity for a select few who meet the grade with academics and character.

CHAPTER 49

What Are Early Action, Early Decision, and Regular Admission?

You can apply to a college in various ways. But don't worry: The process doesn't need to be complicated. One way will probably be best for you and for the majority of students.

Most selective and *more selective* colleges (levels 1 and 2) will offer several choices on the application forms. *Early action, early decision,* and *regular admission* are frequently offered, and most students stop dead in their tracks not knowing which one to choose.

Early Action

The best option is to apply early. If you apply between Halloween and Thanksgiving, you won't need to worry about missing deadlines and getting out of sequence. What sequence? The college admission process has steps that go along in an order. If you stay on schedule, you will have less stress.

If you apply in the fall, you will probably get your letter of acceptance by Christmas, the end of the year, or shortly after. What a great holiday present, right? Then you will begin receiving letters asking you for scholarship essays on various topics. If you are lucky, some requests will be very similar, and you will only have to write a few essays. If you have been writing in your junior year as recommended, chances are good that you have a pool of essays at your fingertips. Because you have the application process out of the way, this is your only assignment.

Note Apply early no matter what plan you select.

If you receive an invitation to attend a scholarship weekend, you will have the time because your applications have been turned in early. It is a great feeling to be ahead of schedule, isn't it? While your friends are scrambling to visit colleges and are in a panic taking ACT or SAT tests late, you can relax and know everything is going as planned.

With Early Action you are under no pressure to commit to any school or make any nonrefundable deposits. You get accepted early and wait for the scholarship competitions and the award letters to arrive in the spring. The grant and scholarship funding has not been given away to anyone. You have not disqualified yourself from anything by applying late.

Early Decision

Be very careful with an early decision. Early Decision speeds up the admissions process. It may seem to be a good choice initially, but it should be used for special circumstances only.

Quote "When possible make the decisions now, even if action is in the future. A reviewed decision usually is better than one reached at the last moment."

–William B. Given, Jr.

An example of Early Decision involves Alexis, a strong student with a college professor parent. Colleges often offer tuition at no cost to children of faculty. If that child does not want to attend the parent's college as is often the case, the college may have a pool of sister schools that the student may attend and still be tuition free. Alexis chose a private college in a neighboring state. Because financial aid was not an issue, she selected Early Decision and was accepted.

Another example of Early Decision is a prepayment tuition plan. States offer a payment plan where parents may deposit money over many years for future use at a state university. The tuition is prepaid and if tuition increases, the student's tuition cost is unaffected. In a case like this, financial aid is not an issue because tuition is already paid.

If you are offered a full tuition as a National Merit Scholarship recipient, you may make the decision to not look further for a college. This illustrates another reason to select Early Decision.

However, if you are still somewhat undecided and the financial aid package will determine where you may attend, do not use Early Decision. Early Decision has some fine print that may not be desirable. Commitment will be required in January or February, before the other schools send out their award letters outlining the cost for attendance. As part of the fine print in an Early Decision commitment, you will be expected to pull applications from all other colleges. Nonrefundable dorm deposits and fees are due immediately. Because the other colleges will not be making offers until March or April, you will never know what school would have been the most affordable. It is not uncommon to see a $7,000 difference between two private college offers.

While some circumstances may justify an early decision, most students should stay away from checking this option.

Regular Admission

Regular admission can be the best option if you apply early. But, if you apply in the spring, you are settling for leftovers. Many colleges have *rolling admission,* and students may apply up through the summer prior to classes beginning. Sounds easy enough, right? Don't do it. Rolling admission means that the college will accept students without a deadline, but it does not guarantee you a good financial aid package or a dorm room.

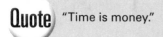 "Time is money."

–Greek proverb

If you plan on attending a junior college, you don't have much to lose financially. You will be accepted and, because the tuition is already less than other college options, you are not out much.

If you are applying late to a state university, you may find yourself accepted but without a place to live. Campus housing at a state university may fill up by Thanksgiving or sooner for the following school year. Finding an apartment—and roommates to help fund the apartment—and buying transit tickets or a car to drive to classes (and dealing with the parking hassles) are not things to relish. It can be very inconvenient to apply late to a large university.

Private colleges are a different ballgame. Private colleges have *priority deadlines*. While there are no guarantees, if you apply prior to this deadline, you are placing yourself in a priority position. If you apply to a private college in the summer because of rolling admission, you will find yourself accepted but probably sitting with loans instead of scholarships and grants.

 "Action may not always bring happiness; but there is no happiness without action."

–Benjamin Disraeli

Many colleges begin earmarking scholarships and grants in January and February. Many colleges have only so many cookies to give away. When they are gone, they are gone. The Johnny Come Latelys may attend classes on campus but will end up paying far more than necessary. Had those same students applied early, they would most likely be paying less.

 "The last of the human freedoms—to choose one's attitude in any given set of circumstances, to choose one's own way."

–Viktor Frankl

Don't Be Late

No matter which plan you select, do not apply late. Applying late disqualifies you from scholarship weekends and other types of scholarship competition. Marlie applied in January and got accepted to a large university. Unfortunately, she and her parents did not fill out the FAFSA early, and they missed the university's early financial aid deadline of February 15. Because of this mistake, she and her family ended up paying $7,000 more than necessary. By missing the deadline, Marlie was disqualified from the university's automatic need-based grant. So a family that truly needed the grant didn't receive it.

There are colleges and universities with deep pockets. They may be far and few between, but they are out there. These colleges have a great funding resource that doesn't seem to run out. If you are accepted late at this college, you may still receive the same financial aid package as if you had applied early. Unfortunately, they are not advertised as generous.

> Lacey's parents were in a transition in their lives. Her father had been a successful insurance agent and felt the calling to go into youth ministry at his church for a fraction of his previous income. In the meantime, the family expenses and house payment remained the same. Mom was a clerk in a convenience store. Dad did not want the family to know the dire straits they were in financially, so he filed the FAFSA with inflated income figures. Of course, Lacey qualified for little to no financial aid, and the family could not afford college for her.
>
> A private college consultant was called to help the family in July and saw the errors quickly. She corrected the figures and contacted a local college that had deep pockets. As a favor to her, they calculated Lacey's financial aid package within 24 hours. The family went from owing $15,000 to $1,500. Lacey attended this private college all four years and graduated, and the family paid what they could afford. This was possible only because the college had deep pockets from endowments.

Applying early is always the better choice. This is why serious research for colleges must be done in the junior year or even sooner. Too many options evaporate when students apply late.

Quote "Dost thou love life? Then do not squander time, for that's the stuff life is made of."

–Benjamin Franklin

CHAPTER 50

How Can You Prepare for Writing Essays?

E ssays can be either somewhat important or very important. They are judged differently by each college. One institution may place much more value on the essay than another college does. The essay may constitute a value of 5 percent or up to 20 percent of your admissions package.

The higher-level universities (level 1 and level 2) may place more emphasis on the essay. Colleges in the mid-range (level 3 and level 4) may place less emphasis on the piece. Either way, you want to write a good essay because a poorly written one could hurt you in the admissions process or in competing for a scholarship.

Write Essays Early

Because essays are important, you should plan ahead. The junior year or the summer before your senior year would be a good time to write your essays. Essay questions usually appear as the last entry on a college application form. You have been working on the application all night, and you are getting tired. You turn the page to the final section, and there it is staring right at you—the essay request. Who wants to start writing an essay at that moment when it is probably a better idea to go to bed? Throwing together an essay at the last minute means not giving it the time it deserves. Start fresh the next evening when you have only the essay to worry about.

Give essays the time they deserve.

Avoid a Laundry List

Because you are submitting a resume that lists other accomplishments, don't include such laundry list items in your essay. The essay should tell something about yourself above and beyond what the college personnel already know about you. They know you attended Space Camp in Houston. They know you graduated in the top 20 percent of your class. Here is your opportunity to say something new that has not been addressed. The admissions form may omit something about you that is worth talking about. The essay is the time to tell it.

 Don't repeat your accomplishments in the essay if they are already known to the college.

Watch Word Count

Essays vary in the required word count. For one, you may be asked to write 500 words; for another, 750 words. Make the adjustments as necessary. This could take some time, so plan on giving yourself that time. Double-check all the directions and details so your essay looks custom fit for this college, not for another school.

Find an Original Topic

Some colleges will ask you to come up with your own topic. What should you pick?

A life experience is one option. It doesn't need to be something that made headlines. It can be something as simple as a family vacation to the Michigan Upper Peninsula or a choir trip to New York City. The Michigan trip could be tied into the importance of preserving nature. The New York City trip could be used to discuss the importance of diversity.

Another option could be a world or national concern. Be careful, though, not to blame countries or politicians for things you see as problems. Merely explain your perspective. You might have a wind farm in your backyard, and this could lead to the topic of developing alternative energy sources. Stay away from criticizing a member of Congress for not doing more. Don't blame anyone or make the issue political.

A significant person in your life is an excellent topic. Perhaps you have a grandparent who taught you life lessons by example. While the focus should be on the effect he or she has had on you, it is appropriate to tell a little about your grandparent as well.

Your personal background could be a very good topic for an essay. If you are a first-generation American, if you are an immigrant who survived Darfur, or if you were adopted into your family, these topics can reveal much about your character and personality if they are treated in a positive way. Did you move from a rural community to a major city or from a major city to a rural community? Be careful not to include horrific details of your experience. Keep it tasteful and place the emphasis on how the experience has made you the person you are and how your values have been shaped by your experience.

Ethical dilemmas are very difficult and tricky, but if you feel you have made a responsible choice that is appropriate for discussion, you could write about it. For example, your friend could be bulimic and perhaps he or she trusted you with that secret. You made the decision to tell the school counselor and get help for your friend. You could tell why you did that and how your values were part of the decision. While offering insight into your character and your ability to solve problems, this topic may be a bit heavy for an essay. You may feel more comfortable in selecting something a bit lighter. Be careful to choose a topic that is appropriate for you.

A risk that you have taken that turned out in your favor is a good topic. Perhaps your advisors did not recommend taking advanced math classes, but you thought you could do it. You were successful. Tell what you had to do to be successful and talk about your belief in yourself.

 "Keep your fears to yourself, but share your courage with others."

–Robert Louis Stevenson

A fictional character is a fun topic to select. Tell why you admire that character or how you are like that character. Perhaps you have something in common. A character from real life is also an excellent topic. Tell why. Perhaps you lost a family member to illness, and you would like to tell what impact this loss had on your life. If the experience altered your life in a negative way, move on to another topic. Select something with a more positive tone. However, if the loss brought about something positive, then go ahead.

Sources

Be careful about looking online for sample essays. It may be very tempting to plagiarize. It is not worth it. However, if you want assistance in writing an essay, you might want to look at *One-Hour College Application Essay* (JIST Publishing) by Jan Melnik. It contains good information on what to do and what not to do with comments from college admissions directors. It shows excellent sample essays and tells why they are quality pieces.

Make Essays a Priority

Whether it is a self-selected essay topic or one selected for you, make the essay a priority and give it the time it deserves. Don't procrastinate in writing essays.

Quote "Putting off an easy thing makes it hard, and putting off a hard one makes it impossible."

–George H. Lorimer

When and Why Will You Be Writing Essays?

You might be surprised by how often you will be writing essays for college-related events. It is a good idea to collect sample questions for the colleges you like. Then ask your English teacher if you could write on these topics during your junior year. This is killing two birds with one stone. Save every essay you write.

Note Essays are used often in the college process.

Applications

You will find that each type of college has a different type of application. Some, but not all, require essays.

Junior Colleges

Junior colleges are not likely to ask for an essay. The admissions procedure is quite simple. If you have a high school diploma or a GED, you will be admitted. Fill out a simple form, pay your application fee, and you will be accepted. (Scholarships often are given for strong academics in high school and for musical or athletic abilities.) However, once you have completed your two years at a junior college and begin searching for a four-year college for transfer, you may be asked to write an essay.

State Universities

State universities are more selective than junior colleges. Universities admit students based on a combination of class rank, grade point average, and ACT/SAT scores. Formulas may be used to determine who is in and who is out. The admissions process does not require essays. Some scholarships may require essays, but some do not.

Private Colleges

Private colleges usually ask for an essay for admission and another essay for scholarship competition mid-year. Just count on it. Private colleges consider high school activities and volunteerism. It all goes into a package that will be evaluated on a competitive basis.

Scholarships

Before you apply to a college, you are likely to be looking for scholarship money, right? You may begin doing so years before you go to college. Some popular Web sites are www.fastweb. com, www.FinAid.com, and http://apps.collegeboard.com.

You will register on these sites and complete a questionnaire to be matched to possible scholarships. Then you will begin to receive applications. Most of these applications require an essay. Sorry. That is just reality. However, each time you write an essay, save it. You may be able to use essays more than once.

Don't get carried away and register for too many sites. Each site has many of the same scholarships, and you may be receiving duplicates, making things a little confusing. Pick a few and call it good. Each site may have billions of dollars in scholarships.

Start checking your counselor's bulletin board, and you will be surprised by just how many local scholarships are offered. Knights of Columbus, Jaycees, Lions, Wal-Mart, Tyson, and American Legion are all likely to require an essay.

The scholarships might stipulate that a parent must belong to a specific organization. The Knights of Columbus organization has a scholarship that applies only to a student who wants to attend a Catholic college and who also is the child of a deceased KC parent. Check on the scholarships with restrictions because the pool of applicants might be smaller.

Of course, a nice touch is to include a resume and a cover letter just because this looks professional—and only a few other applicants will do it.

 Quote "Achieving goals by themselves will never make us happy in the long term: it's who you become, as you overcome the obstacles necessary to achieve your goals, that can give you the deepest sense and most long-lasting sense of fulfillment."

–Tony Robbins

What Do Colleges Want to See in Essays?

Colleges want to see *you* in essays. Your thoughts, your values, and your personality are what the committee members look for as they read your words. That is why the questions seem so personal or strange. A well-constructed essay could be up to 20 percent of your application value and could determine whether you get accepted to the college or whether you receive a scholarship. The more prestigious the college, the more important the essay.

> **Quote** "Sometime in your life you will go on a journey. It will be the longest journey you have ever taken. It is the journey to find yourself."
>
> –Katherine Sharp

A Portrait of You

Your essays should paint a picture of you. ACT/SAT scores, grade point averages, and class ranks are numbers. These only tell part of the story. The essay provides the opportunity for you to set yourself apart from the crowd and emphasize why you would be the smart choice for this college or scholarship.

Your personality gets an opportunity to shine beyond the numbers. Because you already have given academic information on your resume and possibly on the application form, you don't need to repeat it. This is your time to emphasize other positives about yourself.

Quote "The man who speaks the truth is always at ease."

–Persian proverb

The Questions

A common type of question is "Tell about a life-altering event you have experienced and how it changed you." If you haven't had such an event, don't bluff your way through it. A college usually gives you a choice of two or even three essay topics. Always select a topic that you can truthfully write about.

Keep in mind what you are to answer in the question. Don't go off on another tangent and ignore part of the question. For example, consider the question about a life-changing event. Don't spend the entire essay telling about your recovery from a car accident. Leave enough space to address the rest of the question—how this event changed you. That is probably the most important part of the question, and your answer will allow the reader to get to know you well. Actually, how you react to something is often more important than the incident itself. You won't be fooling anyone by skipping over the difficult portion of the essay question.

Note Answer the essay question completely.

The focus should be on you and not on your siblings, parents, or some other significant person in your life. The college doesn't want to know about all the other people. You are the main focus. After all, they are thinking of accepting you and not the others.

Interesting Details

Can you imagine what it would be like to be someone on a scholarship committee and read essays all day? To make it worse, some people are reading responses to the same two or three questions all day, week after week. Give them a break! Make yours interesting. A well-written essay should have an interesting beginning to catch the attention of the reader. Using vivid and descriptive words and phrases brightens the essay and brings it alive. You want the essay to be memorable and placed toward the top of the pile, but not in a shocking way. The essay should not be disturbing or take a bizarre twist bordering on the *Twilight Zone*.

Note Write an interesting essay—express yourself!

Use humor carefully. Make sure the humor is not a put-down of another person or sexual or political in nature.

> Andy's essay choice was to tell of a time that he learned a life lesson. He bought a very used Chevy pickup from a gentleman who said he would trust it on a trip to California. This may have been true, but only if the gentleman had been living two miles from the California border. One week after Andy bought the truck, he took a relaxing drive and found himself nearing a cemetery. He heard a noise. As he looked in his rearview mirror, he saw oil spilling onto the highway in large amounts. The engine had just blown up. Andy turned off the road and into the cemetery. There he was in a graveyard with a dead pickup. To add insult to injury, a Ford towed him home.

This example uses humor without damaging another person. Of course, Andy's lesson was to have a mechanic inspect a vehicle and not take the owner's word. Andy learned what to look for when buying a vehicle.

Writing an essay is not the occasion for therapy. If you were mistreated as a child, save this discussion for a counseling session. Do not vent about such issues in a college essay. Readers will be uncomfortable reading about it. While you may have learned a life lesson, save it for a more appropriate moment.

Note Save shocking events in your life for other occasions.

Variety

Try to not use the same words throughout the essay. If you are writing about a car, vary your essay by using words such as *vehicle, Buick, my wheels*, and so on. Use a thesaurus to assist you in writing more interesting sentences. Using the same words repeatedly is boring and indicates a lack of creativity. However, don't use words that you are not sure of or words that are not commonly used.

Grammar and Spelling

Have an adult or teacher proofread your essay. If you have been working on an essay for a long time, your mind will fill in the missing words because you know what you're trying to say. On the other hand, when others read the essay, they will probably catch your errors. They will see the oversight or misspelling because they didn't create the piece or read it several times. Sending an essay through a spell checker is not enough because an incorrectly used word can be spelled correctly while the word itself is still wrong.

Note There is no room for spelling errors on an essay.

Have an auldt or tcheaer poorf your easay. If you have been wkronig on an easay for a lnog tmie, your mnid wlil flil in het mssinig wdorsbceause you kown what you'er triying to yas. This is an example of the mind filling in letters. Despite the horrible misspellings in the passage, you can still understand the meaning. The two sentences are the first sentences of the previous paragraph. As long as the first and last letters in a word are correct, your mind can quickly reshuffle the other letters to make it readable.

An Outline

Having an outline of the essay before you begin to write is very useful. It may take a long time to come up with an introduction, key points, examples from life experiences, and a closing. But once an outline is formed, the writing becomes easier. "You" are one of the hardest topics there is. Don't make it harder by not having a plan—the outline.

Original Work

While it may be tempting to go to www.EssayEdge.com and pass off an essay as your own, don't do it. Who do you think you are kidding? You are turning in your essay to people who do this for a living. Not only will you not fool them, but you are also likely to not be accepted because of plagiarism. Computer programs allow teachers to take sentences from your work and see whether they are original or copies. You may want to read essays that other people wrote, but make yours an original.

 Try to make your essay the best part of your admissions package.

Deadlines

Meet the essay deadline. Pay attention to when essays are due. Some are due with the application form, and some are due several weeks later. Double-check every date because each college has different guidelines. Post deadlines on the kitchen calendar.

What if you have just one day left? Fax the essay to the college. Better to fax than miss the deadline. You aren't the only student the college is considering for admission or for a scholarship. If you miss a deadline, that makes the pool of qualified students just a little bit smaller.

PART V

How You Can Afford the Best College for You

CHAPTER 53

How Can You Save Money for College?

S aving money for anything is difficult. But you can
save and pay for college in some creative ways not
available in the past. They all sound good initially, but read
the fine print. Some of them have little surprises that you may
not like. Be particularly careful about saving and investing in a
changing economy. Look at all your options and be sure to seek
advice when you have questions.

Mutual Funds

A great way for parents to save for your college is to invest
money in mutual funds. Using automatic withdrawal once a
month from their paychecks into the mutual fund makes it easy
to save. Your family doesn't see the money withdrawn. Your
family doesn't spend it. Yet it is there if you need it. If you are a
parent, start this when children are young, forget about it, and
the money will be there if and when you need it. If you don't
need it, you may spend it on anything you wish or let it grow.
Students aren't locked into spending it on college. The down side
is that, if the stock market is in a slump, you may see the college
fund shrink.

Note Mutual funds may shelter your college fund.

State Education Plans

Many states offer tuition saving plans. When a student is young, parents begin making monthly payments toward college, with the assurance that tuition will be paid in full. If tuition is $10,000 per year when payments begin, you are assured that you will not owe the difference if tuition is up to $15,000 by the time you begin college. The plan covers full tuition. It's like a tuition insurance plan. What could be wrong with this plan?

Note Read the fine print in a state educational fund.

What if you don't want to go to this school? As a student, you could be an introvert who can't sleep just thinking about going to a major university. Or you could learn by the junior year that you are not four-year college material. You want to go to a junior college and major in Manufacturing Technology, a two-year program that the university does not offer.

What if you receive a full-ride scholarship to Harvard or Stanford? Will you attend the local state university and decline an offer from Harvard or Stanford? Do you get your money back from your tuition savings plan? No. At least not without penalties.

The penalties and regulations vary from state to state. Your family should learn the regulations for your state before signing anything. Parents could be better off placing the same amount of money into a mutual fund. There are no penalties there if plans change.

529 Plans

529 Plans have been offered for several years, and they feature tax savings to the donor. The funds are tax free until they are withdrawn. Then, if the withdrawals are used for education expenses, they are federal-income-tax free. They may not be state-income-tax free, however. When the beneficiary receives the fund, it is taxed at his or her tax rate and not at the rate of the owner.

Note The tax benefits for a 529 Plan are tremendous for the donor.

What happens if the beneficiary—the college student—receives generous scholarships and does not need this funding? It is easily transferred to another family member, even a cousin, with no penalties. Another benefit is that the owner of the fund maintains control of the account. It may be earmarked for a student, but the owner has complete control with no tax implications.

Contributions to a 529 are considered gifts for estate tax purposes and count toward the $10,000 annual gift tax exclusion. In fact, if a person wants to set up five accounts in one year, he or she may do so for a $50,000 tax-exempt gift for five beneficiaries.

Is this plan limited to family members? No. As a donor you may name anyone as a beneficiary. Only when the beneficiary changes does it need to be to a family member. How would this work for a grandparent, for example? Each year, a grandparent could set aside $10,000 with no tax implications. If the grandparent is married, the spouse may also set aside $10,000 for a total of $20,000 in one year. If the grandchild earmarked for this fund does not attend college, the fund is easily transferred to another grandchild with no penalties attached.

Are there penalties somewhere in this plan? Yes. If the funds are not used for educational purposes, a 10 percent IRS penalty is assessed when money is withdrawn, and in addition, the funds are taxed at the owner's current rate. The reason the fund is not used is very important. If the beneficiary receives scholarships and does not need these funds, the penalties are waived.

Details vary from state to state, and a 529 is not appropriate for everyone's situation. Your family can contact a financial planner it trusts and learn whether a 529 is right for the family's situation.

Student or Parent

Does it matter whether savings are in a parent's name or in your name? Yes, it does. Let's say your parents are trying to save a little for your college expenses. They put $200 into your college account under your name. At the end of three years, you have $7,200. Of course, you must claim this on the FAFSA in January. As part of the formula, you will be expected to contribute $2,520 because students are assessed at 35 percent of savings.

Let's play this out another way. Let's pretend that your parents take that same amount of money each month and place it under their name to keep for you until you go to college. Parents' savings are assessed at 5.6 percent so the contribution would be $403. Under the first plan, $2,520 went for payment to the college, and you still have to buy books and a laptop. Under the second plan, you contribute $403 to the college and have money for books and laptop with much more left over.

 Note Parents contribute 5.6 percent of savings, and students contribute 35 percent.

Let's now pretend that you have saved $9,000 for a car for college. You plan on buying a car in May as a graduation present to yourself. Good plan? Let's think about this. You will be filing the FAFSA in January or February, and on the FAFSA you must claim money in your savings and checking on the day you file. If that $9,000 shows up in your savings when you file, you will be assessed at 35 percent, and more than $3,000 will be expected from you for college expenses. If you bought yourself the car as a Christmas present, it may work out differently for you.

Note Timing is important when filing the FAFSA so you give accurate financial data.

Time the events so that they truly show your financial status. The financial aid process aims to be fair, but if you miscalculate, you could end up paying much more for college than you deserve to pay.

What if you haven't saved? What can you do?

Second Job

Many parents with students in college don't have much time to miss them because the parents have taken second jobs to pay for college. Unfortunately, this is a Catch-22. It may solve the problem for this year, but the increased income will be used as a basis for financial aid for the following year. Increased income equals decreased aid. If you take a small part-time job to help with monthly expenses, that probably won't make a great impact on next year's package. But, if you take on a significant job, it just might.

You can go to various sites that have estimator links, such as www.act.com. There you will find a form for entering your new income figures to see how much the extra income would hurt you for the following year.

Grandparents' Gift

Grandma and Grandpa just sold a rental property and want to help you with college. They want to give you a large sum of money for a high school graduation gift. Ask them to hold onto their money until you graduate from college. You don't have any debt entering college but will have plenty after graduation. Wouldn't it be better if you could have them pay off your guaranteed student loans with enough left over for a car, too? It is better use of the money to get it at college graduation.

College Payment Plan

Not every family has managed to save for college. Many colleges offer a zero percent interest payment plan for parents who don't want to take on loans or don't qualify. Most of the payments are for eight or nine months, and this allows parents to be debt-free when the student graduates. As you visit colleges, ask whether they have this interest-free option. It could be the deciding factor on where you choose to attend. For families that can easily afford a monthly payment of $500 or $800 a month, this is a great opportunity.

 Note Colleges are offering monthly interest-free payment plans.

Home Equity

A home-equity line of credit is a questionable option that families resort to taking. If college money is not saved or not enough is saved, a family may dip into home equity to pay the difference. The interest is tax deductible, but if the real estate market is soft, it may not be a risk worth taking. Should an unforeseen event happen, a family could lose its home.

You may need to get creative to pay for college. Apply to several schools—four, five, or six may not be too many—and then review the various packages the colleges offer. Reducing the initial price of college by attending a more generous school is a good way to pay for your education, too.

Note Apply to several schools to increase the odds of receiving a generous package.

CHAPTER 54

Can You Afford College?

You are likely to be able to afford college if you know your family EFC (Expected Family Contribution), understand what it means, and know how to find a college that will honor it. Families often pay too much for college because they do not know what their fair contribution should be. The EFC is a critical factor in pursuing an affordable college education. The EFC is discussed in more detail in Chapter 66.

There is a way to estimate what you should pay for college. Each family is different. The family down the street with the same type of house and similar income could pay a dissimilar amount because of circumstances that differ from yours. College costs are on a sliding scale, so you pay according to what you can afford. The less you make, the less you pay. But that is only true if you find a college that will meet your financial needs. The challenge is to find colleges that will do so. Because you won't have that information until late in the senior year, apply to several colleges.

Note Apply to four, five, or six colleges.

Expensive Colleges

Many students make the mistake of avoiding expensive colleges. They think the safe road is to go to a state university for $15,000 instead of a private school costing $30,000. While that may look like a good thought initially, it could cost you more to attend a state university than a private college that is generous. Very few students pay the full sticker price for college. Some students pay 10 cents on the dollar, and many pay even less. Compare financial aid packages between a state university and a private college. You may be very surprised.

Ironically, the colleges with the steepest tuition are often those with the deepest pockets for financial aid. They can afford to be generous because their alumni have been generous. Colleges invest large donations into endowment funds and use the earnings to give as financial aid. One large donation can turn a college that met the financial need of a family at 75 percent into a college that meets financial need at 90 percent or even 100 percent.

 Note Expensive colleges are often the most generous.

Position yourself to be in the upper 50 percent academically at a college. See Chapter 22 for more information. This positioning increases your odds of getting scholarships and grants. Apply to four, five, or six colleges. Colleges will ask you to list the other schools you are considering. This is no random request. Colleges know how generous other schools are and know whether they represent competition. If the other colleges you list are generous, you are more likely to place yourself into a more generous bracket.

 Note Your position among other students on campus makes a huge difference in what you receive in your award letter.

The Real Cost

The real cost of college is based on the FAFSA that you fill out soon after January 1 of your senior year in high school. FAFSA stands for Free Application for Federal Student Aid. This form is used to determine eligibility for all aid: federal, state, and college. However, many private colleges have their own forms and allow additional expenses the FAFSA does not. The cost of each college depends on what your FAFSA outcome is. The best scenario is a high ACT or SAT score and low expected family contribution. If this is the case for you, stand back and let the generous offers roll in.

Note What you really pay for college is in the award letter you receive in the spring.

EFC Is So Important

The EFC is the product of the FAFSA. EFC stands for Expected Family Contribution. Once the FAFSA is processed and produces the EFC, a family knows what its contribution will be toward one year of college. Whether a family has one, two, or three children in college, the EFC is the same because it is not a student contribution but rather a family contribution. In reality, the family that has twins going to college or three children in high school at the same time has an advantage. This family will pay less for college in the end. If your family has three children born over 12 years, you will pay more for college than a family that had three children in four years.

Unfortunately, many families don't know what an EFC is and never realize what could have been.

This part of the book gives many useful tips on how to find the best financial option for you. But it isn't just about getting generous offers. There are many methods to paying off student loans quickly, which is just about as good as getting generous scholarships and grants.

Loan Forgiveness

Getting loans forgiven is the next best thing to receiving a scholarship or grant. Student loans are sometimes forgiven if specific conditions are met. There are several circumstances under which the federal government reduces or eliminates the need to repay loans. Check into these. You may be surprised to learn just where they apply.

Loan forgiveness may apply if these conditions occur:

- If a student is in a car accident after graduation from college and cannot work, and if doctors concur that this condition is permanent, repayment of loans is not expected.

- If a college should close its doors and a student cannot attend another school to finish, repayment is not expected. Loans are made with the assumption that the student will graduate, have a professional career, and be able to repay debt. It is not the student's fault that the college closed, making it impossible for the student to finish school.

- If a student volunteers to work with the Peace Corps or Vista, he or she may qualify for loan forgiveness of up to 70 percent.

- The government wants to entice college graduates to work in shortage areas. If a student agrees to teach in the field of math, science, foreign languages, bilingual education, or another shortage area, up to 100 percent of the loan amount may be forgiven. The government may stipulate that a teacher must work five years to have all loans forgiven.

- A teacher may also have loans forgiven up to 100 percent if he or she works in a government-designated low-income area. Many inner-city schools have severe teacher shortages because of poverty or crime. Teachers who work in these schools for a specific number of years may have all loans forgiven.

- If a college graduate serves in the military during time of war or in an area of hostilities and imminent danger, up to 50 percent of loans may be forgiven. However, if that same student had gone into the military first and signed up for the GI Bill, it is likely that no loans—or few loans—would exist.

- A full-time nurse or medical technician may have his or her loans forgiven if he or she works in a shortage or poverty area. For example, Indian reservations need qualified nurses in the hospitals. Nurses who work in these areas may find that their pay structure is very generous as well.

- A full-time staff member of a Head Start program may qualify for 100 percent of loan forgiveness. Children must qualify financially to be in the Head Start program. Therefore, the Head Start population is considered a low-income region.

CHAPTER 55

What Are Scholarships, Grants, Financial Aid, Loans, and Work-Study?

Scholarships, grants, loans, financial aid, and *work-study* describe programs that address ways to pay for college. But each is different. When award letters arrive from colleges in the spring of your senior year in high school, you will see that the award letters use some or all of these terms. The award letter will inform your family of the financial aid package you will receive.

Scholarships

Academic scholarships are awarded on academic merit and require that a specific grade point average be maintained in college. The requirements are often a 3.0, 3.2, or 3.5 grade point average. Because grade point averages frequently drop from high school to college, a 3.2 high school student should be very careful with a 3.2 GPA requirement for a college scholarship. It could be very difficult, if not closer to impossible, to keep meeting this requirement.

College scholarships are usually larger than local scholarships. College scholarships can range from $1,000 to more than $20,000, while local scholarships are usually in the range of $250–$1,000. The good news is that scholarships do not need to be repaid.

Scholarships may be lost if students don't fulfill the GPA requirements. If a student receives a 3.0 and the scholarship requirement is 3.2, he or she will be placed on probation. Students usually are given one semester of probation. After that, if they don't rise to the occasion, the scholarship is lost. Scholarships are mini-contracts: "If *you* do this, *we* will give you that. If you don't hold up your end of the bargain, we don't deliver."

Grants

Grants are totally different. While like scholarships they do not need to be repaid, grants have no strings attached. You don't need to jump through any hoops. If you maintain a 2.0, like any student in good standing on campus, you keep the grant.

Pell grants are for the most financially needy students. Family income has to come near the poverty level for students to obtain these grants. Many students from lower-middle-class families may qualify for Pell grants.

 "I would never have amounted to anything were it not for adversity. I was forced to come up the hard way."
–J.C. Penney

State tuition grants are given to residents attending college in the home state. Tuition grants are intended to level out the playing field between state colleges and private colleges. The typical range of tuition grants is $2,000–$4,000. The needier you are, the more likely you are to receive the higher amount. The more income your family has, the less you will receive. State tuition grants are far more generous than Pell grants. If your family earns $100,000 in annual income, you may still qualify for some amount in state tuition grant funds.

State tuition grants do not transfer to another state. You are eligible only if you attend in your state of residence. If you live in Missouri, your state tuition grant only applies to Missouri and does not transfer if you attend college in Iowa or Kansas. While state tuition grants do not cross state lines, generous colleges will make up the loss. That way, you may attend an out-of-state college for about the same out-of-pocket expense as you would pay for attending within your resident state. There are really no penalties to cross state lines if you attend a private college.

Consortiums

Many states are forming consortiums, which benefit students financially. Most states expect out-of-state students to pay much more for tuition than students within their home state. But some states are joining in alliance and allowing students to cross the state border without paying a penalty.

Here is an example. Let's pretend that Minnesota, North Dakota, South Dakota, and Nebraska form a consortium that allows students from these four states to cross borders without paying a penalty. If tuition is $6,000 in North Dakota, you, a Nebraska resident, will pay the same amount as a North Dakota resident would pay. You will not pay the $12,000–$23,000 fee often charged for out-of-state residents.

But in the middle of these states sits Iowa. Iowa isn't going to play the little consortium game. Iowa decides that, if it joins the consortium, too many students will leave the state to attend college in Minnesota, South Dakota, and Nebraska. So Iowa students are held hostage by Iowa's refusal to join the consortium. If students leave the state, they pay much more for tuition. Iowa's decision is costing its citizens a great hardship.

On the other hand, Minnesota and Missouri may drop out-of-state penalties along the border to allow Iowa students to attend for the same or nearly the same cost as residents. There is more than one way to play this game.

Inquire whether your state belongs to a consortium so you may cross borders without penalty.

Financial Aid

The award letter you receive in the spring will include most or all of the financial items mentioned in this chapter. Not everyone will receive a scholarship, grant, and work-study, but most students receive a financial aid package of some sort. Colleges take your financial need and try to address it through various means.

If you qualify for a Pell grant, you will receive one automatically. Colleges are more than happy to give you a Pell grant because it does not come out of college funds but instead comes from the federal government. Work-study also comes from federal funds, so most colleges are generous with work-study. State tuition grants come from the state and are automatic as well.

 "Some misfortunes we bring upon ourselves; others are completely beyond our control. But no matter what happens to us, we always have some control over what we do about it."
–Suzy Szasz

Loans

Loans are the least desirable component of a financial aid package, but they are a fact of life. The average student can expect to be in debt $20,000–$30,000 when he or she finishes four years of college. Loans come in three packages: subsidized, unsubsidized, and private.

Subsidized loans come from the federal government, which pays your interest while you are in college. You don't begin paying interest until six months after your graduation from college. Subsidized loans are often called *Stafford* or *Perkins loans.*

The federal government also funds *unsubsidized loans,* but the interest starts as soon as the funds are disbursed. By the time you graduate, you can have four years of interest added to the total of what you owe. The nice thing about federal loans, both subsidized and unsubsidized, is that the interest rates are capped and do not fluctuate.

"Some people use one half their ingenuity to get into debt, and the other half to avoid paying it."

–George D. Prentice

Private lenders fund *private loans*. These companies need to make money from the funds they lend you. The interest rate is usually higher than government loans and not fixed. For many families, private lenders are a necessity, but they are the least desirable of the least desirable.

Work-Study

Jobs on campus are usually funded by work-study money from the federal government. Students must qualify for work-study by demonstrating financial need.

The college may give you $500 to $1,000 in work-study funds, but your schedule has to fit your work-study job. If this is part of your financial aid package, the money you earn must go toward tuition. But if your work-study package is in addition to your financial aid package, you may keep the money as spending money or as savings.

All of the above may appear on an award letter. When you review all your award letters, pay close attention to what types of loans you receive, taking note of the interest rates. Also look closely at the grants, scholarships, and work-study involved. Weigh the loans with scrutiny. Your dream college may offer you the top financial aid package, or it may offer you a financial nightmare for the future.

 "Turn your stumbling blocks into stepping stones."

–Anonymous

CHAPTER 56

Where Can You Find Scholarships?

S cholarships are not that difficult to find because many of them come directly to your high school. Getting a scholarship, though, is a different matter.

Your Counselor's Office

Your counselor receives scholarship applications and posts them on the bulletin board. Make a habit of walking past the counselor's bulletin board daily to check out what's new. Be sure to do this during your senior year and even toward the end of your junior year. Some counselors have a special section on the wall labeled "new" for you to check out. As new applications come in, they go to the main bulletin board, and a fresh application replaces the former new application.

If you qualify for a posted scholarship, consider applying. Read the fine print. One scholarship may require you to hold a 3.5 GPA. Another scholarship may require that you play a certain sport. Some might require a specific ACT or SAT score.

 Note Check your counselor's bulletin board for the latest scholarship applications.

Sources of Information

Be sure to access these sources for scholarship possibilities:

- Community organizations
- High schools
- Colleges
- Internet sites

Community Organizations

Civic organizations have fundraisers throughout the year that allow them to donate to worthy causes in the community. Scholarship funds would constitute one of the worthy causes.

Some well-known groups that offer scholarships are

- State education associations
- American Association of University Women
- Dollars for Scholars
- Knights of Columbus
- Rotary
- Lions
- Kiwanis
- VFW (Veterans of Foreign Wars)

Note Civic organizations are great sources of scholarships.

Some organizations may have many students applying, while some may have very few. You might be competing against 200 other students or against only 3. These scholarships are commonly in the range of $100–$500. In some cases, children of organization members automatically receive a scholarship.

Local employers also are a source of scholarships. Some scholarships are open to anyone in the community, but many offer the applications to employees' children only. You may qualify for the competition only if a parent is employed by the business. These scholarships are usually for one year.

> **Note** Local employers often give scholarships to employees' children.

High Schools

High schools often give scholarships through private donors. In honor of a former graduate, memorials are presented to students who fit the profile. For example, a teacher may have left a sum of money in her will for a scholarship fund for students going into the teaching field. A deceased farmer's estate may offer a scholarship to a student living on a farm who wants to major in the field of agronomy.

Occasionally, donors may leave an entire farm to a small public high school. The annual income is used to give each student going to college an automatic scholarship. If you are going to a junior college, you qualify for a scholarship. If you are going to a school of cosmetology, you qualify. If you are planning to attend four years of college, you qualify. If you are an A student, you qualify; if you are a C student, you qualify.

> **Note** Occasionally donors give scholarships to all graduating students bound for college.

If it is a good farming year and the graduating class is small, students stand to receive a more generous amount. If it is a bad farming year and the graduating class is larger, the rewards are much smaller. The ethanol and biodiesel boom brought great rewards.

Some high schools give the scholarships when students leave college or graduate. This approach helps pay for guaranteed student loans. It's a back-door approach, but it reduces students' college debt more than a scholarship presented at high school graduation time.

Colleges

Colleges are the largest and most generous sources of scholarships. The amount of a college scholarship for a strong student can fall anywhere from approximately $3,000 to a *full ride,* meaning all tuition is covered. Each college has different criteria for qualifying. A college that has the middle 50 percent of students falling in the 19–23 ACT range may begin offering generous scholarships with lower requirements. On the other hand, a college with 50 percent of the students falling in the 25–30 ACT range will have much higher requirements for a scholarship.

> **Note** The largest scholarships are usually given by the colleges.

Many colleges will specifically state that an ACT of 26 will ensure the student of a $5,000 scholarship. This inspires students to take the ACT two and three times to meet that goal. This is why some students who could attend colleges of a much higher academic caliber actually choose schools of lesser standing— these students are far above the average for those schools and, this way, they are more likely to receive a good scholarship.

College scholarships usually have a grade point average attached to them. If you achieve the specified grade point average, the scholarship continues all four years.

> **Note** College scholarships and grants are often for all four years.

Internet Sites

In the past, random scholarships were offered, and it required a time-consuming search to find them. Today, Web sites gather millions of scholarships to their sites and fund the site with advertising banners. Corporations rent banner space with the hope that someone will click and buy their products related to college. Honda, MasterCard, private college loans, cell phones, Dell or Apple, and electronics stores commonly provide advertising banners.

 Fastweb.com is the largest Internet scholarship site.

These sites offer billions of dollars in scholarships. For example, www.fastweb.com offers millions of scholarships worth billions, with new ones added daily. Fastweb boasts of being the largest site in the nation, but it is not the only one. A search for scholarship sites will produce many results, but there are duplications. Many offer the same scholarships, so you don't need to register on five different sites.

You set up your own account on Fastweb with a password and complete a questionnaire. This may take over a half-hour because there are many questions on hobbies, heritage, and other topics. But these questions custom fit you with millions of scholarships. You won't qualify for all of them, but you don't want to qualify for millions of scholarships. Based on the questions you answered, you will receive e-mails with links to specific scholarships. Read about them and learn what you must do to enter. Then decide whether you want to apply. You may receive several each week, so choose wisely or you will burn out. Keep track of which scholarship applications you have submitted, so you don't get confused. You don't want to apply twice.

Ultimately, what really matters is the bottom line, which is out-of-pocket costs. Some students will get scholarships, some will receive both grants and scholarships, and some will only get grants. Don't be disappointed if you don't get many scholarships if you receive great financial aid. It doesn't really matter what kind of aid you get as long as the bottom line decreases.

Quote "Don't wait for your ship to come; swim out to it."
–Unknown

Should You Attend a Scholarship Weekend?

Colleges hold scholarship weekends for prospective scholarship winners. The purpose is to see these students in person and in comparison to one another. You can't show poise, interaction, and problem solving on a transcript or essay.

> **Note** Scholarship weekends are an opportunity to show yourself in a new light.

College Recruitment

Students who are scholarship material are invited to these weekend events, so, if you do not have scholarship potential, you are not likely to be invited. Consider it an honor to be selected instead of an inconvenience that might interfere with your plans for that particular weekend.

You probably plan on working diligently to apply for local scholarships that are valued at anywhere from $250 to $500. Why would you hesitate to attend a scholarship weekend that could yield a $2,500 to $5,000 scholarship just because of a conflicting cheerleading clinic or a basketball tournament game? Some scholarship weekends may result in a scholarship of more than $10,000.

Note Larger scholarships come from colleges.

Why are private colleges so focused on giving generous scholarships? Colleges have a goal to aggressively recruit students to keep enrollment numbers stable. If enrollment dips slightly, it impacts the college financially. Enrollment decreasing by 10–15 students may result in a professor losing his or her job, which colleges want to avoid.

If a college must pay a student a substantial scholarship to maintain enrollment, it will if it can. Tuition plus room and board might cost $30,000. If a college gives a $10,000 scholarship or grant, it will still receive $20,000 in the form of student loans, parent loans, Pell grants, tuition grants, work-study funds, and other funding that comes from state or federal sources. If $10,000 will yield an additional $20,000, it is worth it to keep enrollment stable or increasing.

Note Maintaining enrollment is very important to a small private college.

Weekend Activities

If you are invited to a scholarship weekend, take the opportunity to go. An invitation to attend a weekend is a sign that you have been noticed and that you probably have a chance to earn some financial reimbursement. Colleges see these weekends as a chance to give you a gift in hopes of recruiting you, and they eagerly look for reasons to do so. You will spend two or three days on campus experiencing the climate and determining whether this is the school for you. You might spend your evenings on the town exploring your off-campus opportunities.

Quote "Courage is grace under pressure."

–Ernest Hemingway

Scholarship weekends are fun, but keep in mind that they are competitive as well. Key focus areas for the college may be leadership, academic excellence, and outstanding talents. You will be given a campus tour, and you will be fed, lodged, and evaluated during your weekend stay.

Colleges will send you a list of the types of clothing you are to bring for the various activities. There may be a dance that is casual and a panel discussion that is semi-formal and held before a team of professors. Problem-solving group activities are often included to identify your negotiation and leadership skills. One-on-one discussions with professors are common.

Instructors and admissions staff will score your performance on all these activities. Think of this as the Academic Olympics. Points earned are added to points already given for your essay or essays, standardized test scores, grade point average, and letters of recommendation. The top scorers will receive the top scholarships.

 "You gain strength, courage and confidence by every experience in which you really stop to look fear in the face. You are able to say to yourself, 'I lived through this horror. I can take the next thing that comes along.'"

–Eleanor Roosevelt

It is likely that you will earn a scholarship if you go to a scholarship weekend. It is largely a matter of the amount of the scholarship.

Will you be disqualified from a scholarship if you don't go? Probably not. However, if you want an opportunity to show yourself in areas that don't come through on paper, this is that opportunity. Go for it!

 "The only thing we have to fear is fear itself."

–Franklin D. Roosevelt

CHAPTER 58

How Are Scholarships Applied to College Costs?

Scholarships are wonderful. They defray the cost of college and make you feel proud and recognized for your hard work, right? That's what everyone thinks. However, when colleges accept our scholarships, they are applied to the cost of college in three different ways. There are times where the college costs remain the same after receiving a scholarship. Surprised? Sorry, but this is possible.

Three Methods

Colleges vary in how they apply scholarships that you have received. You have a right to ask the colleges how your scholarship is applied to the bottom line. Most people don't realize that once the money reaches the college, things could go in one of three different ways.

You proudly notify a college that you received a scholarship for $500. Following are three different examples of methods used for applying your scholarship to your college expenses.

> **Note** Scholarships may be credited three different ways.

Method One

One way colleges apply scholarships is at 100 percent. This method is what most people assume will happen to their scholarships. If the out-of-pocket cost of college is $5,000 to the student through loans, a college will credit the entire amount toward the student loan amount. For example, if a student received a $500 scholarship, the cost in loans would be reduced to $4,500 for that year.

Method Two

A second way to apply scholarship money is at the 50 percent level. Again using the $5,000 amount, a $500 scholarship would be applied at 50/50. The college would apply $250 to the student's loan amount and reduce a college-issued scholarship or grant by $250, allowing another student to receive a $250 scholarship. The $500 scholarship just became a $250 scholarship at that college and student loans are reduced to $4,750. Basically, half of your scholarship went to someone else.

Method Three

Yet another method to apply scholarships is at the zero percent level. Some colleges will use the entire $500 scholarship to replace money given in college grants and scholarships. They will reduce the college grant by $500, place your scholarship in the slot to fill it, and give the $500 to another student. They credited the $500 to your account, but you still have loans totaling $5,000. For all practical purposes, your entire scholarship went to someone else. It had no benefit to you financially, because you still owe the same amount of money to the college. You can see that circumstances are different at each college.

 "Circumstances! I make circumstances!"

–Napoleon Bonaparte

You may think that this is totally unfair. Colleges disagree with you. They have policies, and if you don't think to inquire ahead of time, this may happen under your nose. Many families do not realize it has happened.

How to Use this Information

Method three is more likely to occur at private colleges that have already given you generous aid. State universities are more likely to give you 100 percent credit because they don't give generous grants and scholarships like private institutions do. It is very common for students to attend a more expensive private college for less than a lower-priced state university.

Note Apply to a combination of private and state schools to tip the odds in your favor.

The first step in the process is to apply for scholarships. The second step is to learn how these scholarships will be applied to your fees by the colleges in which you have a serious interest. Call the financial aid office at a college and ask if the scholarships will be applied at 100 percent to defray costs dollar for dollar or if they will be applied at 50 percent or 0 percent.

How scholarships are applied may make a big difference in which college you select. If you win a $3,000 scholarship, you certainly want that applied at 100 percent, because you worked hard for it. However, if your college is already generous with aid and you don't think you are scholarship material, you may not want to spend your senior year applying for 20 scholarships.

Take a close look at the award letter before you decide. If college 1 is asking $6,000 and honors scholarships at 50 percent, and college 2 is asking for $4,500 and honors scholarships at zero percent, you are still ahead in selecting college 2.

This consideration is another confirmation of why you should apply to five or six colleges. Some students apply to six or eight schools. The colleges you select may be more important than getting small, independent scholarships. Go into your college search with a clear mind, knowing how the system works.

CHAPTER 59

Are There Guaranteed Scholarships?

A re there guaranteed scholarships? This question has a very short answer: No.

The postcards and e-mails that guarantee large scholarships or promise a full refund if you don't get one are a scam. The refund clause lends credibility to the scam, but it is still a scam. The offers that promise large scholarships typically begin to arrive at the beginning of junior year. The required fees are usually nominal, so the offers may look tempting. The fact is that no one can guarantee you a scholarship.

> **Note** Guaranteed scholarships do not exist.

Scholarship Rule 1: Don't Ever Pay for Scholarships

Companies who want you to pay for scholarships are nothing more than a database of the scholarship information already available on www.fastweb.com at no charge or at colleges, where it is also available at no charge. These scam artists are taking advantage of people who do not realize they can access the information elsewhere. If you don't know this, you could be one of the many victims.

While these companies may not charge very much, the secret to the scam is volume. If enough people give these scam artists $30, it adds up to a nice sum of money.

 Note Never pay for scholarships.

Scholarship Rule 2: Don't Fall for the Guarantee

Many people are seduced by the guarantee. "Gee, we aren't out anything because if we don't get a scholarship, we get our money back." No, you don't.

The fine print states that you must apply to all the scholarships that are matches and that you must have evidence that you have been rejected. Sounds reasonable, right? It isn't. This is why: After you complete the questionnaire, you may receive more than 30 scholarship opportunities.

Let's pretend that you are very proactive and apply to all 30 opportunities. Some of these scholarships are obsolete. You will receive no response from the site. Therefore, you have no evidence that you have been rejected. So your guarantee is null and void.

The e-mail addresses that you receive often are impossible to contact. If you try to reply, you'll get a notice that the site no longer exists.

Six Scam Clues

1. **Guarantees.** There is no such thing as a guaranteed scholarship unless it appears in writing from a college. Until the final decision is made by the organization, no one knows what the results will be. Company-issued guarantees are sure to be scams.

2. **A fee.** If there is money involved, back away from the "too good to be true" opportunity.

3. **Only available here.** Companies that state they hold exclusive rights to information about a scholarship are usually running scams. Scholarship sources rarely give exclusive rights. They want as many students in the competition as possible.

4. **You are a finalist.** Isn't that great? Except you have entered no competition. Your name was selected from a database of millions of students awaiting money from those who don't know it is a scam.

5. **We do all the work.** Sorry. Students do the work. This is another clue that you are being scammed.

6. **No contact information.** You hit reply to the e-mail and get no contact information. This opportunity is a one-way path from your checkbook into theirs.

Colleges

Most colleges have a database accessible online from which you may fill out scholarship forms, or they may steer you to the largest scholarship site in the country: www.fastweb.com.

Scam artists surfaced in large numbers after the 9-11 tragedy and after Katrina in New Orleans. They also appear annually to take on a new crop of high school juniors. Don't be among that crop. Contact a college or Fastweb and save yourself money and frustration.

 "Honesty is the best policy, but there are too few policyholders."
–Anonymous

CHAPTER 60

How Can an Athlete Obtain a Scholarship?

Many good athletes from small high schools hope for large college scholarships. While sports statistics may be impressive for a small high school, the same statistics may not seem that impressive to a college. One way to find out how you compare is to go on the sports pages on college Web sites and check out the records by the athletes on campus. How tall are the members of the team? What are the scoring averages of the team? If you are in that range or close to it, you might have a chance. By comparing yourself online prior to visiting the college, you have an idea of what your chances would be of earning an athletic scholarship.

Note Have a strategy before you begin visiting colleges. Know how you compare to athletes on campus.

Plan for a Scholarship

College athletic scholarships are not easily earned. College standards are much higher than high school standards, and the competition is much tougher.

Note Winning an athletic scholarship requires advanced planning.

Athletic scholarships require advanced planning. If you hope to be in the running for an athletic scholarship, work must begin in the junior year in high school. As a junior, you must register with the NCAA (National Collegiate Athletic Association) Clearinghouse. High school counselors have the forms to fill out so the NCAA may certify you as eligible. A fee is required that equals college admission fees.

The clearinghouse will review your information to see whether the criteria are met. Eligibility standards are not optional. Classes taken in high school, standardized test scores, and grade point averages are all reviewed.

Note Register with the NCAA Clearinghouse in the junior year.

Research NCAA Eligibility

The NCAA has recently changed its initial eligibility rules for freshmen entering Division I and Division II schools. The required number of high school courses has been increased. In the past, students could take 13 core courses to be eligible to practice, play, and receive financial aid. In 2008, the required number was raised to 16. The breakdown is as follows:

- 4 English courses
- 3 math courses, algebra 1 or higher
- 2 natural/physical science courses (one must include a lab)
- 2 social science courses
- 1 additional core course from any listed above or from foreign language, non-doctrinal religion, or philosophy

Note Higher academic standards went into force in 2008.

For more information, visit www.ncaa.org or www.ncaaclearinghouse.net.

Academic Standards

Each division has its own academic standard, so don't assume that if one division standard is met, the other division will have the same requirements. Students are not to be contacted in the junior year of high school. All contact is strictly regulated. Personal meetings are not allowed between college coaches and the high school athletes. However, letters of interest are acceptable. Students may call the college coach with inquiries, but the coach may not call students. After July 1 prior to the senior year in high school, the rules change.

Note Clearinghouse rules change when you become a senior.

Jarod was an above-average high school basketball player. You could say he was the star of the basketball team. He was not an exceptional student academically, but with teachers bending for him, he always played and played well. His school checked grades by the semester, so he was assured of playing. (Other schools check grades weekly, monthly, or quarterly.)

Jarod won a basketball scholarship to a college that was above-average academically. Unfortunately, once Jarod began failing classes, he was not eligible to play. Jerod didn't receive the same breaks as in high school. Compared to high school, the classes were extremely challenging. By January, Jarod was off the team. If he had chosen a college that was lower in academic expectations, Jarod might have been more successful.

Quote "Becoming number one is easier than remaining number one."
–Bill Bradley

Contact

Once you are a senior in high school, college coaches may contact you. However, gifts are not allowed, because this could sway you to select one school over another. College visits are allowed but regulated with time limitations; 48 hours is the limit per visit and the number of visits is limited to five. If your academic performance drops below the acceptable level, the college may stop all contact. If grades are up to the proper level, a letter of intent may be issued and you may accept a one-year commitment to the college.

NCAA and NAIA

Criteria are different for Division III schools. Division III schools fall into two categories: NCAA and NAIA (National Association of Intercollegiate Athletics). NCAA Division III schools may not give athletic scholarships. Students might receive grants and scholarships, but they may not be for athletics. However, NAIA Division III schools may give athletic scholarships. Students who have hope of getting a scholarship in this area need to investigate their schools to make sure they give athletic scholarships.

Note Check to see whether your colleges even offer scholarships.

Regulations

Colleges are held increasingly accountable with enhanced athletic regulations. Whether an athlete plays for a Division I, II, or III college or university, meeting academic requirements is a must. Grade point averages play a major role in being a successful athlete at the college level.

Students who have athletics in mind need to maintain high academic standards not only in high school, but also in college. The need to focus on academic excellence has never been greater.

Quote "Excellence in any art or profession is attained only by hard and persistent work."

–Theodore Martin

CHAPTER 61

Can Arrests Affect Your College Opportunities?

What are the consequences of an arrest? Arrests may be minor or major. Getting a speeding ticket is technically an arrest. You may lose your license, your insurance rates may be raised, and you won't be able to drive your car to college if you lose your license.

Simple Misdemeanor vs. Serious Arrest

Of course, arrests can be more serious than a simple traffic violation. Most parents will not experience that dreaded phone call: "Mom, I've been arrested." Still, high school students are often in the wrong place at the wrong time, and they frequently give in to peer pressure. Some actions and their consequences may impact a student's education. Others will not.

The following are not likely to affect college admission:

- Underage drinking
- OWI (operating under the influence)
- A scuffle in the park
- Trespassing
- Speeding tickets
- Parking tickets
- Seat belt violations
- Breaking and entering

While these offenses do not represent behavior to be proud of, colleges probably will not ask whether a student has had speeding tickets or has repeatedly forgotten to wear a seat belt. Most colleges do not ask students whether they have been involved in a crime, and a minor infraction does not need to be disclosed.

A Trend

However, a slow trend is emerging and, in some cases, questions about arrests are beginning to show up on college application forms. If the student answers yes to the question, then he or she is likely to be asked for more details. Yet most minor infractions are overlooked.

When Jason was 14, he went cruising with three friends. One of the friends wanted to go hunting, and Jason knew his uncle had a rifle cabinet. In fact, his uncle had often let him borrow a rifle. The friends drove to the uncle's house and found that the family was not at home. Jason knew how to get into the house through a basement window, though, and all four boys entered the home to get the rifle.

Jason thought his uncle wouldn't mind, and he was right. However, a neighbor had been left in charge of checking the home while Jason's uncle was on vacation, and this neighbor did mind. He called the police, and the boys were arrested for a long list of serious violations. Because the boys were juveniles, the records were sealed.

Despite this incident, Jason won a full-ride scholarship to Colgate University. Yes, it was a stupid thing for Jason to do. It wasn't his idea. He didn't steal anything. But he should not have gone along with the crowd.

Zero Tolerance

Some colleges are becoming zero tolerant on aggressive crimes such as assaults and robberies. They have had bad experiences on campus and don't want any more. Large state universities are more likely than small private colleges to ask about past crimes.

When a college application arrives, look for questions about arrests. If the question is not on the form, it means that this college does not require that you disclose such information.

Drugs

There is an arrest that can become a parent's worst nightmare. It's the arrest involving illicit drugs, which has a lifelong ripple effect. This type of arrest is a different ball game than an OWI or hanging on the back of a minivan spoiler flying down Main Street shouting, "Hee haw." Any arrest involving meth, marijuana, cocaine, ecstasy, or other illegal substance may severely affect a college opportunity.

The government asks about drug arrests, and the question is on the financial aid application to be filed in January of the senior year in high school. The following is on the FAFSA (Free Application for federal Student Aid):

Have you ever been convicted of possessing or selling illegal drugs? If you have, answer "yes," complete and submit this application, and we will send you a worksheet in the mail for you to determine if your conviction affects your eligibility for aid.

What does aid mean? In this statement it may mean all financial aid:

- Scholarships
- Grants
- Loans

Without scholarships, grants, and loans, most students cannot afford to attend college. The colleges are not asking about drug arrests, but the federal government is asking. If the conviction fits the government's criteria, the student is more than likely to be considered ineligible for any government loans or grants.

Because the FAFSA drives all aid, colleges abide by the FAFSA guidelines. In certain cases, a student may be ineligible for any tuition assistance at all.

> **Note** Aid can be lost temporarily or permanently.

The federal government controls the purse strings at a college. Pell grants and guaranteed student loans are both under federal control. Once students are determined as ineligible by the FAFSA, they must fund college independently. This is nearly impossible for most students and their families, because four years of college can easily cost from $60,000 to $130,000 or more.

The majority of high school students do not realize that a weekend party will affect them not only in the way of legal fees and fines but may affect the rest of their lives by denying college to them.

Could this happen for a first offense? It could. A committee, not the college, makes the decision. There is a possibility that a first offense could be the basis for denying college loans for a year. If there are no new charges, the student could be eligible after that. However, this is not a guarantee.

> **Quote** "Life is not the way it's supposed to be. It's the way it is. The way you cope with it is what makes the difference."
>
> –Virginia Satir

An arrest for illicit drugs justifies hiring a good attorney. If a child is charged with selling, possessing, or using drugs, the ramifications can be disastrous if there is a conviction. The legal fees may be well worth it. The loss in financial aid could be far greater than any legal fees.

> **Quote** "There are two ways of meeting difficulties: You alter the difficulties, or you alter yourself to meet them."
>
> –Phyllis Bottome

CHAPTER 62

Are There Other Ways to Lose Scholarships?

Besides arrests, are there other ways to lose a scholarship? Absolutely, yes. You may have earned a scholarship. That does not mean you can't lose it. You can.

Potential Problems

Colleges look at many items when deciding to admit you and give you a scholarship. After you have been accepted, this is still the case. If things change dramatically, you are no longer the student they accepted.

Grade Point Average

If you hold a 3.6 GPA and plan on taking advanced classes in your senior year, the college is impressed with you. However, you decide to take it easy your senior year after you are accepted and have a scholarship in hand. You drop out of several activities, you don't apply yourself in classes, your grades drop significantly, and you don't feel like taking those advanced classes.

If this happens, the colleges may rescind your scholarship and even your admission. If you are no longer an interesting student to them, they may admit another student instead.

Note If your grades plummet, you are no longer the same student a college accepted.

The Internet

The Internet is a great source for finding generous scholarships. Fastweb.com is a popular scholarship vault holding millions of scholarships for students who qualify. It is free. Students register and complete an online interview, and scholarship applications will begin arriving soon after that.

 Note The Internet is a great place to find scholarships—and to lose them.

Colleges are known for giving the largest scholarships, frequently for all four years. Local organizations give scholarships as well, but usually for the freshman year only.

These scholarships can be easily lost if students post inappropriate profiles on various sites such as

- Friendster
- Facebook
- MySpace
- Xanga
- LiveJournal

Internet Searches

College admissions counselors are beginning to look beyond the usual letters of recommendation as they investigate the students considered for scholarships. Counselors are beginning to google student names and see what is posted on the Internet. Some check students randomly; some check only if students have been brought to their attention. Others are actively researching students online.

 Note Colleges are using Google to investigate the online character of prospective students.

Joan Place, director of guidance counseling at Centerville High School in Dayton, Ohio, said in the *Dayton Daily News* (Nov. 25, 2007), "Every college has raised the bar on what they want from our students academically, and now it's socially as well. What ends up separating you from another student could be how you present yourself online."

For example, a college is strongly considering four students for a very large scholarship. The information on all four is very similar, and there is little data to give one an edge over the other—until the college begins a Google search. To their surprise, two of the four students have unflattering MySpace profiles. One has very politically incorrect comments about females, and another talks about alcohol parties and displays photos. These two students are now disqualified from the scholarship pool, and the college is free to focus on the two remaining students. Chances are slim to none that the two disqualified students will ever know the reason why they were no longer in the competition.

University of Massachusetts Study

How often is this online research happening? The University of Massachusetts–Dartmouth concluded a study in the fall of 2007. They questioned 453 college admissions departments and found that

- 26 percent are actively researching students through search engines.
- 21 percent are checking out social networking profiles such as MySpace and Facebook.

 Note Approximately one-fourth of colleges are using Google and MySpace searches to investigate students.

One-in-four odds for winning the lottery would be great. Unfortunately, these odds are not great when they concern being investigated online.

Elli thought it was so cute as a seventh grader to have seductive pictures taken of her in her bathroom, in her bedroom, and at the local lake. She was mostly nude and had enticing invitations below the pictures. This was all done in fun.

Later, the following year, Elli accused some boys of inappropriate touching. The defense attorney typed her name on Google and found the seductive pictures. This was used against Elli. Elli had a tearful testimony in court, and the charges against the boys were thrown out.

Elli could easily be on porn sites without her knowledge. Her chances for college scholarships were greatly damaged with this information on MySpace. Unfortunately, she can do little to completely erase these images. Removing them from her site is ineffective because so many other people have seen them and passed them on and on and on. Erasing an original picture on the Internet is not as easy as destroying an original photo from a camera.

What Ifs

Keep the following what ifs from the National Association of College Admission Counseling (www.nacac.org) in mind.

What if you posted something unethical online but then took it off? The bad news is that once you put something on the Internet, there is usually no way to take it down. You may delete the inappropriate information from your site, but if it has gone out to friends or visitors to your MySpace site, it impossible to delete because you don't know where else it has gone.

What if you make your files private but post inappropriate things? Friends love to send on juicy bits of gossip. If something is inappropriate, you increase the chance of it being passed on. Some of your "friends" may be waiting for something to bring you down a notch. Don't put it online, and you won't have to worry about it.

What if someone else puts up your picture from a slumber party? If you are at a party with cell phone cameras, there are no guarantees that you will not appear somewhere on the Internet within days. Be careful what you wear at slumber parties. If your friends put your name under your picture, you are on the Internet in an unfavorable light and don't even know it. And, to make things even worse, if you are scantily dressed, owners of porn sites may put your picture up as a billboard to bring people to their site. Your photo could be on a porn site without your knowledge.

Imagine the shock when an admissions counselor types in your name for a Google search and is taken to a porn site.

Note Protect your opportunities for scholarships and carefully post information to the Internet.

Real World Implications

You may be removed from athletic opportunities because of MySpace posts.

Trent was at a drinking party and, unknown to him, someone was taking cell phone pictures. Trent was having a great time hanging on people with a beer in each hand wearing a T-shirt with profanities. The next day, "friends" sent pictures of the party to nearly everyone in high school. Unfortunately, the principal also received the pictures. Trent had just asked the principal to write a letter of recommendation for him because he was competing for a character scholarship. Trent has not only lessened his chances for getting a great letter, but he also got removed from the basketball team. The coach has a drinking policy, and now Trent won't be starting for a while. To make matters worse, other players were identified, and the high school may not even have enough students to play.

An Airtight Online Profile

How can you make sure your online profile is squeaky clean?

- Do not post anything to your site that would be morally or ethically questionable.
- Never post personal information such as your address, daily schedule, or phone number.

- Make your profile private so a selected group can view your information.
- Don't add "friends" you don't personally know.
- Ask friends with Web sites to remove photos of you that could be seen as unflattering.
- Make sure your friends never use your name when they add you to their site.

Note Once something has been online, it is nearly impossible to know whether it has been completely deleted.

Fortune 500 companies have been using Google to investigate future employees for years. Now, colleges are doing the same to select students.

CHAPTER 63

How Can You Increase Your Chances for Receiving a Good Financial Aid Package?

Y ou either increase or decrease your chances for a good financial aid package by the colleges you select.

Pick the Right Colleges

Colleges post the ACT scores of students who attend the college. If the college has the middle 50 percent of students in the 21–25 ACT range and your score is 26, you are in the scholarship range automatically. Even holding an ACT of 23 or 24 will give you an advantage.

Note Select colleges at your academic level.

Colleges also post the percentage of financial need met. This tells you how generous colleges have been in the past in meeting financial need based on the FAFSA results. If a college has historically not funded students well, it is not likely to fund you well, either. The information is posted in the college guides most of the time. You may also call the financial aid office at the college and ask questions if you cannot find this information in the college guide. Some colleges state "N/A" for financial aid information, so inquire before you spend too much time researching these schools.

Ask what the school's policy is for meeting the family EFC (Expected Family Contribution). Colleges may fund from 32 percent up to 100 percent. The higher the number, the better.

> **Note** Find colleges that have been generous in the past.

Also, keep your ears open. Your friends or their older siblings may have shared information about good financial aid packages that they received from colleges. Some schools can afford to be much more generous than others. Listen closely to which colleges are named often as being generous with financial aid. All schools on your list do not give the same funding even if they all receive the same FAFSA results. The FAFSA does not guarantee you the funding you deserve. The EFC is merely a starting point, and then it's up to you to find the best options. Look at state universities and private colleges alike and then see which one offers the best package.

Build Relationships with Admissions Staff

It stands to reason that you have to get to know the college admissions staff and the admissions staff has to get to know you. If you do not call and make an appointment, do not visit the campus, do not make phone calls, and do not ask questions, how is the college to know you are interested in attending? Your application will go to the bottom of the pile.

> **Note** Develop a relationship with your admissions counselor.

Being a college admissions counselor is a difficult job. The admissions office is responsible for keeping enrollment stable. A counselor may be given 400 names of students who have inquired about the college. Out of those, only 75 students may actually decide to attend the college. The students who have repeated contacts are the ones to whom the counselor will give more time and attention. Their actions have shown the counselor that they are the most likely to attend. These same students are more likely to receive better financial aid packages because colleges begin setting funds aside for students who are likely to attend.

Visit Campus During Junior Year

Visit colleges early. If you don't visit colleges in your junior year of high school, you won't be able to make a decision about where to apply in the fall of your senior year. If you don't apply early in the senior year, you may miss out on scholarships and grants that have been given away to those who did apply early.

The early bird gets the worm in many cases, because often colleges don't have a lot of worms to give away. When they are gone, they are gone. There are some very generous colleges that can afford to be generous at all times, but most colleges can't afford to do this.

Note Forget visiting colleges in the senior year—that should be done in the junior year.

Visiting a college in the junior year also allows you to get to know the college better and see whether it is a good match for you. While many colleges look great when you visit, as you begin digging into the offerings they may not look as great.

Jeanette fell in love with a college that sat on the shores of a lake. The buildings were beautiful, and the small size was just right for her. The college was very generous with financial aid, and she was all set. Jeanette even knew that she wanted to be a psychology major and go on to graduate school to earn her master's degree. It wasn't until late in the school year that she learned this college offered only a minor in psychology. She could either change her major or change schools.

(continued)

(continued)

> Jeanette changed her major. She wrongly assumed that, because the college had professors teaching psychology classes, the college offered a major in that discipline. If Jeanette had dug a little deeper during her conversations with the college, this information would have surfaced sooner.

 Note Ask questions. Don't assume everything is available at all colleges.

Highlight Activities

Colleges are looking for students who are involved in activities. If your resume lists several activities—and lists them consistently—this increases your chances for scholarships or grants.

Some colleges offer scholarships to journalism majors who wrote for the school newspaper or participated in the yearbook composition. Students receive football or basketball scholarships because of stellar performance in those sports. Scholarships are given for theater, vocal music, and band. Colleges may offer you a scholarship to be in the marching band and play for football games. Are you a swimmer? Colleges with swim teams offer scholarships in swimming. Even if you are not a star, a small college may give you a scholarship as an incentive to play on the team.

Note Being active in high school increases chances for scholarships.

Write Essays

Colleges offer the largest scholarships. They expect something in return from you to show you deserve it, and this is often an essay. A well-written essay can tip the odds in your favor.

Neil was a fairly strong student and involved in many activities. He was a slam-dunk for scholarships at private colleges. But because he refused to write admission essays to the private colleges that were recruiting him, he received no scholarships.

The state university he decided to attend did not consider him good enough for any academic or athletic scholarships. At smaller schools he was appreciated more; unfortunately, refusing to write the essay disqualified him from being accepted.

 Note Essays are often the tool colleges use to know you better.

Show Volunteer Work

Character is a big buzzword at colleges. It is all over promotional literature and Web sites. Giving to others in a generous manner by being a volunteer shows character. You are giving back to the community that has invested time and money in you.

If two students are competing for a major scholarship and one has a long list of volunteer activities while the other does not, the scholarship is more likely to go to the student with the volunteer work.

 Quote "If you think about what you ought to do for other people, your character will take care of itself."

–Woodrow Wilson

Be a Leader

Colleges want to offer many activities on campus. Weekends especially are the time for activities, because they keep students staying on campus instead of going home. Colleges don't want to be empty on weekends. An empty campus makes things difficult for the remaining students who come from a distance.

"I suppose leadership at one time meant muscles; but today it means getting along with people."

–Indira Gandhi

Activities often require student leaders to create them to make the events happen. Showing leadership qualities in your resume and letters of recommendation throws luck your way. Not everyone is capable of leadership, so the students who have proved themselves may be rewarded for it. Students who get things done look very interesting to a college.

Start Early

Colleges are on a schedule. In the fall of your senior year, colleges hope to receive your application. This allows them to review the information and make a decision on whether to accept you.

If you are accepted, you are then a contender in the winter scholarship competition. In the spring, your scholarship and grants will be included in your financial aid package. These are sequential steps. If you apply late in March, you are out of sequence and less likely to have things work to your advantage. You may receive funding for college, but this funding may be heavy on loans and light on scholarships and grants.

Note Stay in sequence on the college journey. If you get off course, you may hit some dead ends.

If you are truly interested in improving your chances for a good financial aid package, follow these tips and you will be successful.

"Success isn't measured by the position you reach in life; it's measured by the obstacles you overcome."

–Booker T. Washington

What Are the Differences Among Student Loans?

L oans are the least preferred method of paying for college, but most students and some parents end up taking loans to fund an education.

A typical college student graduates with $15,000–$25,000 in loans. When you look at your financial aid letter in the spring, there are some loan characteristics you should know about. There are better loans and worse loans.

Note Some loans are better than others.

Three Categories of Loans

There are three categories of loans:

- Private loans
- Student loans
- Parent loans

Private Loans

Private loans are very fluid from year to year and from financial agency to financial agency. The interest is usually higher and not subsidized, and as a result, these loans are the least preferable of all. For many who do not qualify for government loans, private loans are the only option.

In 2008, many private loan agencies did not offer loans to students because the interest rate was too low to make a profit. The federal government took action to fill in the gap, and the number of available student loans increased. With low interest rates, private companies are not going to take the risk of not making money.

Wells Fargo Student Loans, Sallie Mae, and Bank of America are but a few of the entities that are still offering loans when hundreds of agencies have stopped doing so. Read the fine print carefully. Remember, they are not giving loans to do you a favor. These organizations are making money.

As you review your award letter, look at the labels that identify the loans.

Student Loans

There are several different types of student loans. The most common are Perkins loans and Stafford loans.

Perkins Loans. Perkins loans go to students who show exceptional need on the FAFSA. You can't choose to have a Perkins loan. You must qualify for it. With a Perkins loan, colleges—not banks—serve as the lender. Government funds make the loans possible, and the interest rate cap is 5 percent. This rate is lower than other loans.

While other loans expect repayment to begin within six months after graduation—or after dropping out—the Perkins loan repayment begins in nine months. Students who fall below half-time status must begin repaying loans. The exception would be active military duty.

Award letters from colleges will stipulate which loans the student will receive. Students who qualify for Perkins loans often qualify for Pell grants, too.

 Note Perkins loans have a very low interest rate.

Stafford Loans. Stafford loans are the most common college loans. These come in subsidized and unsubsidized forms. One is much more desirable than the other.

Subsidized loans are preferred because the federal government pays your interest while you attend school. This is a major perk. You must show financial need to be awarded a subsidized Stafford loan. Interest for a subsidized loan begins six months after graduation or when your education ends. You pay no interest from the time the funds are disbursed for your education until six months after you graduate. You are receiving a four- or five-year loan with no interest until you graduate. This is quite amazing, actually.

Unsubsidized Stafford loans are not awarded because of great financial need. Most students qualify for an unsubsidized Stafford loan, but the interest begins accumulating as soon as the funds are disbursed. Interest on Stafford loans is capped at 8.25 percent, and in times of low interest rates can be below 3 percent.

If students have funds set aside that earn more than the Stafford rate, they often borrow the money and use the saved funds only when the Stafford interest rate becomes greater.

Tom had a better job than most high school boys. He worked on construction sites with an uncle and other skilled workers. Tom was paid well on weekends and during the summer. He saved most of the money he made and invested it in mutual funds. Earnings on average were in the 10 to 12 percent range.

Despite saving this money for college, Tom took out Stafford loans. He didn't want to sacrifice his 10 to 12 percent earnings when he could get a loan for 3 percent interest. He was 7 percent ahead in taking out the low-interest loan. However, if the markets go down and interest goes up, Tom may change his mind.

Parent Loans

PLUS loans are available for parents to help fund their children's college expenses. PLUS loans are not part of the award letter, but parents will receive an amount that they are to contribute.

A credit check is required prior to receiving a PLUS loan. PLUS loans do not have a grace period, and payments begin as soon as disbursements occur. The cap is 9 percent interest, but low interest rates can drop the interest to less than half of this amount. Because the interest rates are adjusted frequently, the interest can quickly rise but will not go above 9 percent.

In times of low interest rates, parents often keep their mutual funds intact and apply for PLUS loans. If the interest on a PLUS is 4 to 5 percent and the mutual funds are growing at a rate a greater rate, it makes sense for parents to take out PLUS loans.

Quote "Parents can give everything but common sense."

–Yiddish proverb

Award Letters

When award letters arrive in the spring, you will receive various dollar amounts under different loans. The FAFSA determines how much government assistance will be allowed.

Whether the loans are subsidized or unsubsidized, they are all to be repaid. Failure to do so may result in denial of loans in the future. Deferments are available for special situations, but these are temporary and eventually repayment is expected.

Having student loans is expected, but be watchful on just what amounts you accept. They are loans and must be repaid.

Quote "If you think education is expensive, try ignorance."

–Anonymous

CHAPTER 65

What Should You Know About the FAFSA?

F AFSA stands for "Free Application for Federal Student Aid." All financial aid is based on a student's FAFSA results. Therefore, it is imperative that families fill out the FAFSA. It drives all financial aid.

File FAFSA in January

To file a FAFSA successfully, you must have income tax information. So families should plan on filing the 1040 tax return in January if there is a college student or a high school senior in the family. If it is impossible to file early, use data from last year and then make changes. But, in any case, file early. The latest date to file would be some time during the first part of February.

> **Quote** "The journey of a thousand miles must begin with a single step."
> –Chinese proverb

Why file the FAFSA so early? Colleges have deadlines for financial aid. Each college has a different deadline. Some are as early as February 15. If a family misses the financial aid deadline, they may be disqualified from large amounts of aid at a particular college. No one wants that to happen.

Find out what the deadlines are at the colleges to which you have applied. Some deadlines are in March and some are April, but at many state universities the deadlines are February 15 or February 28.

In many cases, students can attend another college if the deadline is missed. However, if students plan on choosing a major in a specialty area such as engineering or veterinary medicine, those colleges are limited. Deadlines become extremely important in such cases.

 Quote "Don't wait for something big to occur. Start where you are, with what you have, and that will always lead you into something greater."

–Mary Manin Morrissey

FAFSA Data

You will be expected to supply the following information when filing the FAFSA:

- Income tax form 1040 data
- Adjusted gross income
- Wages
- Salaries
- Tips
- Combat pay
- Parents' income tax payment from the prior year
- Exemptions
- Current cash on hand, savings, investments, checking account
- Real estate, not including your home
- Net worth if business or farm owners
- Federal benefits, including SSI (Supplemental Security Income); food stamps; free or reduced lunch; WIC (Women, Infants, and Children program); TANF (Temporary Assistance for Needy Families)

- Child support
- Earned income credit
- IRA (Individual Retirement Account) deductions
- Other income not listed on income tax

Quote "Most people who succeed in the face of seemingly impossible conditions are people who simply don't know how to quit."
–Robert Schuller

In addition to financial aid information, what else needs to be listed on or in place for the FAFSA?

- U.S. citizenship
- Proof of legal residency (for state and college aid only)
- Social Security number
- Compliance with Selective Service registration if male (www.sss.gov)
- High school diploma or GED
- Marital status
- Number of people in the home
- Number of people in immediate family who are attending college
- Parents' e-mail address
- Parents' Social Security numbers
- Parents' dates of birth
- Parents' state of legal residence
- Education levels of parents
- Any dependent children
- Veteran of the U.S. military
- School codes for where you have applied or plan to attend
- Enrolled or acceptance at an eligible college (one that receives federal funding)
- No refund owed on a prior federal grant
- No default on federal student loans
- No record of a serious drug conviction

"Our greatest glory is not in never falling, but in rising every time we fall."

–Confucius

Arrests Involving Drugs

An arrest for drugs is one of the worst things that can happen to you if you need college funding. The drug conviction question does not include illegal sale of alcohol or cigarettes. It does not include an arrest for illegal drug possession or sale for anyone under 18 unless tried as an adult. It does not count any convictions that were removed from your record.

What if you were convicted of a marijuana charge when you were 19? You must fill out the drug conviction worksheet. A panel will determine financial aid eligibility. The panel follows federal criteria and makes one of three decisions:

- **Eligible.** Your eligibility for federal student aid is not affected.
- **Partially Eligible.** You will become eligible for federal aid during the school year. You can become eligible earlier in the school year if you complete an acceptable drug rehabilitation program.
- **Not Eligible.** You are not eligible for federal aid for this school year unless you complete an acceptable drug rehabilitation program. You may still be eligible for state and school aid.

What if you are convicted while in college? You must notify the college immediately, and you will be asked to return all federal aid disbursed to you. That is not a good thing. If the refund date has passed, you need to work with the college to see what can be done. In some cases, little to nothing can be done. You may be liable for the tuition fees without attending classes.

SAR and EFC

When the FAFSA is submitted, a report will be issued to you outlining your financial status in the SAR (Student Aid Report).

At the top of the report, the EFC (Expected Family Contribution) will be listed. The numbers following the EFC will show how much your family can expect to pay for college. However, each college honors the EFC at a different percentage.

Your family may be asked to pay much more than the EFC. For example, a family with an EFC of only $2,000 can be asked to pay $18,000 toward one college. Another college may ask the same family to pay only $2,200. It all depends how generous the colleges are. This is why you want to apply to four, five, or six colleges and see what the offers are. Colleges vary greatly in what they offer. Chapter 66 explains the EFC.

File the FAFSA, know your EFC, and apply to several colleges to tip the odds of financial aid in your favor.

 "The elevator to success is out of order. You'll have to use the stairs...one step at a time."

–Joe Girard

What Is an EFC?

FAFSA, SAR, EFC—what are all these letters and why are they important? Are they making you a little nuts? It isn't all that complicated, but what you don't know can hurt you when it comes to selecting a college.

Expected Family Contribution

FAFSA and EFC are extremely important. FAFSA is the Free Application for Federal Student Aid, and EFC stands for Expected Family Contribution.

College is on a sliding scale—the more you earn, the more you pay. If you go into the final stages of the college search and don't know what your EFC is, you can't make good decisions about financing college. In the spring, if you don't understand your EFC, you won't know whether you could receive a better package.

In fact, knowing the EFC is similar to knowing the blue book price of a car. It gives you a baseline to begin analyzing whether you are getting a reasonable offer. If you don't know your baseline, you can't know whether the award letter is good, bad, or ugly.

The SAR

The SAR is the Student Aid Report that discloses your EFC. After you file the FAFSA in January of the senior year, the results are printed into the SAR. In the top right-hand corner of the SAR are the letters EFC, which stand for Expected Family Contribution.

After the EFC are some numbers. These numbers represent what a family should have to pay for college for the coming year.

The EFC can change if family income or expenses change substantially. If the family's financial situation remains about the same, so will the EFC.

Parents of high school juniors can go to http://testdev.act.org/ finaid/packages.html and use the calculator that will figure their EFC. This way, families can know their EFC before filing the FAFSA.

 Note The SAR is the report that contains the EFC.

Delayed 1040

Although it is ideal to file tax returns prior to filling out the FAFSA, it may not be possible. In fact, it may work against the family if they are rushed into filing a tax return in the month of January. If this is the case, it is better to use the 1040 numbers from the prior year and file early if taxes cannot be filed in January. Adjustments can be made later. If a family has a stable income from one year to the next, the EFC will be similar one year to the next.

Colleges may randomly ask families for a copy of their 1040, so it pays to be honest. Just count on the fact that you may be audited and go ahead and file with that in mind. Giving misleading information on the FAFSA is considered fraud.

Quick Electronic Results

If the FAFSA is filed electronically, the results will be back quickly. In the top right-hand corner are the letters EFC followed by a series of numbers. The smaller the numbers, the better. The numbers represent dollars but will not show a dollar sign. This is why so many people don't realize that the EFC represents what the family can afford. An EFC of 800 means the family is expected to pay $800, and an EFC of 8,000 means the family is expected to pay $8,000.

Colleges and the EFC

The EFC is used by colleges to determine the generosity of their award letters. All state and federal aid is driven by the FAFSA. Some college aid is also determined by the FAFSA. If the FAFSA is turned in late, or not turned in at all, a family could be disqualified from any grants, loans, or work-study. Don't miss the FAFSA deadline, and don't miss the college financial aid deadlines.

Financial Aid

Financial need is the difference between a family's EFC and the school's cost of attendance, which can include living expenses. Colleges have different levels of generosity in how they handle financial need. A college with deep pockets could give thousands of dollars more in student aid than another college is prepared to give. It pays to apply to several schools, because each school will honor the EFC differently.

Keep in mind that each college has a different deadline for financial aid. Some may be in April, and others may be in February. Colleges want families to submit requests for aid by the deadline so they can appropriate money. If a family does not file in time, the funds might be gone.

 Note Don't miss any deadlines.

Individual Policies

Each college has its own policies and amounts of aid it may give. Where does this money come from other than tuition? Colleges have income streams from endowments and taxes.

Public universities and junior colleges rely on taxes, while private universities rely on private donors. Many earmark a certain number of dollars for aid each year. When it's gone, it's gone. If a college runs out of funds, you may be out of luck no matter what your EFC is. This is why it is important to select colleges that have a history of being generous—and then apply early.

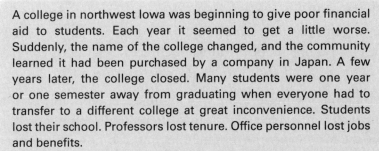

A college in northwest Iowa was beginning to give poor financial aid to students. Each year it seemed to get a little worse. Suddenly, the name of the college changed, and the community learned it had been purchased by a company in Japan. A few years later, the college closed. Many students were one year or one semester away from graduating when everyone had to transfer to a different college at great inconvenience. Students lost their school. Professors lost tenure. Office personnel lost jobs and benefits.

Fortunately, a college less than an hour away honored all the transfer credits, allowing students to graduate. However, this college was not in a solid financial condition, either. Many thought these students jumped from the frying pan into the fire. Miraculously, a very generous donor contributed millions of dollars to the second college, enabling it to be solid far into the future.

This school is now able to offer generous financial aid and can afford to be very aggressive in recruitment of students. This college has recently become very popular with students and families.

 Quote "It's never too late, in fiction or in life, to revise."

–Nancy Thayer

Baby boomers are sending their youngest children to college. When this boom passes, many colleges are going to struggle to fill the desks. Enrollment overall is expected to decline unless large numbers of nontraditional students decide to attend. Programs may need to be cut to balance the smaller budgets. Stable schools will be competitive, while others will close their doors.

Shop Around

It is very wise to apply to five or six colleges, because the cost of attending one college may be 700 percent higher than the cost of attending another school. No, I'm not kidding. 700 percent!

Colleges are not obliged to meet the EFC aid levels set by the FAFSA. The FAFSA is only a guide. Some colleges meet aid at 100 percent, some at 90 percent, some at 70 percent, and some as little as 30 percent. It is up to the family and student to find the best options for financial aid, so it does not pay to have your heart set on one school. You want choices. Wait until you have all offers in hand and then decide where to attend.

Two families with the same style of home, comparable cars, and similar jobs may have drastically different EFC numbers. It is not only the family income that matters but also how many other critical factors are in the equation. Retirement funds, real estate equity, savings, inheritance, stocks, medical expenses, business losses, the number of children in the family, age of the parents, and much more all factor in to the FAFSA formula.

The FAFSA allows for many variables, giving you a much different financial need than the family down the street.

Do not look at the price tags of colleges if you need financial aid. What matters most is how much aid is given in the form of grants, scholarships, and work-study. Don't avoid expensive colleges. Colleges with the highest costs are often the most generous. Keep an open mind until spring when colleges make their offers.

 Note The cost of attending one college may be 700 percent higher than the cost of attending another school.

CHAPTER 67

What Is an Award Letter?

An award letter could be considered your bill for attending college. If you don't like the bill at one college, you may decide to attend another.

Different Letters

Colleges mail award letters in April or May of the senior year. These letters state exactly what the college expects you (and your family) to pay for one year of college. You will see dramatic differences in the offers from various schools. This is why I strongly suggest that you apply to several colleges and not have your heart set on just one school. Your heart could be broken quickly.

Note Wait until spring to decide where to attend.

Quote "Money is like a sixth sense, and you can't make use of the other five without it."

–W. Somerset Maugham

Letter Components

The award letter often begins with the total college costs (tuition, room, and board) and then shows how this cost is decreased by financial aid. Items listed will be scholarships, grants, and student loans. Paying the difference between the total cost and the amount of aid is the parents' responsibility. Work-study may also be listed if the student qualifies.

Work-study may be listed in one of two ways. Some colleges include the work-study opportunity as part of the package. In this case, the money you earn needs to go toward tuition. But some colleges offer work-study in addition to the financial aid package. In cases like this, the student may use the money for personal expenses or books.

Let's pretend a family has an EFC of $4,500, and the student applies to two colleges.

College One

Total Expenses	$32,500
Scholarships	10,000
Grants	12,000
Loans	
Federal Stafford Loan	3,500
Unsubsidized Stafford Loan	2,000
Parent Contribution	$5,000

Because the college had large endowments, it could afford to give this student $22,000 in aid. The student will have $5,500 in loans and the parents will pay $5,000. In this case, the student is eligible for $1,000 in work-study and gets to keep the money for personal use.

 "With money in your pocket, you are wise, and you are handsome, and you sing well too."

–Jewish proverb

The same student could easily receive a different award letter if the college cannot afford to be generous.

College Two

Total Expenses	$30,500
Scholarships	5,000
Grants	5,000
Loans	5,500
Work-Study	500
Parent Contribution	$14,500

This college not only gave less aid but also placed the Work-Study opportunity in the financial aid package. The student will not have the money to use for personal expenses. Instead, this money will have to go toward tuition, room, and board. What if this were the only college to which the student had applied? You can see why it is much more preferable to have four, five, or six award letters in your hands before making a decision on where to attend.

Individual Policies

Each college has its own policy on how it funds aid. The level of endowments a college has invested determines the policy. Endowments are alumni and community-funded contributions that are invested for future needs. The more generous the donors, the more generous the college.

Ivy Leagues

It is common knowledge that an Ivy League education is very expensive. It is also understood that Ivy League schools have deep pockets. The Ivies have recently announced that any family with an annual income below $60,000 will pay absolutely nothing for college. Of course, the trick is to be accepted by Harvard or Stanford. These colleges turn away more than 80 percent of those who apply. But, before you get too impressed with the generosity of Ivy League schools, there is a good reason why they are suddenly more generous than in the past. The government was going to investigate each college, calculate endowments, and mandate the colleges to give more aid. The Ivies decided to keep the government out of their business by controlling their own money. It was also a great public relations move.

Reaching for the EFC

Colleges try to meet the family EFC (Expected Family Contribution) in the best possible way. The EFC is the most important number calculated from the FAFSA. If the EFC is $4,500, colleges will come as close to this number as they can. Here is where the generosity of a college comes into play. If the college doesn't have the endowments to reach this number, the family in the earlier example will be asked to pay more than $4,500. In fact, most families are asked to pay more than the family EFC. How much more is determined by what the college can afford.

Quote "Money is to be respected; one of the worst things you can do is handle another person's money without respect for how hard it was to earn."

–T. Boone Pickens, Jr.

Colleges know which schools are their competition because you, as an applicant, have told them. On the college application and/or the FAFSA, you listed other colleges to which you have applied. Colleges know which schools have the endowments to be more generous and which schools do not. If you have generous colleges listed, each one knows they must be in the ballpark to get your consideration. Of course, if a college just doesn't have the funding to be competitive, it will give a poor financial aid offer by default.

Note Colleges know their competition.

Asking for More

Can you ask a college to give more aid? Yes, you may certainly try if you are working with a private college—but don't miss the acceptance deadline. If you suspect your college is generous, you might be successful in receiving $300, $500, or even $5,000 more. If you are trying to negotiate with a large state university, you might want to save yourself the frustration and not try. You are already receiving a discounted education at a state university because this institution is funded mostly by tax dollars.

If special circumstances are not reflected on your FAFSA, ask the college if you may write a special needs letter. You might get some additional assistance from the college. Your FAFSA numbers will not change, but the college might honor the EFC more generously.

Quote "I'm proud to pay taxes in the United States; the only thing is, I could be just as proud for half the money."

–Arthur Godfrey

It is becoming common to see students attend a private college for slightly above the EFC while the award letters from a large public university would ask the students to pay $5,000 more to attend. If the families did not apply to both private and public colleges, they could pay more for college and never know that they could have saved a substantial amount of money with a private school.

Note The best formula to have in your possession is a high ACT/SAT and a low EFC. Both generate aid.

Good News

Parents with two or three children in high school are concerned about funding college for more than one child. The good news is that the EFC is not a per-child rate but rather a per-family rate. If your family has two children enrolled in college, your family's

$8,000 EFC is not $16,000 for two but rather remains $8,000 total. Families that have children entering college every one or two years spend less money for college than those that have children five years apart.

Financial Aid Offices

The financial aid departments at colleges are more than happy to answer any questions you might have. They want you to choose their college. Even if they have to give your family generous aid, in many cases you will bring much more than that in federal grants and loans.

 Be honest and fair when working with a college.

Some people think that college should be free, and they are not happy with any offer from a college. Be reasonable. The FAFSA helps colleges assess what is affordable for you to pay. If the FAFSA has determined that you can afford to pay $15,000 per year, that is what you will probably be asked to pay. If your EFC is $550, you will be expected to pay $550 based on your financial need.

You need a college and colleges need students. It is truly an "I'll help you and you'll help me" situation.

> **Quote** "Invest in yourself, your family, your friends, your planet, if you want a HIGH return."
> —Sharon Riddell

CHAPTER 68

Which Award Letter Is Best?

The best award letter should make college affordable for both students and parents, but the details can get a little confusing.

Components of the Letter

This section explains how to analyze the parts of an award letter.

Work-Study

If you receive work-study, look to see whether it is included in the financial aid package or offered in addition to financial aid. If you received a $20,000 package with work-study in addition to financial aid, that could be considered a $21,000 package in its entirety. Work-study as part of the financial aid package is not the same as work-study on its own. If the money is earned as part of financial aid, it goes toward tuition, room, and board.

> **Note** Work-study may appear in either of two places in the award letter.

Grants

Review the grant amounts listed. Grants are gifts and do not need to be repaid. The bottom line isn't the only thing that is important. Study the items that create that bottom line.

> **Note** Grants are gifts and are not repaid.

Loans

Study the loans carefully. Is your award letter heavy with loans and light on grants and scholarships? Are you receiving subsidized loans?

Subsidized loans accumulate no interest while you are in college because the federal government is covering that cost. Interest on your subsidized loans begins six months after you graduate. Unsubsidized loans pile on interest the entire time you are in school. It can really add up.

Note Loans come subsidized and unsubsidized.

Scholarships

While scholarships are a great thing, check out the grade point average that is required for you to keep the scholarship you are granted.

Some scholarships are given for exceptional academics in high school. In such cases, high academics in college are expected. A 3.5 GPA is not easy to maintain in college. If you drop below a 3.5 GPA, you will be placed on probation for the following semester. Then, if your GPA returns to 3.5, you will keep your scholarship. If not, you will lose it.

Some colleges will try to replace a lost academic scholarship with some other aid, but many will not.

Note Look for the GPA attached to the scholarships.

Some academic scholarships are based on an ACT or SAT score and require a 2.0 GPA. Others may require 3.0 or 3.2. Check into the GPA required for scholarships. If two colleges have a similar financial aid package but one requires a 3.0 and another a 2.0, the college asking for 2.0 would be a safer bet.

Some athletic scholarships are lost because the athlete did not maintain the required grade point average. Many athletes are not interested in attending a particular college if they can't play their favorite sport. The loss of a scholarship may mean a transfer for athletes like this.

Parents' Responsibility

While you may be happy with your great loan package, your parents could be going in debt for $50,000 to send you through four years of college. Don't let the glamour of your favorite school darken the financial future of your family. The best award letter should be fair to both parties.

If parents take on a PLUS loan, payments begin within one or two months. Make sure you know what the payments will be and what the interest rate is before taking on a PLUS loan.

Private Lenders

In the past, private lenders have picked up the difference between what parents and students could get from colleges and what the government offers. Financial instability has caused a large number of companies to not offer education loans in recent months. If the student loan industry becomes profitable again, business may resume. Look for caps on interest rates and deferments when exploring private lenders.

Note Be careful with private loans.

Other Perks to Consider

Other perks may make it worth paying a little more for college. Paying $500 more a year could be worthwhile when you consider some of the extras.

- **The quality of food** may become an issue very quickly. Eat in the cafeteria on your visit to the college and talk to students. Do they eat all their meals here regularly or only rarely? Is food available after hours? Are the hours extended to meet class schedules? The students will be glad to tell you about the food.

- **Laptop computers** at a low price are a trend. Some colleges are providing students a laptop for half the price they would ordinarily pay. Yes, there is a fee, but you wouldn't be able to buy a laptop for that price.

- **Laundry service** is occasionally a perk. You place your clothes in a bag with your room number, and it returns, clean, at the end of the day. Very few colleges offer this service. At most colleges, you will have to do your own laundry. Some schools charge only 75 cents for a load of clothes, and some offer free usage of washers and dryers. Other universities charge $1.50 or more per load. This adds up quickly.

- **Tutoring** can get expensive. Some colleges allow students to complete work-study hours by being tutors. It is a win-win situation. The tutor earns money, and the student saves money.

- **Air-conditioned dorms** may be worth a little more in a warmer climate. Studying and sleeping can be very difficult in a hot and humid environment.

- **Free parking** is a great perk. This is especially true when you consider that some students must walk several blocks to a paid parking lot. Is the parking close to the dorms? If so, that's another perk.

Study college perks and pay close attention to the details in your award letter. Some perks are worth more than the slightly higher college costs.

CHAPTER 69

What Do You Need to Fill Out the FAFSA?

File the FAFSA in January of your senior year in high school. What do you need to gather so you are ready to file? Months ahead of time, get a worksheet that lists all the needed information. Your high school may have a paper copy of it, or you can go online at www.ed.gov/studentaid to find the information. Print it and gather all the items necessary for your filing in January. If you have unanswered questions, you may call 1-800-433-3243 from 8 a.m. through midnight eastern time. Pencil in data and keep it until you can file electronically on www.fafsa.ed.gov.

Many of the questions on the FAFSA are quite easy to fill in. But some are not. This chapter explains those questions.

Investments Data

The investments category is often confusing. Investments include

- Real estate, but not the home you live in
- Trust funds: parents and student
- Money market funds
- Certificates of deposit
- Stocks
- Stock options
- Bonds
- Securities
- Education IRAs

- College savings plans
- Installment and land sale contracts
- Commodities

If any of these items are under your name or under your parents' names, specific values dated Dec. 31 will be needed for the FAFSA.

If assets or investments are listed under your name, they will be included in the award letter at the rate of 35 percent. However, if the same assets or investments are held in your parents' name, the contribution is 5.6 percent.

Parents may think it's tempting to place property or investments in a child's name, but they should be prepared to pay the consequences. Many families shelter assets for children for this very reason.

Note It is better to have assets under the parents' names than the student's name.

Business and Farming

Business and/or investment farm value includes the market value of land, buildings, machinery, equipment, inventory, and more, minus debt. Therefore, farming operations and businesses with substantial debt are not a large liability. In fact, families with businesses that are running in the red often receive more financial aid.

Checking and Savings

A statement of parents' and student's savings and checking totals are required.

Life Insurance

Life insurance is different. Life insurance is exempt from being reported on the FAFSA. Parents are not expected to cash in life insurance to pay for college. However, there are many creative options that fall under the umbrella of life insurance. Some policies allow payments into mutual funds that may be withdrawn with no penalties to pay for a computer, apartment, car, or tuition.

Note Life insurance is a way to shelter funds.

Family Ties

The number of people in a family is a factor on the FAFSA. The more individuals the family is supporting, the lower the amount a family is expected to pay. These items are needed for the FAFSA:

- W-2s
- Untaxed income
- Mortgage information
- Social Security numbers
- Income tax returns for both student and parents

Note A larger family will pay less for college.

Colleges of Interest

The FAFSA will ask you to list colleges of interest. Each college has a code available in college literature or on the Web site—or you can call the admissions office.

Your SAR (Student Aid Report) will be sent to the colleges you list with your EFC (Expected Family Contribution). List the colleges you have found interesting. Why? You want colleges to know you are interested in them. You also want to apply to a large pool of colleges so you have more options when the financial aid letters arrive.

But the downside is that some colleges will not admit you if you need substantial aid. Need-blind colleges are in the majority, and these schools accept students no matter what their financial status. However, some colleges discriminate against students who need substantial aid. You can talk to colleges and ask whether they are need-blind. If they are need-blind, they don't discriminate.

Note The FAFSA drives all financial aid. Complete it early in January of your senior year.

Are You Eligible for Federal Student Loans?

If you are male, you must register with the Civil Service to be eligible for federal student loans. Federal student loans make up the majority of loans. It does not mean you will be drafted into military service by registering, but if our nation is faced with an extreme circumstance, males could be drafted into military service. The government wants to know the location of all males in case of emergency.

If you have been arrested for selling or buying illicit drugs, your chances of receiving college aid diminish. You will be required to answer this question on the FAFSA, and you will be in limbo until you receive a decision from a committee. Traffic tickets, speeding tickets, and disorderly conduct will not affect your student loans, but a drug arrest will.

Note An arrest for drugs will impact your college education like nothing else.

CHAPTER 70

Why Is the Timing of the FAFSA Filing Important?

The FAFSA needs to be filed in January to meet college deadlines for financial aid. Colleges operate on a sequential calendar. Many colleges stop taking applications for admission in the fall so they can remain on a timeline. Competition for scholarships and admission decisions occur in the winter. Award letters are sent in the spring, and enrollment is finalized in the summer.

When students don't follow this timeline, it throws things off a bit, but colleges make it work. If students miss deadlines, however, they are disqualified. You need to stay on the same sequential calendar as the colleges to be in step with them.

Note File the FAFSA in January or you can lose aid.

Financial Aid Deadlines

Most colleges set February, March, or April as deadlines for financial aid information. Because the FAFSA is the mainstream of funding for colleges and students, the FAFSA must be filed prior to those deadlines.

While the FAFSA may be filed on January 1 of the senior year, few students file at that time because W-2s and completed 1040 forms are not available. However, this deadline does stress the importance of filing early. Try to file as soon as possible after January 1.

Each college may have a different financial aid deadline.

Because the colleges' financial aid deadlines may vary greatly over several months, you don't want to take the chance that your favorite colleges have a deadline of February 15 and you don't know.

The deadlines are posted on the college Web sites and are also available in guides such as *U.S. News and World Report Ultimate College Guide* or *College Handbook* by the College Board.

Two Deadlines

Many colleges have two deadlines for financial aid information: the priority deadline and the final deadline. The priority deadline should be your goal because you, of course, want priority for financial aid. Who doesn't want to be first in line?

Colleges often have their own financial aid forms that are due in addition to the FAFSA. The college financial aid forms may address items not considered on the FAFSA, such as large medical expenses or credit card debt. Because the financial aid deadlines vary greatly, you need to research this information early in your senior year.

Note the deadlines at the following colleges:

- The University of Michigan at Ann Arbor has a priority deadline of February 15 and an overall deadline of April 30.
- Harvard University lists February 1 as the priority date and as the only deadline.
- The University of Notre Dame lists February 15 as the deadline for the institution's financial aid form and as the overall deadline.
- Coe College in Cedar Rapids, Iowa, lists March 1 as the only deadline.
- McPherson College in McPherson, Kansas, lists March 1 as the deadline for the institution's financial aid form and April 1 as an overall deadline.

- Liberty University in Lynchburg, Virginia, sets March 1 as the only deadline.
- Eckerd College in St. Petersburg, Florida, sets the priority deadline as February 15.
- The University of Colorado at Boulder sets the priority deadline as April 1.
- Buena Vista University in Storm Lake, Iowa, sets the priority deadline as June 1.

You can see that knowing only one deadline can disqualify you from aid at many colleges. What if you only looked at Buena Vista's June 1 deadline and assumed all colleges had the same deadline?

Note Stay in sequence with the college timeline.

By filing the FAFSA in January, you automatically comply with all college deadlines. It is a safety net of sorts. If you file in January, you don't miss the Harvard deadline or any other college deadline. Yes, it puts you quite early for Buena Vista's deadline but that's better than missing one, right?

What if you just can't file in January? Use last year's data until your family files its taxes and then make adjustments later. It is better to use last year's data than miss the deadline. As long as you file by the deadline, you are not disqualified. Many families have similar incomes from year to year, so the EFC will probably be quite similar from year to year as well.

Note You may file last year's data but file early.

Generous Colleges

Most students do not know which college is more generous than another. Harvard is known for meeting financial need at 100 percent, as is the University of Virginia. Other schools are also very generous but aren't as well known.

Buena Vista University has the ability to offer a great financial aid package in late August within a few days of the beginning of classes. If you are applying to a college that can't afford to do this, you need to meet the priority deadline to increase your chances of getting the biggest cookies before the cookie jar is empty.

> **Note** Don't count on getting aid if you miss the deadline.

Making Wise Choices

Families in the top 5–10 percent pay only 6 percent of their annual income for college. The middle class pays approximately 20 percent of their income for college. Selecting the wrong college may plunge a middle-class family deep into debt. College tuition has risen faster than inflation over the past 30 years. Families today are paying a much higher percentage of their income than families from a generation ago. And tuition is rising each year. Tuition at public universities is increasing more than tuition at private colleges, but both are rising annually. Research your options and choose carefully.

> **Note** Colleges vary greatly in the amount of aid they give.

Apply early in the fall, compete for scholarships early, and don't miss the deadline for filing financial aid. While it is true that college costs are on a sliding scale, it does matter which college is holding the scale. Selecting the wrong college can dramatically affect the financial health of a family. Paying too much for college can be avoided.

> **Quote** "Destiny is not a matter of chance, it is a matter of choice; it is not a thing to be waited for, it is a thing to be achieved."
> –William Jennings Bryan

CHAPTER 71

How Can Enlisting in the Military Help You Pay for College?

There are several paths for receiving a college education through the military. Chapter 48 explains military academies, ways in which you can receive your education first and serve in the military later, and the option of serving with active duty first and receiving your education later.

> **Note** Each branch of the military has different benefits.

Service and Benefits

There are obvious risks involved in joining the military, but many people choose to enlist despite these risks, and they do get a college education. Some recruiters state that high school students are choosing the military option in large numbers. The climbing college tuition costs may be a factor.

There are three main options when it comes to military service:

- Joining the National Guard
- Attending a military academy
- Enlisting in one of the military branches

> **Note** Benefits vary from state to state.

National Guard

National Guard enlistees participate in boot camp and specialty training. They make a six-year commitment to military service one weekend each month.

They face the possibility of being called for active duty. Keep in mind that 80 percent of the military personnel in Iraq in 2008 were National Guard troops. The possibility of being called for active duty is very strong.

Educational benefits for the National Guard vary greatly from state to state:

- California offers no educational benefits to the National Guard—zero.
- Missouri pays at 100 percent for newer recruits and 50 percent for those enlisting prior to 2001.
- Minnesota varies with partial tuition and textbook reimbursement.
- Nebraska pays at 75 percent but only at state universities and technical schools.
- South Dakota pays at 50 percent but only at state universities.
- Illinois supports at 100 percent at state schools.
- Iowa pays at 50 percent at state universities, community colleges, and selected private universities. Iowa is one of only three states that allow funding at private colleges.
- Rhode Island residents are allowed to attend one undergraduate course per semester free of charge at a state college or university.
- North Carolina residents are allowed $2,000 per year for a total of $8000 in benefits.
- Texas residents are paid at 100 percent for 12 credit hours per semester.
- West Virginia pays at 100 percent for undergraduate degrees at any West Virginia state school or equivalent funds for in-state private schools.

Note The Midwest boasts of the largest percentage of recruits into the military branches.

U.S. Army

The Army has several tiers of education benefits. It may pay up to $72,900, but recruits must pay $100 a month during the first year of service. With that sum, the recruit is eligible for $72,900 in education benefits. $1,200 earns $72,900. That's a great interest rate, isn't it? It varies with enlistment time and the specialty chosen.

The Army Reserve may pay in the $11,000–$23,000 range. What if you already have some college hours before you join the Army? You may receive up to $65,000 as part of a college loan repayment program. If you enlist full-time for three years or more, you could qualify.

What about ROTC (Reserve Officers' Training Corps)? There are 700 campuses that offer an ROTC program in which students may compete for full-tuition scholarships, generous textbook allowances, and a stipend of up to $5,000 for living expenses.

U.S. Marines

The Marine Corps is considered the right arm of the president. The Marine Corp helicopter lands on the lawn of the White House to whisk away the President. The Marines also have the longest training period. How do they measure up for education benefits?

Tuition is paid at 100 percent up to $4,500 per year. The Marine Corps also will fund instructional fees, laboratory fees, computer fees, and mandatory enrollment fees combined for postsecondary education, from vocational certification through graduate study.

U.S. Navy

The Naval Education and Training Command's Advanced Education Voucher (AEV) program is designed to provide advanced education opportunities for senior enlisted personnel in ranks E-7 through E-9. The Advanced Education Voucher program is aimed at superior performers who have the potential for continued upward mobility. It specifically targets assistance for postsecondary, Navy-relevant degree programs.

The program, which is part of the recently announced Professional Military Education Continuum, supports baccalaureate and master's degree completion in designated areas of study through off-duty education.

AEV for baccalaureate degree completion will cover 100 percent of tuition, books, and related fees. Each participant will be limited to $6,700 per year for a maximum of 36 months from the date of enrollment. AEV for the master's degree will cover 100 percent of tuition, books, and related fees up to a maximum of $20,000 per year. Total program costs per participant will not exceed $40,000.

All branches of the military are recruiting and changing benefits. The situation is very fluid. Check the benefits carefully prior to signing on the dotted line. Once you sign, you don't have options.

CHAPTER 72

What Are Some College Scams to Watch For?

Some scams will cost you more embarrassment than money, but others can cost thousands of dollars.

Student Loans

The most recent scandal involves college student loans. New York's attorney general is investigating conflicts of interest in the college loan business. More and more evidence is showing that the interconnections between colleges, banks, and loan officers are too self-serving.

What is being uncovered is a little arrangement of kickbacks promoting higher interest loans to students and parents. For example, a college might promote a private lender such as Sallie Mae instead of government student loans. A student might just sign the student loan agreement without investigating to determine that substantially lower interest could be available with the U.S. Department of Education.

In a different scenario, the loan officer handling a parent PLUS loan at a bank might receive a kickback when suggesting a particular private lender.

Such scandals have occurred at Washington University in St. Louis and at DeVry University in Chicago. In cases such as these, schools list preferred lenders. Unfortunately, these lenders do not necessarily offer a better package but may instead offer perks and kickbacks to the college or financial aid officer. This situation is more likely to occur with families who do not qualify for lower interest loans.

Which companies are being watched carefully? Sallie Mae is one. With congressional calls for caps on student loan interest, Sallie Mae stock has recently taken a dive. Some in government want to cut student loan interest in half.

Scholarships

Another scam centers on paying for scholarships. Students might receive a postcard or e-mail stating that an insider can guarantee thousands in scholarships for only $59.95. The guarantee is for at least $500 in scholarships, and it may extend to $20,000. With a guarantee, how can you lose? Easily.

The guarantee is good only if students apply for all scholarship opportunities. The company might send each student 75 opportunities. The students then will be required to fill out all applications, write essays, respond to long questionnaires, and keep a copy of each document sent to every company. If the students don't do this, the guarantee is null and void.

With busy high school schedules, it is difficult to find any high school student who would have the time to do all of this. Of course, if they don't, they don't get their money back. Unfortunately, students often don't realize that sites such as www.fastweb.com have endless sources for scholarships at no cost.

 "A fool and his money are soon parted."

–Anonymous

Athletics

Good athletes often hope to play their way through college. Unfortunately, some recruiters might mislead athletes about the requirements.

Students are told by counselors to take challenging classes. Of course, this might lead to a lower grade point average. Unscrupulous recruiters might tell students that they don't need those entire math and science credits to attend their college. This sounds great; however, what the students don't know is that when they select a major in college, they might not be admitted into a selected program without important math, science, foreign language or English credits. So the students might get into the college but not the program.

The students might also find that the lack of preparation at the high school level will result in poor grades in college. Poor grades in college equal being benched. Being benched means losing the scholarships.

Transferring Credits

"All our credits transfer everywhere." Online colleges and junior colleges often make this statement. However, it is not always true. If a student plans on attending a higher-level college and needs to transfer hours, the higher-level college may refuse to accept the hours. Colleges such as St. Olaf, Grinnell, and Carleton require prior approval.

For example, if you are going to pursue a degree in psychology, a college might want all psychology credits to be earned there so it can be assured of consistency in the theories taught. The college may refuse to accept sociology and psychology classes from any other college. On the other hand, the college might have accepted English classes without a problem. Prior approval is a must before signing up for any college credit classes if the hours are going to be transferred.

Be wary of promises made verbally and not put in writing. Even if statements are put in writing, can you jump through the necessary hoops?

Using the *Best College for You* CD-ROM

The CD-ROM included with this book compiles the advice from the *Best College for You* into checklists, examples, and timelines to help you get ready for college.

To use the CD-ROM contents, insert the CD-ROM into your CD-ROM drive. If your computer does not automatically open the CD-ROM and display the files, navigate to your CD-ROM drive and double-click it to open the CD-ROM.

You may wish to print or save the documents to your computer. For tips on using the CD-ROM's documents, please read the file on the CD-ROM called "About This CD-ROM and Table of Contents (Read First)."

The CD-ROM includes the following files:

- About This CD-ROM and Table of Contents (Read First)
- Sophomore Year Checklist
- Junior Year Checklist
- Senior Year Checklist
- Summer Before College Checklist
- Preparing for the ACT and SAT Checklist
- College Preparation Timeline
- Narrowing Down Your College Choice Checklist
- College Folder Cover Template
- Sample Resume 1
- Sample Resume 2

- Writing an Essay Checklist
- Sample College Application Essay
- College Visit Checklist
- College Interview Checklist
- FAFSA on the Web Worksheet
- Sample College Award Letter

Software Licensing Agreement. This is a legal agreement between you, the end user, and JIST Publishing, regarding your use of the *Best College for You* CD-ROM ("Software"). By installing or using the Software, you agree to be bound by the terms of this agreement.

1. **Grant of License.** JIST hereby grants to you (an individual) the revocable, personal, non-exclusive, and nontransferable right to use the Software on one computer solely for your personal and non-commercial use. Sharing this Software with other individuals, or allowing other individuals to view the contents of this Software, is in violation of this license. You may not make the Software available on a network, or in any way provide the Software to multiple users.

2. **Copyright.** The Software is owned by JIST and protected by United States and international copyright law. You may not remove or conceal any proprietary notices, labels, or marks from the Software.

3. **Restrictions on Use.** You may not, and you may not permit others to copy (other than one back-up copy), distribute, publicly display, transmit, sell, rent, lease, or otherwise exploit the Software.

4. **Term of Agreement.** The term of this Agreement begins upon installation of this Software and shall terminate 3 years from the date of purchase.

5. **LIMITED WARRANTY**

(A) FOR A PERIOD OF 30 DAYS FROM THE DATE OF PURCHASE, THE CD-ROM THAT CONTAINS THIS SOFTWARE IS WARRANTED TO BE FREE FROM DEFECTS IN MATERIAL AND WORKMANSHIP. IF THE MEDIA IS DEFECTIVE OR FAULTY IN WORKMANSHIP, YOU MAY RETURN THE MEDIA TO JIST WITH A WRITTEN DESCRIPTION OF THE DEFECT, AND JIST WILL REPLACE THE MEDIA WITHOUT CHARGE OR MAKE THE CONTENT AVAILABLE TO YOU ONLINE. REPLACEMENT OF THE MEDIA IS YOUR SOLE AND EXCLUSIVE REMEDY AND JIST'S SOLE LIABILITY:

(B) EXCEPT FOR EXPRESS PROVISIONS IN PARAGRAPH (A), THE SOFTWARE AND ACCOMPANYING WRITTEN MATERIALS ARE PROVIDED ON AN "AS IS" BASIS, WITHOUT ANY WARRANTIES OF ANY KIND, INCLUDING, BUT NOT LIMITED TO, ANY IMPLIED WARRANTIES OF MERCHANTABILITY OR FITNESS FOR ANY PARTICULAR PURPOSE. NO ORAL OR WRITTEN INFORMATION OR ADVICE GIVEN BY JIST, ITS DEALERS, DISTRIBUTORS, AGENTS OR EMPLOYEES, SHALL CREATE A WARRANTY, OR IN ANY WAY INCREASE THE SCOPE OF THIS WARRANTY, AND YOU MAY NOT RELY ON ANY SUCH INFORMATION OR ADVICE. JIST DOES NOT WARRANT, GUARANTEE, OR MAKE ANY REPRESENTATIONS REGARDING THE USE OR THE RESULTS OF USE, OF THE

SOFTWARE OR WRITTEN MATERIALS IN TERMS OF CORRECTNESS, ACCURACY, RELIABILITY, CURRENTNESS, OR OTHERWISE, AND THE ENTIRE RISK AS TO THE RESULTS AND PERFORMANCE OF THE SOFTWARE IS ASSUMED BY YOU. IF THE SOFTWARE OR WRITTEN MATERIALS ARE DEFECTIVE, YOU, AND NOT JIST OR ITS DEALERS, DISTRIBUTORS, AGENTS, OR EMPLOYEES, ASSUME THE ENTIRE COST OF ALL NECESSARY SERVICING, REPAIR, OR CORRECTION OTHER THAN EXPRESSLY DESCRIBED ABOVE.

(C) NEITHER JIST NOR ANYONE ELSE WHO HAS BEEN INVOLVED IN THE CREATION, PRODUCTION, OR DELIVERY OF THIS PRODUCT SHALL BE LIABLE FOR ANY DIRECT, INDIRECT, CONSEQUENTIAL, OR INCIDENTAL DAMAGES (INCLUDING DAMAGES FOR LOSS OF BUSINESS PROFITS, BUSINESS INTERRUPTION, LOSS OF BUSINESS INFORMATION, AND THE LIKE) ARISING OUT OF THE USE OR INABILITY TO USE SUCH PRODUCT OR RELATED TO THIS AGREEMENT, EVEN IF JIST HAS BEEN ADVISED OF THE POSSIBILITY OF SUCH DAMAGES. JIST SHALL NOT BE LIABLE TO YOU FOR ANY INDIRECT, SPECIAL, INCIDENTAL, OR CONSEQUENTIAL DAMAGES OR LOST PROFITS ARISING OUT OF OR RELATED TO THIS AGREEMENT OR YOUR USE OF THE SOFTWARE AND/ OR THE RELATED DOCUMENTATION, EVEN IF JIST HAS BEEN ADVISED OF THE POSSIBILITY OF SUCH DAMAGES. IN NO EVENT SHALL JIST'S LIABILITY HEREUNDER, IF ANY, EXCEED THE PURCHASE PRICE PAID BY YOU FOR THE SOFTWARE AND BOOK.

6. **General.** This Agreement and any dispute under it will be governed by the laws of the State of Minnesota and the United States of America, without regard to their conflict of laws principles. Both parties consent to the exclusive jurisdiction and venue of the federal and state courts in the county of Ramsey and the state of Minnesota. This Agreement constitutes the entire agreement between you and JIST with respect to its subject matter, and supersedes other communication, advertisement, or understanding with respect to the Software. This Agreement may not be amended or modified except in a writing executed by both parties. If any provision of this Agreement is held invalid or unenforceable, the remainder shall continue in full force and effect. All provisions of this Agreement relating to disclaimers of warranties, limitation of liability, remedies, or damages, and JIST's ownership of the Software survive termination.

ACKNOWLEDGMENT. BY INSTALLING THE SOFTWARE, YOU ACKNOWLEDGE THAT YOU HAVE READ AND UNDERSTAND THE FOREGOING AND THAT YOU AGREE TO BE BOUND BY ITS TERMS AND CONDITIONS. YOU ALSO AGREE THAT THIS AGREEMENT IS THE COMPLETE AND EXCLUSIVE STATEMENT OF AGREEMENT BETWEEN THE PARTIES AND SUPERSEDES ALL PROPOSED OR PRIOR AGREEMENTS, ORAL OR WRITTEN, AND ANY OTHER COMMUNICATIONS BETWEEN THE PARTIES RELATING TO THE LICENSE DESCRIBED HEREIN.

Index

B

biology majors, 180

boyfriends, following to college, 154, 258

brochures, college-produced, 216

Burchers, Sam and Bryan, 71–72

business majors, 179

businesses, FAFSA information, 358

C

campus life
changes from parents' time, 211–213
college catalog information, 219
college guide listings, 147
determining college choice, 196
observing during college visits, 199–202

campus services, 197

campus visit questions, 200–202

careers
traditional, 8
workforce demographics, 7–8

cars on campus, campus visit questions, 200

catalogs from colleges, 218–221

character, qualities colleges look for, 107

childhood interests, choosing majors from, 223–225

civic organizations, sources of scholarships, 300–301

Civil Service, registering with for financial aid, 360

classes
advanced, sophomore year, 25
AP (Advanced Placement), 45–48
challenging, taking to prepare for ACT/SAT, 74–75

college
choosing majors from, 230
college catalog information, 219–220
college visit questions, 201
remedial classes, 214
favorite subjects, choosing majors from, 225
IB (International Baccalaureate), 48–49
registering for, 5
sophomore year, 22–23

clothing
campus visit questions, 200
changes from parents' time, 212–213
college interviews, 207

college
alternatives to, 97–101
consequences of arrests, 317–320
saving for, 89–91
versus high school, time management, 9–14

college applications, 38–40, 241
requesting learning-disability assistance, 185–187
updating awards information, 41–42

education majors, 180
EFC (Expected Family
Contribution), 148–150, 292,
341–346, 350
electives, 55
elementary education majors,
180
English majors, 181
Enterprising personality
category, 227
essays
applying to college, 242,
275–276
college requirements, 40, 239
increasing financial aid due
to, 330–331
polishing, 35
scholarship requirements,
276–277
writing, 29–30, 271–274,
278–282
experience
adventure, 113
distance from home when
choosing colleges, 109–110
extracurricular activities
determining college choice,
196
freshman year, 16

F

faculty
faculty-to-student ratios, 112,
144–145, 195–196
help in choosing majors, 229
FAFSA (Free Application for
Federal Student Aid)
completing forms, 42–43,
337–341, 357–360

filing timing, 361–364
lowering costs with, 291–292
Fair Test Web site, 76–77
family
gifts of money, 288
pressure for college choice,
108–109, 114–116
reasons to not choose
colleges, 157
farming, FAFSA information,
358
Fastweb Web site, 36, 89, 303
financial aid, 297
costs versus college generosity,
259, 344
EFC (Expected Family
Contribution), 342–346
good package, increasing
chances for, 327–332
help from admissions
counselors, 163–164
need met, average percentage,
148–150, 196
reasons for early college
applications, 231–232
scholarships. *See* scholarships
student traits looked for,
102–107
financial aid offices, contacting
about award letters, 352
financial information, college
catalog information, 219
Fogg, Neeta, 228–229
food
before tests, 84
college visits, 152, 204–205
weighing college costs,
355–356

W–Z